Liminal Landscapes

Ideas and concepts of liminality have long shaped debates around the uses and practices of space in constructions of identity, particularly in relation to different forms of travel such as tourism, migration and pilgrimage, and the social, cultural and experiential landscapes associated with these and other mobilities. The ritual, performative and embodied geographies of borderzones, non-places, transitional spaces, or 'spaces in-between' are often discussed in terms of the liminal, yet there have been few attempts to problematize the concept, or to rethink how ideas of the liminal might find critical resonance with contemporary developments in the study of place, space and mobility.

Liminal Landscapes fills this void by bringing together a variety of new and emerging methodological approaches of liminality from varying disciplines to explore new theoretical perspectives on mobility, space and socio-cultural experience. By doing so it offers new insight into contemporary questions about technology, surveillance, power, the city, and post-industrial modernity within the context of tourism and mobility.

The book draws on a wide range of disciplinary approaches, including social anthropology, cultural geography, film, media and cultural studies, art and visual culture, and tourism studies. It brings together recent research from scholars with international reputations in the fields of tourism, mobility, landscape and place, alongside the work of emergent scholars who are developing new insights and perspectives in this area.

This timely intervention is the first collection to offer an interdisciplinary account of the intersection between liminality and landscape in terms of space, place and identity. It therefore charts new directions in the study of liminal spaces and mobility practices and will be valuable reading for range of students, researchers and academics interested in this field

Hazel Andrews is a Senior Lecturer in Tourism, Culture and Society at Liverpool John Moores University, UK.

Les Roberts is a research associate in the School of the Arts at University of Liverpool, UK.

Contemporary geographies of leisure, tourism and mobility
Series Editor:
C. Michael Hall
Professor at the Department of Management, College of Business & Economics, University of Canterbury, Private Bag 4800, Christchurch, New Zealand

The aim of this series is to explore and communicate the intersections and relationships between leisure, tourism and human mobility within the social sciences.

It will incorporate both traditional and new perspectives on leisure and tourism from contemporary geography, e.g. notions of identity, representation and culture, while also providing for perspectives from cognate areas such as anthropology, cultural studies, gastronomy and food studies, marketing, policy studies and political economy, regional and urban planning, and sociology, within the development of an integrated field of leisure and tourism studies.

Also, increasingly, tourism and leisure are regarded as steps in a continuum of human mobility. Inclusion of mobility in the series offers the prospect to examine the relationship between tourism and migration, the sojourner, educational travel, and second home and retirement travel phenomena.

The series comprises two strands:

Contemporary Geographies of Leisure, Tourism and Mobility aims to address the needs of students and academics, and the titles will be published in hardback and paperback. Titles include:

Routledge Studies in Contemporary Geographies of Leisure, Tourism and Mobility is a forum for innovative new research intended for research students and academics, and the titles will be available in hardback only. Titles include:

Forthcoming:

Slum Tourism
Edited by Fabian Frenzel, Malte Steinbrink and Ko Koens

Tourism and War
Edited by Richard Butler and Wantanee Suntikul

Sexuality, Women and Tourism
Susan Frohlick

Gender and Tourism
Social, cultural and spatial perspectives
Cara Atchinson

Backpacker Tourism and Economic Development in the Less Developed World
Mark Hampton

Adventure Tourism
Steve Taylor, Peter Varley, and Tony Johnson

Liminal Landscapes

Travel, experience and spaces in-between

**Edited by Hazel Andrews and
Les Roberts**

Routledge
Taylor & Francis Group

LONDON AND NEW YORK

First published 2012
by Routledge
2 Park Square, Milton Park, Abingdon, Oxon OX14 4RN

Simultaneously published in the USA and Canada
by Routledge
711 Third Avenue, New York, NY 10017

Routledge is an imprint of the Taylor & Francis Group, an informa business

British Library Cataloguing in Publication Data
A catalogue record for this book is available from the British Library

Library of Congress Cataloging in Publication Data
A catalog record has been requested for this book

ISBN: 978-0-415-66884-2 (hbk)
ISBN: 978-0-203-12316-4 (ebk)

Typeset in Times New Roman
by Wearset Ltd, Boldon, Tyne and Wear

For Ella and Marc

Contents

Figures and table

Figures

Table

Contributors

Hazel Andrews is a Senior Lecturer in Tourism, Culture and Society at Liverpool John Moores University, UK.

Emma Cocker is a writer and Senior Lecturer in Fine Art at Nottingham Trent University, UK.

Ivan Costantino is a doctoral candidate at the Institute of Social and Cultural Anthropology, University of Oxford, UK, and a member of Magdalen College, UK.

David Crouch is Professor of Cultural Geography and Senior Research Fellow at the University of Derby and Associate of the University of Nottingham, UK.

Pietro Deandrea is Associate Professor of English Literature at the University of Torino, Italy.

Emma Fraser is a postgraduate research student in the Transforming Cultures Research Centre (TFC) at the University of Technology, Sydney (UTS), Australia.

Anita Howarth worked as a journalist for ten years and now lectures in political communication, advocacy and campaigning at Kingston University, London, UK.

Yasmin Ibrahim is a Reader in International Business and Communications at Queen Mary, University of London, UK.

Kevin Meethan is Associate Professor in Sociology in the School of Social Science and Social Work at Plymouth University, UK.

Emily Orley is a Researcher-Practitioner and Lecturer in the Drama, Theatre and Performance Department at Roehampton University, UK.

Piret Pungas is a doctoral candidate in the Department of Geography, University of Tartu and Researcher at Tallinn University, Estonia.

Les Roberts is a Research Associate in the School of the Arts at University of Liverpool, UK.

Tom Selwyn is Director of Studies of the Masters in Travel, Tourism, and Pilgrimage and Professorial Research Associate in the Department of Anthropology and Sociology at the School of Oriental and African Studies (SOAS), University of London, and Professor of Anthropology at San Xia University, China.

Bjørn Thomassen is Associate Professor at the American University of Rome, Italy.

Ester Võsu is a Researcher in the Department of Ethnology, University of Tartu, Estonia.

Simon Ward is a Lecturer in Film & Visual Culture and German at the University of Aberdeen, UK.

1 Introduction

Re-mapping liminality

Hazel Andrews and Les Roberts

Lim·in·al: Of or pertaining to the threshold or initial stage of a process.

Land·scape: a) A view or prospect of natural inland scenery, such as can be taken in at a glance from one point of view; a piece of country scenery; b) A tract of land with its distinguishing characteristics and features, esp. considered as a product of modifying or shaping processes and agents (usually natural).

(Oxford English Dictionary)

The finitude into which we have entered somehow always borders somewhere on the infinitude of physical or metaphysical being ... life flows forth out of the door from the limitation of isolated separate existence into the limitlessness of all possible directions.

(Simmel 1994: 7–8)

While we would not wish to launch this collection of essays on liminality and landscape by proposing an 'authoritative' definition of the book's two overarching concepts, we nevertheless feel it instructive to consider for a moment the 'general' meanings ascribed to these terms in order to get a sense of how we might go about negotiating understandings of the ways they are enacted, performed or theorised in practice. 'Of or pertaining to a threshold', the liminal already in some way connotes the *spatial*: a boundary, border, a transitional *landscape*, or a doorway in Simmel's sense of a physical as well as psychic space of potentiality.[1] The liminal is also, we note, the 'initial stage of a process'. It therefore exhibits *temporal* qualities, marking a beginning as well as an end, but also duration in the unfolding of a spatio-temporal process: liminality as a generative act, a psychosocial intentionality of being. But what of landscape? A view or prospect, a piece of inland scenery (as long as it is not urban), we take from this the idea of landscape as image, vista, representation: a visual index of an area of land (the countryside) as viewed from a given perspective. But also, as a 'tract' of land we can infer a certain materiality and locatedness: a space one can inhabit and navigate one's way through in an embodied sense. By extension, landscape is understood as something that is 'shaped' and 'produced', and which is thus contingent on human or natural 'processes and agents'. Insofar, then, as, ontologically, landscapes are processual and in a constant state of transition and becoming is there not a case for suggesting that landscapes themselves are intrinsically liminal? Indeed, as David Crouch enquires in the afterword to this volume, 'can landscape be anything but liminal?' Or is this to over-stretch the conceptual parameters by which articulations of 'liminality' and 'the liminal' might (should?) otherwise be framed?

These are questions that the multi-disciplinary contributions to this book in their different ways seek to confront. Conceptually, liminality, like landscape, fares none too well if restricted to what we can glean from the OED. So far, so obvious. Yet in approaching landscape through the prism of liminality (and vice versa) a 'back-to-basics' stripping down of the complex and in many ways plenitudinous structures of meaning that have coalesced around these concepts might be a fruitful way, for the purposes of this introduction, of taking stock of the 'place' of the liminal (rhetorically and spatially) in contemporary theory and debate. It is not our intention here to over-anticipate the rich imbrication of ideas of liminality, space and mobility as explored across and between the disciplinary fields of study represented in this collection, preferring instead to steer the reader towards the chapters themselves; it is rather to chart a provisional topography by which to identify and explore some of the common themes and preoccupations that present themselves for consideration at this historical moment. In this vein, the broader intent of *Liminal Landscapes* is, to borrow from the title of the 2010 symposium from which this book has evolved, to 're-map the field' of debates in the social sciences and humanities around concepts of the liminal and liminality.

Accordingly, what we set out below is a triangulation, of sorts, between three landscapes – two English and one Welsh – each of which harbours qualities, affects, or characteristics that may in some way be described as 'liminal': Margate beach in Kent, Morecambe Bay in Lancashire, and Mostyn on the Dee Estuary in Flintshire, North Wales. Along the way we identify some of the common theoretical and thematic threads running through the different contributions to the book. Our rationale for this approach is to purposefully avoid a state-of-the-art appraisal of liminality, or mapping a theoretical overview of the concept, or even tracing its intellectual provenance. Our altogether more cautious aim is to sketch a discursive landscape of the liminal, a three-fold process in which we set out to explore: a) the ways the concept is being applied and theorised in a contemporary context; b) the inherent spatialities of the liminal; and c) the extent to which current theories of liminality are still anchored in – or perhaps burdened by – some of the foundational ideas in anthropology from which they have developed. The other, more modest aim of this introduction is to chart the evolution of our own process of critical engagement with ideas of liminality; a journey which begins in the seaside resort of Margate.

Dahn to Margate

Over a decade ago we used to visit Margate beach on the north-east coast of Kent for day trips out of London. The town was a popular holiday destination for thousands of people until, like many UK coastal resorts, it saw a downturn in its fortunes as a result of the development of cheap charter tourism holidays abroad. Although our visits to Margate were primarily to unwind after a week spent at the academic coal face, the ability to switch off our faculties of critical engagement and resolutely don our leisure hats was often tested by a curiosity with regard to the spectacle on offer in the resort. One of the first things that struck us was the complexity of its marginal nature. Margate is marginal in terms of physical loca-tion on the edge of the land, marginal to holiday-taking practices in terms of its decline in popularity as a seaside resort, marginal as a cultural landscape in rela-tion to dominant narratives and geographies of nationhood, and marginal in the sense of playing host to groups who are in some way marginalised from the fabric of mainstream society. The dispersal policy introduced as part of the Immigration and Asylum Act in 1999 made it incumbent on authorities to house asylum seekers and refugees in 'areas in which there is a ready supply of accommodation'[2] whilst their applications for leave of stay in the UK were being considered. This particu-larly impacted on the coastal towns of the southern UK given the abundant supply of hotels and guest house accommodation, but more pointedly the concentration of points of entry into the country both in terms of legal and illegal border cross-ings. Margate was one such destination and attracted a certain amount of notoriety when in 2003 asylum seekers resident in the Nayland Rock Hotel staged a hunger strike in protest at the proposal to evict them following their alleged failure to comply in time to Section 55 of the Asylum, Immigration and Nationality Act 2002.[3] In this respect Margate was home to marginal people, those on the edge, betwixt and between structures of place and identity.

Figure 1.1 View from Nayland Rock Hotel, Margate, 2003.

The concept of liminality has particular bearing in this context because of its association with marginality, and is brought into sharp focus in relation to coastal areas by Rob Shields (1991). Shields explores the way by which the UK south coast resort of Brighton emerged as a place associated with transgressive behaviours and the carnivalesque. However, in terms of Margate the concept does not neatly transfer from Brighton and the associations of the carnivalesque and ludic are accompanied by tensions in the form of different kinds of power relations and ideas of surveillance. This can best be illustrated with the example of a beach party we observed one afternoon in the summer of 2001. In an exuberant display of the carnivalesque members of the local asylum community in Margate had hauled giant bass bins onto the beach near to Arlington House, the Brutalist tower block which houses many asylum seekers and refugees and which dominates the seafront skyline. With the speakers thumping inland towards the town the dancers and revellers were also facing landward, many beckoning towards the crowds of curious onlookers who had gathered on the promenade to observe the spectacle, inviting them to join in the party. Behind the spectators, parked by the central reservation on Marine Terrace, stood a mobile police CCTV van; its camera, fixed atop a tall telescopic pole ascending from the roof, was angled down towards the rhythmic sway of partygoers on the beach. Yes, the beach without doubt qualifies as a 'liminal landscape' insofar as it plays host to the carnivalesque, but by the same token we got the impression that the apparent 'freedoms' and licence ascribed to the partying migrants were so circumscribed, and subject to such intensive degrees of surveillance and control, that whatever Bakhtinian attributes the beachscape might display, in practice these are rendered all but meaningless. Reflecting on these disparities, the validity of the use of the concept of liminality applied to coastal areas and beaches was thrown into question; even more so when considered in light of the fact that, notwithstanding Shields's well-worked consideration of the term, 'liminality' had nevertheless become somewhat de-coupled from its original theoretical underpinnings and dislodged from its anthropological moorings.

Around the time of our weekend sojourns to the east Kent resort in the early 2000s the film *Last Resort* (Pawel Pawlikowski 2001) appeared on UK cinema screens to much critical acclaim. A film which was not only shot in Margate, but which also seriously grappled with the liminal experience of migrancy – of suspension, limbo, transit, non-places, marginality, of human 'matter out of place' (Douglas 1966) – *Last Resort* provided an insightful focus of reflection on some of the spatial contradictions and dynamics of liminality; tensions which the ethnographic example of the beach party had also brought to the fore. In the film, Tanya, a young Russian woman and her son Artiom arrive in Britain from Moscow. Upon questioning and detention by the immigration officials at Stansted Airport, Tanya decides to claim asylum. Transported to a 'designated holding area' – a bleak seaside town called Stonehaven (in actuality Margate) where they are to be detained pending the outcome of their asylum application – the passage between the airport and 'resort' resembles a somewhat grimmer version of the transfer journey undertaken by the tourist under the stewardship of the tour-operator (Andrews 2011: 156; see also 2009: 12). This blurring of travel narratives, like other ironic juxtapositions in the film, presents a microcosmic snapshot of *fin de siècle* displacement, where the human flotsam of Tony Blair's Britain rub shoulders with its new outsiders: migrants and refugees from countries such as Afghanistan, Iraq, the former Yugoslavia, Iran, Turkey, Somalia, Sri Lanka.[4] Subverting the metonymic signification of the 'typical' British seaside resort, Stonehaven/Margate both literally and metaphorically exists as a 'place on the margin' (Shields 1991) of nation and identity.

As Andrew O'Hagan observes, '[*Last Resort*] is a film about journeys' (2001: 25), yet despite, or because of this, much of what constitutes the action of the central characters is punctuated by long periods of waiting and enforced sedentariness. Tanya and Artiom are shown waiting in the airport lounge for immigration to let them enter the country; waiting for the immigration service to process their asylum claim (and subsequent withdrawal); waiting for the phone box to call Tanya's fiancé (who she is waiting to be rescued by); and waiting for the tide to rise so as to secure a safe, undetected passage out of the resort. In this Godot-like atmosphere, Stonehaven represents the most immediate of quotidian constraints on endeavours to establish or attain a sense of place. Prevented from leaving the holding area, the detainees' movements throughout the resort are under constant surveillance and restriction. The railway station is closed 'until further notice', and the grey, imposing presence of the sea provides a natural barrier of containment and exclusion.

Framed in these terms, the liminal landscapes of Stonehaven/Margate – shabby, desolate, marginal (and unequivocally 'off the map' of the tourist gaze) – connote less a sense of the carnivalesque – 'a free zone, betwixt and between social codes ... a liminal zone of potential carnival' (Shields 1991: 108–109) – than an affective zone of *stasis* (Roberts 2002a: 82–83); a poetics and politics of entropy; a de-actualising 'any-space-whatever' (Deleuze 1986: 109). As dual snapshots of time and place (Margate in the early 2000s), for us the dialogic correspondence between the cinematic geographies of the fictional Stonehaven and the ethnographic spaces of Margate brought the contradictory structures of liminality – the dialectics of movement, transition, and stasis – more sharply into play. Which is not to suggest that, as a 'Margate film' (if it can be referred to as such), *Last Resort* is avowedly realist in its depiction of the resort – the director Pawel Pawlikowski notes that 'the location was chosen because it wasn't quite real, or real but not real' (Roberts 2002b: 97) – but rather that, like Margate itself, the film provides an insightful case study for problematising understandings of liminality, mobility and space in twenty-first century Britain.

As many of the chapters in this book show, ideas and concepts of liminality have long shaped debates around the uses and practices of space in travel, tourism, and pilgrimage. Victor Turner's writings on ritual and communitas (1967, 1969, 1982, 1987; Turner and Turner 1978), Graburn's (1989) theory of tourism as a sacred journey, or Shields's aforementioned discussion of 'places on the margin' have secured a well-established foothold in theoretical discussions on mobility. The unique qualities of liminal landscapes, as developed by these and other writers on the subject, are generally held to be those which play host to ideas of the ludic, consumption, carnivalesque, deterritorialisation, and the inversion or suspension of normative social and moral structures of everyday life. While these arguments remain pertinent, and their metaphorical appeal ever more attractive, the extent to which liminal spaces provoke counter ideas of social control, terror, surveillance, production and territorialisation, invites an urgent call to re-evaluate the meanings attached to ideas of the 'liminal' in studies of mobility. One aspect of liminality that has become somewhat detached from the term's application in relation to spaces of pleasure is that of *danger*.

On Morecambe Sands

The sea represents both a natural barrier and a potential threat; a reminder that landscapes, symbolic or otherwise, undergo a process of constant change. Indeed, we need look no further than the vast expanse of sandflats and mudflats at Morecambe Bay on the north-west coast of England to find an example of a landscape whose very changeability and unpredictability has taken on wider significance following the death of 23 Chinese migrant workers in 2004 who were trapped by the incoming tide while picking cockles in the Bay. The area is notorious for its fast moving tides and treacherous quicksand, yet the lucrative cockle beds have continued to attract low-paid migrant workers ignorant of, or resigned to the dangers posed by this stretch of coastline. This tragic event (dramatised in Nick Broomfield's 2006 docu-drama *Ghosts*) has prompted a sobering re-assessment of the coastal resort as a site of tourism, leisure, pleasure and consumption. The shifting social geographies associated with these land-scapes has meant that the example of the beach may equally be looked upon as a space of transnational labour, migrancy, racial tension, death, fear, uncertainty and disorientation. In this instance, the precarious and un-navigable natural land-scape of Morecambe Sands becomes a metonym for the increasingly de-stabilising landscapes of trans- or post-national capitalist mobility. Moreover, the settlement of asylum seekers and refugees in UK coastal resorts such as Margate has exposed the underlying tensions and social divisions between repre-sentations that play on the ludic, touristic heritage of these resorts and those which address the marginality and exclusion that characterises the other set of mobilities and meanings evoked by these spaces.

It is not the purpose of this introduction to re-rehearse the discussion of the notion of liminality as it was originally laid out by Arnold van Gennep (1960) and later developed by Victor Turner. This task has already been undertaken in Thomassen's (2009) lucid paper on the uses and meanings of liminality and the development of these arguments in his chapter in this book. What we would wish to note, however, is that both van Gennep and Turner have discussed ideas of the liminal in relation to ritual practices and the psychosocial processes involved in these. What we are concerned with is the specific landscapes that give rise to practices of liminality, and what characterises these landscapes *as* liminal. Evidently, as many of the chapters in this book demonstrate, liminal landscapes and spaces do exist, many of which are tinged with death, connected to transformation and processes of becoming, and often functioning, as sites of artistic practice (Crouch 2010):

> I am interested in liminal places – borderline landscapes, the places in-between. I live and work on that great seductive sprawl of estuary, Morecambe Bay, which is literally the borderline between earth and sea. The Bay inspires me to tell stories.[5]

Made in 2004, the same year as the cockle pickers' deaths, the film *Frozen* tells the story of a young woman's return to Morecambe Bay where her sister had mysteriously disappeared two years earlier. Juliet McKoen, who wrote and directed the film, describes Kath, its central character, as '[inhabiting] a border-line world – somewhere in between past and present, living and dying, waking and dreaming, reality and fantasy, sanity and madness'. The site (or sight) of the sister's disappearance is also framed in terms of the liminal: she vanishes in the blind spot between two CCTV cameras. The pixellated landscape of the digital video footage, endlessly and obsessively replayed by Kath, becomes a transcend-ent and potentially transformative space of affect. Like the Bay, no less a liminal landscape, but one that is deterritorialised: time and memory spiralling into 'a centrifugal vortex of nonspace' (Roberts 2012: 40). The haunted spaces of absence which the low-resolution images invoke are those 'whose affective potency lies in the conjunctive irresolvability of time and space' (ibid.). These and other liminal landscapes incite psychogeographic journeys – quests, pilgrim-ages, divinations, exorcisms, *excavations*: a cultural archaeology of trauma, hope, or oblivion. Moreover, the liminality of death and oblivion also invites consideration as to the attraction (if that is the right word) of certain landscapes as sites of suicide. Richie Edwards, the missing-presumed-dead guitarist and co-lyricist of the Welsh rock band Manic Street Preachers, disappeared without trace in February 1995. Only declared legally dead in 2008 it is widely assumed that he committed suicide. His car was found at a motorway service station (a quintessential non-place in the terms elaborated by Marc Augé) near to the Severn Bridge, the crossing over the Severn Estuary which marks the border between England and South Wales.[6]

In his book *Ghost Milk*, the writer Iain Sinclair describes a guided walk he took across Morecambe Bay 'in quest of other ghosts, the drowned cockle pickers' (2011: 313). As with Margate, Morecambe exudes something of an ambivalent and contradictory sense of place. For Sinclair, 'half-resuscitated, half-choked on the karma of the drowned Chinese cockle pickers, [Morecambe is] an unresolved argument between entropy and aspiration' (ibid.: 260–261). Not surprisingly, the uncertain and treacherous topography of Morecambe Sands demands the acquisition (or hire) of local geographical knowledge. An official guide, known as the Sandpilot of Morecambe Bay, leads parties of curious way-farers on a six-mile trek across the sands. Cedric Robinson, now in his late sev-enties, was appointed as the 25th official Queen's Guide to the Sands in 1963.[7]

Figure 1.2 View towards Morecambe Bay from Grange-over-Sands in Cumbria.

As Sinclair notes, '[the] gnarled prophet … marshalled his strung-out flock with a whistle … [sounding] a shrill blast, to line us up, on the edge of a channel where the sea had rushed in' (ibid.: 313–314). Indicating to the writer the location of the cockle picker deaths, the Sandpilot pointed with his stick: '[they] were on a high sandbank with a fast-flowing river on either side. They had no chance' (ibid.: 314).

The Tarkovskyan, Stalker-like figure of the guide highlights another common attribute of liminal landscapes insofar as initiates (like Sinclair) are required to place their trust in the knowledge of a 'ritual elder' or 'master of ceremonies' so as to ensure safe navigation and transit(ion). Analogies here may be drawn with the relationship between psychotherapist and patient, the former often held to be providing a form of 'ritual leadership' (Moore 1991: 25). In *From Ritual to Theatre*, Turner casts the experimental theatre director Jerzy Grotowski in the role of ritual guide-cum-psychotherapist: 'Let us create a liminal space-time "pod" or pilgrimage centre, [Grotowski] seems to be saying, where human beings may be disciplined and discipline themselves to strip off the false personae stifling the individual within' (1982: 120). It is important to note, however, that the ritual leader is not the *master* or *controller* of transformative space. Such space, as Moore observes, 'cannot be commanded – it can only be invoked' (1991: 27). As such, liminality 'is always within a context of containment in which the boundaries are not tended by the ego of the individual involved' (ibid.: 29), but nor, by the same token, are they overly determined by the intervention of the leader or guide.

Insofar as liminal landscapes can only be invoked but not 'commanded' (in the military and territorial sense) we might then question the extent to which they are or can be 'mappable' in cartographic terms. The requisite geographical knowledge for navigating liminal landscapes is that which is generated and engaged with ritually and experientially: i.e. *in practice* and *in situ*. In the words of Tim Ingold, knowledge is 'ambulatory ... we know *as* we go, not *before* we go' (2000: 229, 230, emphasis in original). It is not the map, therefore, that guides the initiate through these landscapes, but situated practices of *wayfinding*:

> Wayfinding depends upon the attunement of the traveller's movements in response to the movements, in his or her surroundings, of other people, animals, the wind, celestial bodies, and so on. Where nothing moves there is nothing to which one can respond: at such times – as before a storm, or during an eclipse – the experienced traveller can lose his bearings even in familiar terrain.
>
> (ibid.: 242)

But there is also the need for the traveller or wayfarer to attune their bodies to the movements or transformations that are operative on a much slower and molecular scale: the subtle degradations of landscapes otherwise defined in terms of the *absence* of movement and vitality; the zones of stasis referred to above; the entropy of industrial decay and economic decline; the sublime patina of ruins, and so on. How, then, do ideas of liminality relate to the 'deadzones' of social, cultural, or economic 'in-between-ness'. To explore these and other issues we travel south from Morecambe to the Dee Estuary.

Mostyn

Mostyn is a small village in Flintshire, North Wales. It lies about half a kilometre inland from the south side of the River Dee. Running between the village and the foreshore is the A548, the road that links the main built-up areas along this section of coast. As such the village itself is by-passed and despite its connections to one of the oldest families in Wales – the Mostyn family – and to industrial heritage that has roots in the 1200s (O'Toole 2002), there is little that would draw attention. However, the village is linked to two other key features of this stretch of coast. On the river side of the A548 lies the Port of Mostyn and just over three kilometres upstream at Llanerch-y-Mor is the Duke of Lancaster ship. These two sites are distinctly different and bring into focus some of the issues that we wish to explore in our consideration of liminality.

Patricia O'Toole (2002) has provided a rich and detailed history of Mostyn Port (which also touches on some of the history of the village of Mostyn), noting its development and its various fortunes as it evolved into an important channel of mobility during the industrial revolution. Its function as an exporter of coal and the links to the iron works that were founded at the site made the port a key provider of employment and industry in the area. At the same time 'throughout most of the nineteenth century Mostyn enjoyed some brisk business in the passenger service trade' (O'Toole 2002: 18), providing a link to Liverpool and the leisure site of New Brighton on the Wirral. In its role of receiving and despatching goods the port is linked into a global network of commodity exchange sending and receiving ships to the Azores, Finland, South Africa, Greece and Italy to name but a few destinations. The port, designed as a NAABSA port,[8] has survived the ups and downs of changing technology, the complexities of the shifting sands and channels of the River Dee and its canalisation (see Roberts in this volume), and issues relating to de-industrialisation, conflicting interests in terms of land use,[9] and the changes in the working practices of dock workers as a result of the National Dock Labour scheme. Today it no longer processes passenger services and the main business of the port relates to the off-shore wind farm industry and the shipping of wings made in the Airbus factory based about 24 kilometres upstream.

The purpose in thinking about the port and sketching some of its history and present functions is to illustrate that, although it occupies a literal (or indeed littoral) edgeland location, that in itself does not confer the status of liminal. The port has been and remains a central feature of the landscapes and fortunes of the local area and beyond. Indeed the practices that the port has facilitated make it central to key developments in British history. For example, both Henry Bolingbroke (later Henry IV) and Henry Tudor passed through Mostyn Port at key points in their fights for the Crown. The former landed at Mostyn Quay (as it was then known) with troops that marched on Flint Castle and subsequently defeated Richard II. And Henry Tudor evaded capture by Richard III by escaping through Mostyn Quay disguised as a peasant woman (O'Toole 2002). By mining the history of the area and the port's role within that we can say that the port's physical location has not detracted from its centrality in the politics of power struggles or the development of coastal capitalism which places it at the very heart of mainstream socio-cultural practices.

Perhaps to the casual observer passing along the A548 such observations as those made above would go unremarked; access to the port is not 'free' (that is, unless one has business there one has no business being there) and the village, as already observed, is by-passed by the road. What might draw a visitor or cause a passer-by to stop and stare is the presence of the Duke of Lancaster ship moored further upstream from the port at Llanerch-y-Mor. The Duke of Lancaster (latterly also known as the Mostyn Fun ship) was at one time a car ferry and cruise ship. The ship arrived in the vicinity of Mostyn in 1979 where it was to be converted into a floating leisure complex and indoor market. The venture was short-lived and no longer operative by the mid-1980s. The ship remains the property of a north-west UK based businessman who has been in dispute with the local authority – Flintshire County Council – for a number of years.[10]

The presence of the ship in stasis appears incongruous with the working, fluid, mobile port downstream and yet both are connected by the ebb and flow of

Figure 1.3 The Duke of Lancaster, Llanerch-y-Mor, Flintshire, North Wales.

the River Dee and its sands. It goes without saying that the port relies on the river and it was the river that brought the Duke of Lancaster to its current resting place. The Dee requires dredging to make it navigable, and because of the many sandbanks it requires careful navigation. Both the Duke of Lancaster and ships for the port needed and require piloting to safety. In addition the sandbanks have been integral to the current resting place of the Duke of Lancaster as upon its arrival sand was pumped from a bank in the river to around the ship to secure it in place.[11]

When driving along the A548 it is impossible not to notice the hulking presence of The Duke of Lancaster, squatting oddly as it does on the foreshore. Despite its distance from the village of Mostyn the ship's image is used on the two tourism websites for the village.[12] The ship is something of a local curiosity and attracts regular sightseers. It is possible to walk up to the ship but visitors cannot legally board it. However, this has not deterred groups of urban explorers similar to those discussed by Fraser (in this volume). For example, members of 28dayslater – The UK UE Urbex Urban Exploration Forums[13] – have boarded the ship both during the day and at night, running the risk of being caught by the private security guarding the vessel. The Duke of Lancaster is clearly in a state of decay, streaks of rust run down its sides and hull, and with no apparent purpose or function it is slowly wasting away. The ship is held in suspension: it is betwixt and between the land and the river and its decay doubtless poses a threat to the natural environment in which it is situated.

The Duke of Lancaster thus embodies a number of characteristics which, for the purposes of this introduction, we have provisionally identified as 'liminal'. First, it occupies a liminal position inasmuch as it straddles the ambivalent border between river and land. Second, the ship exists in a state of suspended transition. Its industrial life cycle has seen it pass through several stages: from passenger liner to static 'fun ship' to dereliction and decay to (presumably) eventual scrappage. Third, in its current form the site is attractive as a potential leisure or pleasure zone partly on account of its association with danger and illegality: clambering over the barbed wire fencing to board the ship carries with it the seductive allure of transgression but also the threat of injury or death. Danger is also inherent in the ship's corrosion and disintegration; an environmental ticking time bomb, the rusting behemoth poses the potential threat of pollution and ecological degradation. Fourth, at a micro or molecular scale this very state of entropy at the same time represents a liminal flux of becoming. New organic forms flow, secrete, propagate: tumescent and vascular; lichenous flecks of brown and yellow; rhizomic meanderings of bindweed, tendril, and root. Micro-cosmologies effervesce and make themselves known to the naked eye, spreading like a canker across the surface of landscapes otherwise categorised as 'dead' or 'stagnant'. One of the meanings ascribed to the word stagnant in the OED is fluid 'that is at rest in a vessel'. The fluidities and entropic energies that are sustained by and emanate from the malignant colossus of The Duke of Lancaster are most decidedly not at rest. Far from it, they are restless, even imperious in their advance, slowly but surely wresting back nature from a degraded vestige of culture.

In his afterword, David Crouch makes the connection between liminality, ritual and Buddhism.[14] This observation strikes a chord with our foregoing discussion of entropy. In instances where a liminal landscape may be characterised as a 'zone of stasis' the emphasis shifts from reflections on the synchronic attributes of space and place to the subtle variegations of *time*. In one sense entropy *is* time insofar as the radical impermanence that forms the core of Buddhist teachings and philosophy translate to the innate *becoming* of landscapes conceived of as material and symbolic entities undergoing constant processes of change and transformation. We have elsewhere defined a 'zone of stasis' as 'a temporal unfolding of spatial restriction' (Roberts 2002a: 82) where movement or transition is inhibited. For example, time spent waiting in the departure lounge of an airport or in immigration detention areas (such as the fictional Stonehaven). Dialectically working against this spatially-inhibited temporal liminality, 'zones of transition' represent the spatial enactment of potentiality and temporal mobility: 'the unfolding potential of as yet unrealised goals, hopes or desires' (ibid.: 85). It is important to stress, however, that this more agential space-time could also be applied to the examples of the airport and the detention centre. 'Stasis' or 'transition' are not fixed, absolutist properties that are in some way engineered into the architectural DNA of these landscapes (although they *could* be). Liminal landscapes, in the terms we have sought to elaborate in this introduction, reflect not so much an ontology of 'liminalness' (as if we merely need to describe a landscape *as* liminal in order for it to *be* liminal). That much, we would suggest, is a given. The imbrications of liminality, landscape, and mobility prompt and enact more processual, epistemological and anthropological understandings of what we might mean by a liminal landscape: in what ways are given landscapes liminal (or *liminoid*)? How are they liminal? What are the mechanics and processes by which liminalities work or function in relation to landscape? What are the temporal geographies of liminal landscapes? What are the politics of liminal landscapes? What are their affects? These and other questions are variously addressed in the discussions that unfold in and across the chapters of *Liminal Landscapes*. In the end, perhaps it is less a question of what makes a landscape liminal that is the issue, but rather the much broader question of what makes a landscape a landscape. Liminality provides a compelling, illuminating and above all productive framework by which to further these theoretical investigations.

The book

Liminal Landscapes is organised into four parts, the first of which is 'Navigating liminality: theory, method, strategy'. The opening chapter by Bjorn Thomassen is a reflection on the intellectual history of the concept of liminality and a critical analysis of the development of its link with the ludic and carnivalesque. To this end he draws attention to the often missed connection between danger and liminality, a link that other chapters in this book also pick up on. Thomassen also explores the idea of a 'permanent liminality' which arises through the practices and experiences found in some forms of social setting. Emily Orley further explores themes of practice and experience by linking them to places as anthropomorphised entities. Ideas of moving through places yet leaving a trace – imprints of a future past – raise questions about our responses to particular places insofar as these are not fixed but liminal and in a constant state of transition and becoming. Orley argues that such an understanding of place invites us to think differently about how we encounter and remember everyday landscapes, a process of re-envisioning the ethics and aesthetics of place and memory. Emma Cocker's chapter again links the concept of liminality with practice. Focusing on the performance art of Heath Bunting and Kayle Brandon, Cocker examines a specific kind of liminal landscape: that of the border. Through their work Bunting and Brandon explore a creative response to places characterised by certain dominant ideological expectations in the guise of customs officials, border police and immigration officials. The dominant discourses associated with the border are contested in the practice of fluidity and porousness invoked by the artists.

In Part II, 'Gleaning and liminality: edgelands, wetlands, estuaries' the various contributors again examine the importance of the experiential nature of landscape. In this respect Kevin Meethan's chapter takes the reader on a journey along a stretch of Devon coastline in the south-west of England. Using photography as a method of gleaning images and traces of the landscape he encounters, Meethan examines the betwixt and between nature of the beach. Through the practice of walking, observing and photographing Meethan draws attention to the rhythms of the beaches and foreshore along the coast of the Exe Estuary, exploring the liminal nature of these landscapes in terms of both their physical and socio-cultural structures of liminality. In Chapter 6 Piret Pungas and Ester Võsu discuss the liminality of the bogs and mires that make up a high percentage of the land cover of Estonia. Mires represent liminality in terms of their marginal nature and precarious topography and wetlands environment. However, liminality is understood to have different features and these are presented alongside the embodied practices and knowledges that inform the symbolic geography of mires of which *gleaning* – gathering, collecting, extracting – is one such activity. By exploring the changing practices and experiences related to mires, Pungas and Võsu chart a rich cultural and historical geography of Estonian mires as liminal landscapes. Les Roberts' chapter is also rooted and routed in the liminal zones of wetlands, namely the marshes, sandbanks and reclaimed territories of the Dee Estuary which mark the border between Cheshire in England and Flintshire in North Wales. Roberts explores three interlacing liminalities that define this borderland region: its place betwixt and between national-cultural boundaries of identity; the marginality and ambiguous geographies of its physical landscape; and the liminal hinterland between the living and the dead, the latter forming the basis of a psycho-topographic mapping of the Dee Estuary as a real-and-imagined space of embedded memory.

Part III, 'Urban liminalities: ritual, poesis, experience', shifts our attention away from landscapes embedded in rural settings to urban environments. Ivan Costantino's chapter is based on ethnographic fieldwork undertaken in the Tibetan city of Lhasa. Costantino focuses in on a detail of Tibetan life, the ritual circumambulation routes in the pre-1949 areas of Lhasa that bring together and mark the boundaries of the city as a site of modernity, a site of religious power and pilgrimage, and as a site of tourist consumption. A key element of this chapter (as in many of the others in this volume) is that of practice; it is the actions and dispositions associated with place which help inform the idea of a landscape as liminal. The experiential nature of liminal landscapes is further explored in Emma Fraser's chapter by an examination of the practice of urban exploration of (otherwise off-limits and forbidden) sites of ruin and decay, such as sewers and tunnels. Such places are infused with risk and danger. Based on periods of participant observation Fraser demonstrates that the practice of urban exploration in places and landscapes that are off the conventional tourist map do nevertheless constitute a form of adventure tourism. The liminal nature of these landscapes is demonstrated in their falling 'betwixt and between the structural past and structural future' (Turner 1986: 41). In Chapter 10 Hazel Andrews draws attention to another link between the industrial and the liminal. Focusing on Crosby Beach in north-west England, Andrews assesses the role that 'Another Place', an art installation by Antony Gormley, has on the uses of and meanings attributed to the beach from the perspective of visitors drawn to the site by the artwork, as well as local people for whom the beach is part of their everyday experiences. Andrews questions whether geographical location is enough to warrant a landscape being labelled liminal. She suggests that the liminality of a landscape is dependent on *who* the actors are within that place. She also questions the validity of the concept of the liminal in this particular case suggesting that Victor Turner's term *liminoid* is at times more apt.

Tom Selwyn's chapter opens the final part of the book: 'Liminality and nation: marginality, negotiation, contestation'. Selwyn, like Meethan, explores a particular area of the foreshore by foot. In this case the landscape is that which extends along the south-east coast of England around the ancient town of Rye. Again, by observing and recording the features of this area Selwyn examines the symbolic role that such a place can have in forming a narrative about the nature of contemporary Britain which he argues is one characterised by, amongst others, the defence of the British state, class distinctions, and distinctive individualism, all intermixed with the ideas, values and symbols of seaside holidays. In Chapter 12 Simon Ward examines the cultural geography of the British road movie to discuss the state of the nation. Concentrating on three British set films, Ward examines the marginal characteristics of the landscapes depicted in the films as the various protagonists – all people who can be identified as marginal in some way – travel along coastal areas and towards the edge of the land. He concludes by asking what place the different films envision for the marginal in British society and if at the same time the marginal is a landscape conceived as a site for the suspension of normative social structures. The final two chapters of the volume continue the theme of marginal groups. The first of these, by Anita Howarth and Yasmin Ibrahim, considers the fate of those migrants, refugees and asylum seekers caught in the so-called 'Jungle' encampment outside Calais. This chapter focuses on the representation of the people caught in this 'in-between' place of national (un)belonging as well as their 'place' in socio-legal discourses and British tabloid newspapers. The various narratives form a moral discourse which de-sensitise human suffering associated with immigration. Howarth and Ibrahim conclude that such a process makes immigration in so-called 'en-lightened societies' a liminal space between rationality and atavism. Chapter 14 by Pietro Deandrea also explores the fate of immigrants; not those held in suspension but those who have found their way into the UK. Alluding to the reality of the estimated 25,000 enslaved peoples in contemporary Britain, Deandrea explores aspects of such 'non-people' through three fictional works and situates these alongside the theorising of Giorgio Agamben about concentration camps. Finally, David Crouch's afterword pulls together some of the conceptual and thematic threads running across the different chapters. Paying close attention to the ways landscape is performed and enacted, and pointing to the problematised nature of 'landscape' within recent cross- and multi-disciplinary debates, Crouch explores the affective and embodied 'spacings' of liminality, drawing the fitting conclusion that 'landscape is full of liminalities'.

Notes

1 The anthropologist Victor Turner, whose seminal writings have laid much of the theoretical foundations for understandings of liminality and ritual, describes liminality as 'cunicular' – like being in a tunnel between the entrance and the exit (Turner 1974: 231, quoted in Hall 1991: 35).

2 www.legislation.gov.uk/ukpga/1999/33/pdfs/ukpga_19990033_en.pdf. See Section 97 (b). (Accessed September 2011).

3 http://news.bbc.co.uk/1/hi/england/kent/2973512.stm (accessed September 2011).

4 Nationalities representing the highest number of asylum applications to the UK in 2000. Source: Home Office statistics reproduced in the *Guardian*, 'Welcome to Britain: A Special Investigation into Asylum and Immigration', June 2001: 22–23.

5 Juliet McKoen, quoted in the press kit for the film *Frozen* (Juliet McKoen, UK, 2004): www.movementonscreen.org.uk/pictures/frozen_presskit.pdf (accessed September 2011).

6 www.telegraph.co.uk/news/obituaries/3514147/Richey-Edwards.html (accessed September 2011). A service station is also the site of disappearance in George Sluizer's unsettling film *The Vanishing* (*Spoorloos*, Netherlands/France, 1988). In the film a man is haunted by the disappearance of his girlfriend while on holiday together in France. It is later revealed that she was abducted from the service station and buried alive in a coffin, a fate the man only learns about by experiencing the same horror. A space of transition, the claustrophobic interior of the coffin becomes an inescapable liminal landscape: a space in-between the worlds of the living and the dead.

7 http://news.bbc.co.uk/1/hi/england/4628390.stm (accessed September 2011).

8 Not always afloat but safe aground.

9 O'Toole (2002) describes the issues relating to the contestation surrounding the expansion of the port in relation to environmental issues concerning the Dee Estuary's significance in terms of wildfowl.

10 www.dukeoflancaster.net/page2.html (accessed August 2011).

11 ibid.

12 www.stayinwales.co.uk/wales.cfm?village=Mostyn   and   www.aboutbritain.com/towns/mostyn.asp (both accessed August 2011).

13 www.28dayslater.co.uk/forums/showthread.php?t=18739 (accessed August 2011).

14 This connection is also noted by the Jungian psychiatrist James Hall in reference to the traditional Zen ox-herding pictures, which he describes as 'an analogy of the interaction of the ego with the natural mind [or the radical emptiness of Buddha-nature]' (1991: 39).

References

Andrews, H. (2009) 'Tourism as a "Moment of Being"', *Suomen Antropologi*, 34 (2): 5–21.

Andrews, H. (2011) *The British on Holiday: Charter Tourism, Identity and Consumption.* Clevedon: Channel View Publications.

Augé, M. (1995) *Non-Places: Introduction to an Anthropology of Supermodernity.* London: Verso.

Crouch, D. (2010) *Flirting with Space: Journeys and Creativity.* Farnham: Ashgate.

Deleuze, G. (1986) *Cinema 1: The Movement-Image.* London: The Athlone Press.

Douglas, M. (1966) *Purity and Danger: An Analysis of Concepts of Pollution and Taboo.* Harmondsworth: Penguin.

Graburn, N.H.H. (1989) 'Tourism: the Sacred Journey', in V. Smith (ed.), *Hosts and Guests: The Anthropology of Tourism* (2nd edition), Oxford: Blackwell.

Hall, J.A. (1991) 'The Watcher at the Gates of Dawn: the Transformation of the Self in Liminality and by Transcendent Function', in N. Schwartz-Salant and M. Stein (eds), *Liminality and Transitional Phenomena*, Wilmette, Illinois: Chiron.

Ingold, T. (2000) *The Perception of the Environment: Essays in Livelihood: Dwelling and Skill.* London: Routledge.

Moore, R.L. (1991) 'Ritual, Sacred Space, and Healing: the Psychoanalyst as Ritual Elder', in N. Schwartz-Salant and M. Stein (eds), *Liminality and Transitional Phenomena*, Wilmette, Illinois: Chiron.

O'Hagan, A. (2001) 'Review of *Last Resort*', *Daily Telegraph*, 16 March 2001: 25.

O'Toole, P. (2002) *Sea Change: History of the Port of Mostyn*. Chester: Cheshire County Publishing.

Roberts, L. (2002a) '"Welcome to Dreamland": From Place to Non-place and Back Again in Pawel Pawlikowski's *Last Resort*', *New Cinemas: Journal of Contemporary Film*, 1 (2): 78–90.

Roberts, L. (2002b) 'From Sarajevo to Didcot: An Interview with Pawel Pawlikowski', *New Cinemas: Journal of Contemporary Film*, 1 (2): 91–97.

Roberts, L. (2012) *Film, Mobility and Urban Space: a Cinematic Geography of Liverpool*. Liverpool: Liverpool University Press.

Shields, R. (1991) *Places on the Margin: Alternative Geographies of Modernity*. London: Routledge.

Simmel, G. (1994 [1909]). 'Bridge and Door', *Theory, Culture and Society*, 11(1): 5–10.

Sinclair, I. (2011) *Ghost Milk: Calling Time on the Grand Project*. London: Hamish Hamilton.

Thomassen, B. (2009) 'The Uses and Meanings of Liminality', *International Political Anthropology*, 2 (1): 5–27.

Turner, V.W. (1967) *The Forest of Symbols, Aspects of Ndembu Ritual*. New York: Cornell University Press.

Turner, V.W. (1969) *The Ritual Process: Structure and Anti-Structure*. New York: Cornell University Press.

Turner, V.W. (1982) *From Ritual to Theatre: the Human Seriousness of Play*. New York: PAJ Publications.

Turner, V.W. (1986) 'Dewey, Dilthey, and Drama: An Essay in the Anthropology of Experience', in V.W. Turner and E.M. Bruner (eds), *The Anthropology of Experience*, Urbana and Chicago: University of Illinois Press.

Turner, V.W. (1987) *The Anthropology of Performance*. New York: PAJ Publications.

Turner, V.W. and E. Turner (1978) *Image and Pilgrimage in Christian Culture: Anthropological Perspectives*. New York: Columbia University Press.

Van Gennep, A. (1960) *The Rites of Passage*. Chicago: Chicago University Press.

Part I
Navigating liminality
Theory, method, strategy

2 Revisiting liminality

The danger of empty spaces

Bjørn Thomassen[1]

Never before in the history of the world have non-places occupied so much space.

(Benko and Strohmayer 1997: 23)

Introduction

Liminal spaces are attractive. They are the places we go to in search of a break from the normal. They can be real places, parts of a larger territory, or they can be imagined or dreamed. Liminal landscapes are found at the fringes, at the limits. However, there is more to it than that. Had we just been talking about the peripheral, or the far-away, we would be dealing with marginality: that which is the furthest away from the centre. Liminal landscapes are in-between spaces. Seasides and beaches are archetypical liminal landscapes. The seaside is something more than just the end of dry and inhabited land: it is a coast*line* with something on the other side of the threshold. Liminality implicates the existence of a boundary, a *limes*, the Latin word for threshold from which the concept of limitality derives. This limit is not simply there: it is there to be confronted. The ancient Greeks had two words for the sea. *Pelagos* was the standard word used to refer to the sea as a simple 'fact'. *Pontos* indicated something else: it was the sea facing the human being, a trial to overcome, a threshold to pass, an open sea to be crossed, a danger, a challenge. The etymology speaks to this, as *pontos* belongs to a group of significant words with roots in Proto-Indo-European (**pent*) 'to go, to pass; path, bridge', also related to *pateo* 'I step'. When asked who were the most numerous, the living or the dead, Anacharsis (the sixth century BC Scythian sage) is supposed to have retorted, 'where do you place those who are sailing the seas?' (as quoted in Endsjø, 2000: 370).

The Greeks knew very well that the middle stage in a ritual passage had its own spatial reality. The Athenian *ephebes* (neophytes) were sent out to the uncultivated mountainsides to have their civic status altered in a rite of passage. Mythology confirmed geography: the adolescent Odysseus was sent to the mountain slopes of Parnassus to undergo his rite of passage to manhood, with Autolycus, his maternal grandfather, acting as ceremony master (Endsjø

2000: 358). The Ndembu that Turner studied for so many years also knew their liminal geography. When the neophytes were thrown into the ritual passage, this happened initially by a spatial separation from their village as the ceremony master took them into the wilderness, and brought them to a sacred site where they were subjected to a series of tests and personality transforming ordeals.

For a variety of Stone Age peoples caves almost surely functioned as spaces of liminality (Barnatt and Edmonds 2002). Caves were certainly used for funerary and ritual purposes in the majority of Neolithic cultures. Upper Paleolithic and Neolithic caves typically took the shape of dangerous passage ways, quite literally. It is likely that these passage-type caves represented passages to another world: the world of the gods or/and the world of the dead. Caves have been, in many cultures, crucial liminal spaces where shamanistic ekstases occurred, bringing humans into contact with the spirits or the beyond. For the Maya, caves were the entrances to the underworld, not pyramids. It is now a well-accepted hypothesis that cave paintings, such as the famous ones at Lascaux, must be interpreted as being part of ritual passages and actual liminal experiences.

Liminal spaces are evidently part of any culture. The purpose of this chapter is to open up a question: what is happening to liminal spaces in contemporary, 'Western' and 'modern' societies? Such a question is much too big to be addressed, let alone answered, in a single chapter. Rather than answering the question, the aim will be to search for a meaningful formulation of the problem. My discussion will depart from a short introduction to the concept of liminality via Arnold van Gennep and Victor Turner. A typology of liminal experiences will be presented, followed by a discussion of current applications of the liminality concept which will end on a warning note: that the very dominant tendency in postmodern and poststructuralist literature to take a celebratory stance toward the 'interstitial' is a critical development that does not really enable our analysis of liminality and that does not, ultimately, pay respect to the original analysis offered by van Gennep. I argue that Victor Turner's proposal to see the modern world as 'liminoid' is not the best starting point in our attempts to capture the role of liminal space in the world of today. While it is to the merit of Victor Turner that we can think with liminality, in taking up the concept of liminality today we have to step carefully. This is especially the case as the term is increasingly used to talk about almost *anything*. I will instead argue that Turner's own observation that liminal states may at times become institutionalized provides a key toward understanding both temporal and spatial liminality in modernity. In this context, the work of the contemporary social theorist, Arpad Szakolczai, will be discussed.

The history of a concept: from Arnold van Gennep to Victor Turner

The concept of liminality is today experiencing a revival. This revival takes place 100 years after the concept was introduced by the French anthropologist, Arnold van Gennep, in an indeed remarkable book, *Les Rites de Passage*, published in 1909. In *Rites of Passage* van Gennep started out by suggesting a meaningful classification of all existing rites. He distinguished between rites that mark the passage of an individual or social group from one status to another from those which mark transitions in the passage of time (e.g. harvest, new year), whereupon he went on to explore 'the basis of characteristic patterns in the order of ceremonies' (1960: 10). Stressing the importance of *transitions* in any society, van Gennep singled out *rites of passage* as a special category, consisting of three sub-categories, namely *rites of separation, transition rites*, and *rites of incorporation*. Van Gennep called the middle stage in a rite of passage a *liminal period* (ibid.: 11). He called transition rites *liminal rites*, and he called rites of incorporation *postliminal rites*. The ritual pattern was apparently universal: all societies use rites to demarcate transitions.

The universality of the tripartite structure is not to be underestimated. Anthropological claims to universality have been few indeed. There were therefore good reasons to expect that van Gennep's study and careful classification of rites would become an instant classic. However, the framework proposed by van Gennep was not taken up in subsequent scholarship. Especially Durkheim and the Durkhemian school in anthropology/sociology neglected van Gennep's approach (for further details, see Thomassen 2009).

It was Victor Turner who re-discovered the importance of liminality. During his fieldwork, Turner had read about van Gennep via the work of Henri Junod (Turner 1985: 159). Turner stumbled upon van Gennep's *Rites of Passage* almost by chance during the summer of 1963 at a moment when he was himself in a liminal state, having resigned from Manchester and sold his house, but still waiting for his US visa which was delayed because of his refusal to undertake armed military service during the Second World War. The Turners were staying at Hastings on the English Channel, living in 'a state of suspense' (E. Turner 1985: 7). Turner literally lived at a threshold when he encountered van Gennep. Turner *experientially* recognized the importance of van Gennep's insight. The reading inspired him, on the spot, to write the essay 'Betwixt and Between: The Liminal Period in Rites of Passage', the famous chapter in his 1967 publication, *The Forest of Symbols*. Turner presented the paper once in the US, in March 1964. This would be the first of his explorations into liminality.

In his analysis of Ndembu ritual, Turner (1967, 1969, 1974) showed how ritual passages served as moments of creativity that freshened up the societal make-up, and argued that rituals were much more than mere reflections of social order. Van Gennep's framework complemented the term already introduced by Turner: 'social drama'. Turner had been trained in functionalist anthropology. Van Gennep's book further helped him to redirect his work beyond the functionalist paradigm.

Types of liminality

In Turner's own words, liminality refers to any 'betwixt and between' situation or object. This understanding opens up for possible uses of the concept beyond

Turner's own suggestions. Single moments, longer periods, or even whole epochs can be considered liminal. Liminality can also be applied to both single individuals and to larger groups (cohorts or villages), or whole societies, or maybe even civilizations. As I have previously suggested (Thomassen 2009), experiences of liminality can be related to three different types of *subjecthood*:

1   single individuals
2   social groups (e.g. cohorts, minorities)
3   whole societies, entire populations, maybe even 'civilizations'

The *temporal* dimension of liminality can relate to:

1   moments (sudden events)
2   periods (weeks, months, or possibly years)
3   epochs (decades, generations, arguably even centuries)

These different dimensions can function together in a variety of combinations as indicated in this model:

Model 1. Types of liminal experiences: temporal dimensions

It should, of course, be stressed that these are analytical distinctions of a somewhat arbitrary nature. There is no definitive way of distinguishing 'moments' from 'periods', and the dimensions invoked could also be thought of as a continuum. Moreover, while this scheme identifies types of liminal *experience*, it by no means follows that all these experiences are demarcated with a transition *rite* – at least not the same kind of clearly recognizable and institutionalized rites with identifiable ceremony masters, as studied in the work of van Gennep.

Dimensions of spatial liminality

Applications of the concept of liminality have arguably privileged the temporal dimension. This is so despite the fact that van Gennep started his own analysis of ritual passages with a full chapter on 'the *territorial* passage', the title of Chapter II which followed immediately upon his initial classification of rites. Van Gennep clearly saw territorial border zones or border lines, thresholds or portals, as structurally identical with the intermediate period of a ritual passage: spatial and geographical progression correlates with the ritual marking of a cultural passage. Moreover, van Gennep even indicated that perhaps the physical passage of a threshold somehow *preceded* the rites that demarcate a symbolic or 'spiritual' passage: 'A rite of spatial passage has become a rite of spiritual passage' (van Gennep 1960: 22).

Van Gennep discussed in this context both concrete thresholds such as portals or doorways, but he also included demarcations of tribal societies, villages and towns, and neutral zones between countries and larger civilizations. In other

Table 2.1 Types of liminal experiences: temporal dimensions

Subject time	Individual	Group	Society
Moment	Sudden event affecting one's life (death, divorce, illness) or individualized ritual passage (baptism, ritual passage to womanhood, as for example among the Ndembu)	Ritual passage to manhood (almost always in cohorts); graduation ceremonies, etc.	A whole society facing a sudden event (sudden invasion, natural disaster, a plague) where social distinctions and normal hierarchy disappear Carnivals Revolutionary moments
Period	Critical life-stages Puberty or teenage	Ritual passage to manhood, which may extend into weeks or months in some societies Group travels	Wars Revolutionary periods
Epoch (or life-span duration)	Individuals standing outside society, by choice or designated Monkhood In some tribal societies, individuals remain 'dangerous' because of a failed ritual passage Twins are permanently liminal in some societies	Religious fraternities, ethnic minorities, social minorities, transgender Immigrant groups betwixt and between old and new culture Groups that live at the edge of 'normal structures', often perceived as both dangerous and 'holy'	Prolonged wars, enduring political instability, prolonged intellectual confusion (the Thirty Years War) Incorporation and reproduction of liminality into social and political structures Modernity as 'permanent liminality'?

words, liminal places can be specific thresholds; they can also be more extended areas, like 'borderlands' or, arguably, whole countries, placed in important in-between positions between larger civilizations. Staying with the above threefold classification, I suggest that the spatial dimensions of liminality can relate to:

1   specific places, thresholds (a doorway in a house, a line that separates holy from sacred in a ritual, specific objects, in-between items in a classification scheme, parts/openings of the human body)
2   areas or zones (border areas between nations, monasteries, prisons, sea resorts, airports)
3   countries or larger regions, continents (meso-potamia, medi-terranean; Ancient Palestine, in between Mesopotamia and Egypt; Ionia in Ancient Greece, in between the Near East and Europe).

In introducing this third dimension I am perhaps going beyond van Gennep's own suggestions. But there are strong grounds to suggest that even Karl Jaspers' famous theory of the axial age can be meaningfully understood with the notion of liminality (Thomassen 2010). Karl Jaspers' description of the axial age at places used a vocabulary which is almost identical to the one originally proposed by van Gennep. Jaspers described the axial age as an in-between period between two structured world-views and between two rounds of empire building (1953: 51); it was an age of creativity where 'man asks radical questions', and where the 'unquestioned grasp on life is loosened' (ibid.: 3); it was an age of uncertainty and contingency: an age where old certainties had lost their validity and where new ones were still not ready. It was a period where individuals rose to the test and new leadership figures emerged. In particular, the axial age gave birth to a new sub-stratum of persons: 'free-standing' intellectuals; these were often wandering ascetics and therefore spatially uprooted. Finally, and import-antly for our purpose here: referring to the spatial co-ordinates, the axial 'leaps' all happened in in-between areas between larger civilizations, in liminal places: *not* at the centres, nor outside reach of main civilizational centres but exactly at the margins, and that quite systematically so in the Eastern Mediterranean, China and India (Thomassen 2010).

Thinking with liminality: words of caution

In contemporary literature liminality is being applied to a growing number of sub-fields. In anthropology, the liminal has in recent decades been connected to the widespread notions of fluid or hybrid culture (Gupta and Ferguson 1992). Liminality is productively adopted by a growing number of scholars within International Relations (see Malksöo 2010; Yanik 2011). Liminality is also applied to analyse a diversity of minority cultures. Trans-sexuality, or any form of 'trans-gender', may be seen and experienced as liminal (Wilson 2002). Minority groups may be seen as occupying liminal socio-spatial positions. Certain minorities may indeed resemble quite closely the neophytes as described by

Turner: 'The neophytes are sometimes said to "be in another place". They have physical but not social reality, hence they have to be hidden, since it is a paradox, a scandal, to see what ought not to be there' (Turner, 1967: 97). This would be particularly evident for groups like stateless people or illegal immigrants.

To write from the interstices, from the in-between, can be recognized as a strategy in much postmodern or postcolonial literature and contemporary writing. For Homi Bhabha (1994), for example, liminality relates to cultural hybridity. In much postmodern literature, the liminal positively has come to represent an interstitial position between fixed identifications. Liminality represents a possibility for a cultural hybridity that entertains *difference* without an assumed or imposed hierarchy, and in a very general way it is this position that has been embraced in literature, cultural studies and anthropology. The general tendency here is to positively assert liminality as a vantage point from which to think, write and represent otherness and articulate diversity. In many ways, these understandings of liminality are a continuation of Victor Turner's work on the liminoid.

While recognizing the importance of Victor Turner's insights, I argue that we should hesitate to simply follow him (and his followers) here, and that we need to re-address the question: How exactly can we employ the concept of liminality toward an understanding of social, cultural and political processes in modernity? In his ethnographic accounts, Turner repeatedly identified parallels with non-tribal or 'modern' societies, clearly sensing that what he argued for the Ndembu had relevance far beyond the specific ethnographic context. At the level of empirical application, Turner provided two concrete suggestions:

a   In a famous article, 'Liminal to Liminoid, in Play, Flow and Ritual: an essay in comparative symbology' (1983[1974]), Turner suggested that liminal experiences in modern consumerist societies to a large extent have been replaced by 'liminoid' moments, where creativity and uncertainty unfold in art and leisure activities.
b   In his work on the Christian pilgrimage (1978), Turner argued that pilgrimage shares aspects of liminality because participants become equal, as they distance themselves from mundane structures and their social identities, leading to a homogenization of status and a strong sense of *communitas*.

The suggestions proposed in 'Liminal to Liminoid' had by far the largest effects on anthropology and neighbouring disciplines, as several of Turner's students would draw inspiration from Turner to study art, theatre, literature, leisure and tourism as examples of the liminoid. In art and leisure we recreate 'life in the conditional', the playful. Turner became even more of a reference point in the 1980s and 1990s, as anthropology and the wider social and human sciences went through a performative turn with a focus on process. 'Process' and 'performance' were always crucial terms to Turner, so his work was certainly open to all sorts of elaborations in that direction. The two easily most critical aspects of his work were exactly the ones that became 'codified' and that are now dominating academic and popular discourses on liminality.

First, the understanding of the liminal as relating in modern society primarily to art and leisure sidelines some of the clearly dangerous or problematic aspects of liminality. It is not irrelevant that Turner's ideas first started to spread around 1968, and then became more widely known and used with the postmodernist turn of the 1980s. Turner's (albeit hesitant) self-identification with the post-modernist turn certainly opened up a space for a usage of the term that he would, or should, have warned against.

Second, in his attempt to turn liminality into a more applicable term for modern consumer societies, Turner distinguished between 'symbolic systems and genres which developed before and after the Industrial Revolution' (1982: 30). While in itself a much oversimplified dichotomy, the problem is also that in contrast to liminal experiences, liminoid experiences are optional and do not involve a resolution of a personal crisis or a change of status. The liminoid is a break from normality, a playful as-if experience, but it loses the key feature of liminality: *transition*.

I would like to be very explicit here: I do not think that Turner's notion of the liminoid is an analytical step forwards. The notion of the liminoid has allowed for an indiscriminate application of liminality. On *that* account I suggest that we ought to be slightly conservative and return to the starting point of van Gennep: liminality has to do with transition, the ritual forms such transitions take, and the way in which transitions shape both persons and communities. This, however, does not mean that all transitions go smoothly. They do in fact not. And it is here that Turner's less discussed work on pilgrimage may in fact blaze the trail for us in a much more meaningful direction. Turner here caught a crucial mechanism involved in the liminal process: the temporal and spatial fixation of liminal conditions. It was this insight that brought the social theorist, Arpad Szakolczai, to diagnose modernity as a peculiar form of 'permanent liminality'.

The fixation of spatial and temporal liminality

Turner introduced this idea referring to a situation in which the suspended character of social life evidently takes on a more permanent character (Turner 1978). The pilgrimage is an emblematic case of liminality because it so evidently represents both a spatial and temporal (and moral/social) separation from the ordinary. This was much in line with what Turner himself had suggested earlier, namely that in the monastic and mendicant states of the world religions, transition had become a *permanent condition* (1969: 107). Here again, however, we have to be more than cautious about Turner's very positive description of liminality and the creative energies released in liminal spaces. Evidently, the fixation or permanentization of liminal conditions *somehow* relate to the disciplinary mechanisms of modern society. As argued by Szakolczai (2000, 2003), in order to grasp this connection the work of Turner must be brought into contact with social and political theory.

Turner was in fact, unbeknownst to himself, moving close to Max Weber with his insights. In his attempt to diagnose the particularity of the West, Weber had suggested (1963, 1978) that this particularity somehow resided in the 'everydayinization' of the 'extra-ordinary'; in particular, Weber argued that the world religions somehow problematized the basic self/world relations, leading to what Weber termed the 'religious rejections of the World'. These different world relations offered to Weber a clue to the development of a specific Western trajectory based on the social/historical elaborations of Christianity, epitomized in the monastic experiences, and how the search for salvation eventually led to what Weber termed 'this-worldly asceticism'. Weber argued that the kind of life style and the ascetic techniques that had developed within the closed institution of the monastery, in a clearly liminal spatio-temporal setting, eventually spread to the wider society: and in Protestant Europe this happened exactly as the monasteries were closed down and prohibited. In this process, the liminal, secluded and highly (self)regulated life style of monks turned into the ethical code set and life style of the ordinary Protestant in the this-worldly realm, which to Weber represented the underlying spirit of capitalism.

The concrete spatiality in which those forms of conduct developed needs to be stressed here. In fact, a series of thinkers came up with parallel observations while focusing their analysis on other 'closed institutions'. Besides Norbert Elias and his analysis of life conduct in court society (and how it, according to him, came to shape modern bourgeois life style), one must of course mention the works of Foucault, which until the late 1970s focused on another series of closed institutions (the clinic, the madhouse, the prison) whose regulatory mechanisms somehow had come to function within the wider social fabric – and indeed in the creation of modern subjectivity itself. The notion that liminality can become permanentized is of course close to another of Weber's concepts, namely 'routinization of charisma'. This concept refers to a deeply paradoxical but again *real* social process, lying at the very heart of practically any social or political or religious movement. Turner had himself introduced the term, 'institutionalization of liminality' in reference to monastic orders (1969: 107).

At one level of analysis, the point seems to be quite general: the institutions that make up a society (the military, priesthood, arguably even the city itself) have been created to deal with an extraordinary situation only in order to become permanent. While this in a way is 'normal', the experience of being 'stuck in liminality' is also highly critical and can take on peculiar and highly problematic forms that can indeed be identified. Using again van Gennep's tripartite structure, Szakolczai argued (2000: 220) that there are three types of permanent liminality, critically originating in the three phases of the rites of passage. 'Liminality becomes a permanent condition when any of the phases in this sequence [of separation, liminality and reaggregation] becomes frozen, as if a film stopped at a particular frame' (ibid.). He invoked a salient example for each type of permanent liminality: monasticism (with monks endlessly preparing the separation from the world), court society (with individuals continuously performing their roles in an endless ceremonial game), and Bolshevism (as exemplifying a society stuck in the final stage of a ritual passage). The two first suggestions build on insights by Turner himself, Weber (and his study of the Protestant ethic) and Elias (and his study of court culture). The understanding of communism as a specific 'third stage' type of permanent liminality can be sustained by pointing to the fact that 'communism was a regime in which the Second World War never ended' (ibid.: 223). Rather than healing the wounds and looking to the future, communist regimes sustained themselves by playing continuously on the sentiments of revenge, hatred and suffering, preventing the settling down of negative emotions (see also Horvath 1998).

In other words, without a proper re-integration, liminality is pure danger. The even larger claim made by Szakolczai was that modernity is itself a kind of permanent liminality: a continuous testing, a constant search for self-overcoming, an incessant breaking down of traditional boundaries, and an existential sense of alienation and loss of being-at-home that in the modern episteme establishes itself as normality.

Permanent liminality and the modern world

The contemporary scene seems to be characterized by an increasingly ambivalent attitude toward liminality: on the one hand a fear of liminal experiences as truly personality transforming events; on the other hand a celebratory stance towards any kind of liminality. On the one hand, and as stressed very much by Foucault, the modern world was always characterized by closing off everything that lay beyond the boundaries of rationality. This hallmark of modernity as excluding limit experiences was perhaps expressed most clearly by Kant. On the other hand it has also been argued, by a series of thinkers, writers and artists, that the modern world is somehow a 'carnival', a grotesque,[2] never-ending comedy, where limit experiences turn into norm, a frenzy that never really cools down (Thomassen 2012a).

The diagnostic effort by Szakolczai suggests that the modern episteme somehow represents a temporal permanentization of liminal conditions that at a given moment 'freeze' and turn into structure. But this temporal fixation of liminal conditions is paralleled by a spatial dynamic; it is increasingly evident that the modern world is characterized by a constant proliferation of empty spaces or non-spaces, a movement whereby the liminal becomes central and establishes itself as normality (Augé 1995). Surprisingly enough, this danger was signaled with great clarity by Plato (1995), in his discussion of the *Khora* in Timaeus. The question relates to one of Plato's main concerns in his later writings, namely the productive powers of nothingness, and how non-being turns into being. Here Plato reluctantly had to go beyond Parmenides, who had always insisted that nothing can grow out of nothing, and that one should therefore not talk about nothingness. Evidently Plato sensed that the end of the classical world critically had to do with exactly such a proliferation of non-space – a space in which the Sophist thrives. *Khora* is a void, an abyss, in which things can reproduce themselves infinitely, it 're-flects' like a mirror that is not affected by the image it reflects. *Khora* is without limit, without bottom, without ground. Like the number zero, which the Greeks dreaded so much and therefore never used, the *Khora* is nothingness and infinity at the same time. Plato, the founder of Western epistemology, somehow saw this implosion of nothingness as a lurking threat to the ordered world around him. But in that recognition Plato makes himself a theorist of the contemporary.

The temporal fixation of liminal conditions into social, political and cultural structures as recognized by Szakolczai is arguably paralleled by a spatial implosion of liminality. This critically involves a gradual loss of the distinction between liminal and ordinary spaces. The proliferation and celebration of liminal spatiality has become connected to the commercialization and intensifying social and political control of exactly such spaces, annulling their transformative potential while flattening our mental and physical landscapes. It is also this process that, far from deleting the playful and carnivalesque from the modern world, actually turns the world itself into a permanent carnival. This involves, as pointed out by Andrews (2009), a constant but often also hopeless search for 'experience'. In a world where an increasing number of people are in constant search for excitement and stimulation of the senses, boredom is always lurking around the corner. A carnival that never ends stops being fun; it turns into mechanical role play. Liminality cannot and should not be considered an end-point or a desirable state of being; when this happens, creativity and freedom lose their existential basis and turn into its opposites: boredom and a sense of imprisonment.

By simply taking a celebratory stance towards liminality in our attempts to go beyond modernity we are indeed celebrating the perhaps most critical aspect of that very modernity: the ceaseless drive toward overcoming traditional boundaries, or, using the expression of Giesen (2009), the constant 'lure to transgression'. This pressure toward constant transformation, the seeking for hybridity, intimately relates to a sense of exile and homelessness, which many a postmodern writer has positively identified as a condition of being; it also seems an attitude that is currently underwriting an emerging global cosmopolitanism. Any effective response to this development must entail a reconsideration of human experiences in liminality and how such experiences can and *must* be channelled back into meaningful 'background structures' and a feeling-at-home in the world. It is impossible simply to feel at home everywhere if one does not feel at home *somewhere*. The recognition of the liminal characteristics of modernity was certainly what brought Szakolczai in the 'opposite' direction, leading him to introduce the concept of 'home' as central to social and political theory (Szakolczai 2008). It does in fact seem that there is no other remedy to permanent liminality than to re-establish some notion of background in which individual action can be understood and measured, and in which frenetic movement finds a rest. We need to turn to the concreteness of lived space.

Conclusion: on being-at-home in a meaningful world

This chapter has attempted to open a debate on how we think and live with liminality today. The tendency in the reception and application of liminality in the social and cultural sciences, in art and performance is that liminality represents an unordered, chaotic element of creativity and freedom in a modern world that was drowning with (Kantian) rationality. It is particularly clear that many writers see liminality as fitting within a larger framework of social constructivism, or as resonating with poststructuralist theories, positing themselves against more structural or nominalist philosophies or world-views. There are, however, strong grounds to reject this reception. Social constructivism developed as a paradigm in order to stress human agency in the meaningful construction of the 'World', positing itself as an alternative to more dominant rationalist-positivist scientific views, as rational choice theory in political science or Realism in International Relations. What is rarely recognized is the extent to which rational choice theory and social constructivism share a foundational epistemology: namely that the world itself is essentially unordered, and that human beings impose their order upon it via their (rational or not) choices, ideas and acts. Rationalism and social constructivism alike predicate upon a prior distancing to the world. They thus perpetuate a kind of epistemic homelessness which goes to the heart of modern thinking.

Turner's work can instead be pushed in a different direction, and to some extent this direction had indeed been indicated by van Gennep himself, and was taken up by Turner in his later work. Turner realized that liminality served not only to identify the importance of in-between periods, but also to understand the human reactions to liminal experiences: the way in which personality was shaped by liminality, the sudden foregrounding of agency, and the sometimes dramatic tying together of thought and experience. Turner saw the parallels between his own project and the philosophy of Dilthey for this reason (see for example Turner 1982: 12–19; 1988: 84–97). This was indeed an important and momentous intellectual encounter, made late in Turner's life (Szakolczai 2004: 69–72). The recognition made by Turner was quite simply that experiences are in a formal sense ordered sequences. This of course does not mean that liminality is *simply* structure and order – to make such a claim would be meaningless: liminal spaces and moments are indeed characterized by contingency and uncertainty. However, liminal *experiences* do have a 'form' or a recognizable 'pattern'. It is important to stress that van Gennep did not really launch a theory of ritual, as much as he claimed to have detected the underlying *patterns* in rites. Where Durkheim established a priori categories as the units of his taxonomy, van Gennep inferred these units from the tripartite structure of the ceremonies themselves.

I think it is possible to take van Gennep's framework even one step further here – and a further step away from any social constructivist interpretation that invariably will end up stressing the freedom of human creativity: for van Gennep the basic fact of transition did indeed somehow tie the human being to nature.

Nature must here be understood in the best of Hellenic-classical traditions as a meaningfully ordered *cosmos*, an animated universe, rather than a chaos upon which we, human beings, must impose our order. Transitions from group to group or from one social situation to the next are a 'fact of society', van Gennep said (1960: 3). However, for van Gennep transitions are also a 'fact of existence' that ties our individual and social life to nature: 'The universe itself is governed by a periodicity which has repercussions on human life, with stages and transitions, movements forward, and periods of relative inactivity' (ibid.: 3). Van Gennep returned to the parallel to nature in the conclusion where it inspired him to the beautiful and significant closure of the book:

> Finally, the series of human transitions has, among some peoples, been linked to the celestial passages, the revolutions of the planets, and the phases of the moon. It is indeed a cosmic conception that relates the stages of human existence to those of plant and animal life and, by a sort of pre-scientific divination, joins them to the great rhythms of the universe.
>
> (ibid.: 194)

Here again the contrast to Durkheim (and contemporary social constructivism) is very stark: for Durkheim human beings bestow order on nature from their self-created social order, a clearly neo-kantian position. The style and content of Van Gennep's closing paragraph much more closely resembles the cosmology found in Plato's *Timeus*, the work in which Plato most clearly posits the recognition of the beauty and order of the natural world as the condition for living and *thinking* rationally. This can also be said differently: the role of human beings in the universe is not to erect order, create schemes, concepts and models and then impose these upon an unstructured chaos, to 'build the world' from scratch. This tendency was exactly what Eric Voegelin would come to recognize as the Gnostic nature of modernity (Thomassen 2012b). Instead, our role in this universe and on this planet – the only one we have – should rather be to humbly 'tune in' to the beauty of the world. Or, as van Gennep said, join the great hymns of the universe.

Notes

1 This chapter is a revised version of a conference paper first presented at the Symposium on 'Liminal landscapes: re-mapping the field', John Moores University, Liverpool, July 2010. Parts of the chapter are elaborations of a previously published article, 'The Uses and Meanings of Liminality' (Thomassen 2009) which appeared in a special issue dedicated to liminality in *International Political Anthropology*.
2 The word comes from 'grotto', e.g. cave.

References

Andrews, H. (2009) 'Tourism as a "moment of being"', *Suomen Antropologi: Journal of the Finnish Anthropological Society*, 34(2): 5–21.

Augé, M. (1995) *Non-places. Introduction to an anthropology of supermodernity*, London: Verso.

Barnatt, J. and Edmonds, M. (2002) 'Places apart? Caves and Monuments in Neolithic and Earlier Bronze Age Britain', *Cambridge Archaeological Journal*, 12(1): 113–129.

Benko, G. and Strohmayer, U. (eds) (1997) *Space and Social Theory. Interpreting Modernity and Postmodernity*, Oxford: Blackwell.

Bhabha, H. (1994) *The Location of Culture*, London: Routledge.

Durkheim, É. (1967) *The Elementary Forms of Religious Life*, New York: Free Press.

Endsjø, D. (2000) 'To lock up Eleusis. A question of liminal space', *Numen*, 47: 351–386.

Giesen, B. (2009) 'The three projects of modernity', *International Political Anthropology*, 2(2): 239–250.

Gupta, A. and Ferguson, J. (1992) 'Beyond Culture: Space, Identity and the Politics of difference', *Cultural Anthropology*, 7(1): 6–23.

Horvath, A. (1998) 'Tricking into the Position of the Outcast: A Case Study in the Emergence and Effects of Communist Power', *Political Psychology*, 19(2): 331–347.

Jaspers, K. (1953) *The Origin and Goal of History*, New Haven and London: Yale University Press.

Malksöo, M. (2010) 'The challenge of liminality for International Relations Theory', paper presented at the annual meeting of the 'Theory vs. Policy? Connecting Scholars and Practitioners', New Orleans, 17 February 2010.

Plato (1995) *Timeo*, Traduzione di F. Acri, Milano: Principato Editore.

Szakolczai, A. (2000) *Reflexive Historical Sociology*, London: Routledge.

Szakolczai, A. (2003) *The Genesis of Modernity*, London: Routledge.

Szakolczai, A. (2004) 'Experiential Sociology', *Theoria*, 103: 59–87.

Szakolczai, A. (2008) 'Citizenship and Home: Political Allegiance and its Background', *International Political Anthropology*, 1(1): 57–76.

Thomassen, B. (2009) 'The Uses and Meanings of Liminality', *International Political Anthropology*, 2(1): 5–27.

Thomassen, B. (2010) 'Anthropology, Multiple Modernities and the Axial Age Debate', *Anthropological Theory*, 10(4): 321–342.

Thomassen, B. (2012a) 'Anthropology and its Multiple Modernities: When Concepts Matter', *Journal of the Royal Anthropological Institute*, 18: 160–178.

Thomassen, B. (2012b) 'Reason and religion in Rawls: Voegelin's Challenge', *Philosophia*, forthcoming.

Turner, E. (1985) 'Prologue: From the Ndembu to Broadway', in V. Turner (edited by E. Turner), *On the Edge of the Bush*, Arizona: The University of Arizona Press, 1–15.

Turner, V. (1967) 'Betwixt and Between: The Liminal Period in *Rites de Passage*', in *The Forest of Symbols*, New York: Cornell University Press.

Turner, V. (1969) *The Ritual Process*, Chicago: Aldine.

Turner, V. (1974) *Dramas, Fields, and Metaphors*, Ithaca: Cornell University Press.

Turner, V. and E. Turner (1978) *Image and Pilgrimage in Christian Culture*, Columbia: Columbia University Press.

Turner, V. (1982) *From Ritual to Theatre*, New York: PAJ Publications.

Turner, V. (1983[1974]) 'Liminal to Liminoid, in Play, Flow, and Ritual: An Essay in Comparative Symbology' in J.C. Harris and R. Park (eds), *Play, Games and Sports in Cultural Contexts*. Champaign: Human Kinetics Publishers, 123–164.

Turner, V. (1985) *On the Edge of the Bush* (edited by E. Turner), Arizona: The University of Arizona Press.

Turner, V. (1988) *The Anthropology of Performance*, New York: PAJ Publications.

Van Gennep, A. (1960) *The Rites of Passage*, Chicago: Chicago University Press.

Weber, M. (1963) *The Sociology of Religion*, Boston, Mass.: Beacon.

Weber, M. (1978) *Economy and Society*, Berkeley: University of California Press.

Wilson, M. (2002) ' "I am the Prince of Pain, for I am a Princess in the Brain": Liminal Transgender Identities, Narratives and the Elimination of Ambiguities', *Sexualities*, 5(4): 425–448.

Yanik, L.K. (2011) 'Constructing Turkish "exceptionalism": Discourses of liminality and hybridity in post-Cold War Turkish foreign policy', *Political Geography*, 30(2): 80–89.

3   Places remember events

Towards an ethics of encounter

Emily Orley

James Joyce scribbled the words 'places remember events' in the margin of his notes for *Ulysses.*[1] It is an intriguing idea and one that I would like to take seriously in this chapter. Indeed, I suggest that it can be actively employed as a method to encounter the places that we pass through every day. This raises a number of interesting questions: What if these places, as anthropomorphised entities, really could remember? What impact would this have on our own behaviour, as visitors in those places? How might this serve as the stimulus for the production of artistic and critical work in and about a particular place? And, finally, how might it affect how we, in turn, remember the place ourselves? I will begin my enquiry by drawing on writings from a range of disciplines, including those of cultural geographer Doreen Massey, philosopher Emmanuel Levinas, art historian Lucy Lippard and anthropologist Keith Basso. My argument unfolds in six parts. Parts one to four offer an analysis of the concept of place. I begin by examining the idea that 'places remember events' and go on to juxtapose this notion with Massey's definition of place as 'unfixed, contested and multiple' (1994: 5). Parts five and six of the chapter outline a method of encountering place, which is broken down into two stages. Here I suggest a series of contemporary place-specific artworks which I feel exemplify the method that I put forward. Quiet, transient and open-ended, these are works which do not seek to fix or restrict the places that they engage with. Rather, they offer up the various landscapes they inhabit as liminal, and in this way inspire new, creative and responsible ways of encounter elsewhere.

3.1 Places remember events

What might it mean to take the notion that places remember events at face value, to approach sites as embodied? To say that a place remembers is to endow it with anthropomorphic qualities, to suggest that it is an entity that has the capacity to remember. This is not a new idea. Ecologists, for example, often refer to the earth as a single living organism with human attributes.[2] Also, travel writers have been representing places as if they were people with their own distinctive characteristics for many years. Sociologist John Eade presents a study of the way London has been personified in tourist guide-books (2001).[3] He demonstrates how viewing the city as a person can be a useful and evocative, although potentially problematic, way of achieving an understanding of it.

Anthropologist Keith Basso examines the phenomena of anthropomorphising places in more depth. He asserts that not much is known of the ways in which diverse populations across the world understand place, how they comprehend or make themselves aware of the world around them, but observes, however, that 'places possess a marked capacity for triggering acts of self-reflection' (1996: 53–4). By drawing on the writings of Martin Heidegger and Jean-Paul Sartre,[4] he describes what he calls a process of 'interanimation' that occurs between individuals and specific places. This transpires when the individual begins to pay attention to a place, which causes it to generate its own field of meaning 'through a vigorous conflation of attentive subject and geographical object' (Basso 1996: 56). As the place animates the thoughts and feelings of the attentive visitor, these same thoughts and feelings animate the place in turn, in a reciprocal and dynamic process. Places, which he calls 'human constructions par excellence', are thus brought to life, so that 'even in total stillness, [they] may seem to speak' (ibid.). But, although places are animated in this way, they express only what their animators allow them to say. Basso writes: 'their disembodied voices, immanent though inaudible, are merely those of people speaking silently to themselves' (ibid.). While I would encourage us to think of a place as an entity that remembers, I would also encourage us to understand that, while they retain traces of their past in their make-up, these traces are animated by the individual people that encounter them. In other words, a place remembers only when we animate it to do so by actively sensing it and paying attention to its physical details.

The concept of memory is widely contested and has been extensively theorised, emerging as an influential field of study in its own right in the 1990s. It is generally agreed, however, that it is 'a set of cognitive capacities by which humans and other animals retain information and reconstruct past experiences, usually for present purposes' (Sutton 2003).[5] It involves a complex but fallible system of storing information. Although 'memory' has become a leading term in cultural discourse, however, historian Wulf Kansteiner (2002) argues that memory studies have not done enough to establish a clear conceptual and methodological basis for memory processes, particularly when it comes to collective memory.[6] Memory is too often referred to as a nebulous idea that exists without agency. Writers on the subject have a tendency to not attend to *who* is doing the remembering at any one time. I would like to assert here, therefore, that I am not talking about memory in a vague sense, but the memory held in places, animated by the people who visit those places. (The remembering is done *by* the places even if it is set in motion by the people in those places.) Places retain the traces of what has happened there, within their physical make-up. However much a wall is whitewashed, evidence of previous activity remains underneath. Places hold their own histories. And this holding-of-histories, this remembering that they 'do' can stretch from the banal (the crack in the wall above my desk: however much I try to cover it up or fill it in, traces of it will always be there, underneath) to much more profound realities (the site of a massacre for example).

There is a body of work spanning a range of disciplines on memory and sites of trauma (much of which comes under the umbrella of memory studies). Recent work includes, for example, Maria Tumarkin's examination of six epicentres of national trauma and tragedy across the world (including New York, Sarajevo and the Kuta region in Bali) in order to unearth and examine the psychological investments that these places hold (2005). There is also Malcolm Foley and John Lennon's investigation of the concept of 'dark tourism' (2000) and, in a similar vein, Laurie Beth Clark's examination of 'trauma tourism' (2006).[7] Although this is a rich and fascinating field of enquiry, what I am interested in here are places that we might encounter every day, that are generally more 'ordinary' or commonplace and less immediately provocative; I propose that all places remember, and all places warrant our attention. Although some places (such as sites of trauma) might remember in more raw and conspicuous ways, and often invite more extreme responses, I am interested in places that we might encounter in everyday contexts.

3.2 Places as events

One way of thinking about place, then, is as an anthropomorphised entity that is able to remember. Another way, which is, I think, equally important, but may seem rather contradictory at first, is to see place as a 'constellation of traject-ories', in Massey's words. She calls for a progressive sense of place, one that is 'unfixed, contested and multiple ... [and] open and porous' (1994: 5). She argues that we cannot, or rather must not establish boundaries around, or attempt to secure identities of, place (or places).[8] She shows how place has been conceptu-alised as singular and bounded, and that any search for place reveals a desire for fixity and security in a world of fast-paced living and change. While she recog-nises that a sense of place, of rooted-ness can provide stability, she also demon-strates that it can be problematic, and can encourage what she calls 'reactionary nationalisms, competitive localisms and introverted obsessions with "heritage"' (ibid.: 151). For Massey, therefore, to want to fix the identity of a place is an essentialist tendency that reinforces past traditions and staid ways of thinking.

For her, to associate a 'sense of place' with stasis, memory and nostalgia is neither creative nor productive. Any claims to internal histories or to timeless identities of place can therefore be seen as romanticised and narrow-minded, and delving into the past for internalised origins of place is an isolating and confin-ing practice. To want to establish boundaries around place is to be unwilling to change, to move on, to be open. Seeking to define place also becomes problem-atic then, for the same reasons. Instead, for Massey place needs to be seen as something with no inside or outside, but as something that is both porous and unfixed. She writes:

> Instead then, of thinking of places as areas with boundaries around, they can
> be imagined as articulated moments in networks of social relations and
> understandings, but where a large proportion of those relations, experiences

and understandings are constructed on a far larger scale than what we happen to define for that moment as the place itself.

(Massey 1994: 154)

Thus, a history of a place is accumulated, made up of layers and layers of 'different sets of linkages' (ibid.: 156) to both the local and to the wider world.[9]

Like Massey, Lippard also sees places as articulated moments made up of connections, although she makes more of the layering of histories that accumulate in place and become the bedrock of future action. She writes: 'A layered location replete with human histories and memories, place has width as well as depth. It is about connections, what surrounds it, what formed it, what happened there, what will happen there' (1997: 7). Massey seems to echo this idea, albeit in a slightly different way:

> What is special about place is not some romance of a pre-given collective identity or the eternity of the hills. Rather, what is special about place is precisely that throwntogetherness, the unavoidable challenge of negotiating a here-and-now (itself drawing on a history and geography of then and theres); and a negotiation which must take place within and between both human and nonhuman.
>
> (Massey 2005: 140)

By emphasising that place is about the encounter with the here-and-now, about a coming-together of trajectories on all sorts of levels, Massey is also showing how time becomes a key factor in our relationships with place. Place is an event. The present, the now, becomes all important, as this is the only time that place exists as it is. Place is 'irretrievably, here *and* now. It won't be the same "here" when it is no longer "now"' (ibid.: 139). Tomorrow's 'now' is not the same as yesterday's, and this applies to 'here' too. Place is therefore relative and nowhere is stable. Seen in this way, all landscapes are liminal, transitory by their very nature, constantly suspended in a state of in-between-ness. Massey uses a range of geological examples (such as the gradual shifting of mountains, tides and the poles) to illustrate this spatially (ibid.: 138, 139). But these changing sets of linkages that make up place stretch backwards and forwards in time as well as geographically 'outwards'.

So place can also be seen as an event.

3.3 Places as events that remember other events

On the one hand we can view places (this place, where you find yourself reading these words) as anthropomorphised and able to remember. On the other hand they are constellations of trajectories – yours, mine, all those people that were here (in this place) before. They constitute an ever-changing set of networks which are thrown together and dispersed again and again over time. They are events. But there is a contradiction. A place cannot be an event and an anthropomorphised entity at the same time. Indeed to see place as having human qualities may lead us to bind or fix it (in the way that Massey warns against), and to forget that it is constructed through social, cultural, political and economic processes. If we say that a place remembers there is the danger of viewing it as a self-contained entity that exists independently of the people living or passing through there (Eade 2001: 5). I suggest, however, that it is useful to bring together these two apparently contradictory ways of viewing place: to approach it as embodied (and able to remember), but to understand that its 'body' is unfixed and ever-changing. This might make us begin to see the places we inhabit in a new light. Despite the risks inherent in regarding places as anthropomorphised, there is nevertheless something to be gained from it, as long as is it done in a spirit of self-reflexive awareness.

So, while being a complicated and unfixed set of networks, place might also have the capacity to remember, to hold traces of past activity, in the loosest sense. While it remembers, it does not necessarily do this in a human way. The memory of place may then be thought of as fluid, transitory, and open-ended, activated only by those who pass through. The memory of place is not bound to one particular social group or time. I propose then, that places are events that might remember other events. And if we can see a place like this, it might (I hope) affect how we behave towards it.

3.4 Ethics

If place is a throwntogetherness, we are part of what is being thrown together. We are all implicated in the places that we pass through and inhabit. This implication in place involves, by necessity, a participation, whether we are witting (and willing) or not. In whatever way we behave in the places that we find ourselves, our actions (and inactions), even the most ephemeral, can leave traces.

Other people have passed through and influenced how we experience the places we find ourselves in now. In the same way, we can influence how others will experience these places later. This argument has wider political and environmental implications: we are part of larger interrelated and interdependent processes or ecosystems. By becoming aware of our involvement in these processes (or constellations), we can become aware of how, individually, we can maintain, repair or even change them. We are part of place and place is part of us. By first and foremost making places the object of our awareness and reflection, we begin to think about our own position in the world and our own modes of behaviour towards it. The implication here is that this way of seeing and being in place encourages us to become conscious of ourselves as moral agents, capable of reflecting on our situations.

I will underpin this idea by juxtaposing two broadly construed ethical perspectives: Emmanuel Levinas' writings (1985, 1989, 1996, 2001) and deep ecology's emerging holistic orientation toward moral value and human identity (Gottlieb 1994; Light and Rolston 2003; Sessions 1995; Witoszek and Brennan 1999). Although these two perspectives are not compatible in many ways, they provide a useful basis for my argument here, as I take from them both a call to equality and responsibility – to the other, in one instance, and to the planet, in another. I do not propose to provide an in-depth analysis or critique of Levinas' thought here, or the philosophy of deep ecology, but rather, I will borrow ideas from both frameworks to suggest a specifically ethical approach to place.

Levinas' general position, centred on the self in its performance of a respectful relationship with alterity, provides an important frame for thinking about an ethics of encounter (Levinas 2001). This mode of ethical encounter must necessarily recognise that we cannot know the other and must not attempt to fix their identities with our own narratives. We must be open to their understanding of themselves. As we come face to face with the other, in a recognition of our mutual vulnerability, this encourages relationships of openness, dialogue and respect for difference (Levinas 2001: 200). Levinas puts forward a non-reciprocal relation of responsibility that I believe we can bring to our encountering of place. While we are in a place (any place for that matter, the space you occupy now), we can pay attention to others' stories and practices of place. In this way, in the moment of encounter, in the moment of being here, we can engage in a relationship of care toward this place, the others that have been here before us and those that will be there after us. With this attitude, we hold a long view of how our actions and inactions affect the life possibilities of others. And so, we accept an ethical responsibility. We ready ourselves to question our own identity, our own narratives, our own spatial claims.

This model of ethical encounter overlaps in interesting ways with the philosophy of deep ecology, introduced in the 1970s by Norwegian philosopher Arne Næss.[10] Deep ecology considers humankind to be an integral part of its environment, and stresses the complex interrelatedness of all that is. It proposes that there are no isolated 'things' but an interlocking web of relations in a constant state of flux. Individuals are 'centers of interaction' or 'knots' in this web, constituted by their relationships.[11] It is a holistic movement, therefore, that recognises the inherent value of all living beings and the ecological and cultural diversity of natural systems. Species and ecosystems are classified as entities in their own right, with their own ethical interests. Deep ecologists advocate the use of this view in shaping environmental policies. The philosophy has been developed since the 1970s by a wide range of philosophers and environmentalists and puts forward a radical ethics, which is not without its critics[12] but for the purpose of my argument here it provides a useful, egalitarian frame of reference, calling, as it does, for a particularly heightened degree of moral sensibility and therefore responsibility on the part of any individual engaging with place as an entity in itself. By reflecting on, and being aware of, her engagement with place, the individual becomes conscious not only of her physical position in the place, but how she is implicated as part of a wider 'web', in which others are and have been equally implicated, over time.

By bringing these two different perspectives together here, I am saying that while we are implicated in the places we pass through, these places also exist outside of us, as other. This theory encourages an ethical and creative mode of encounter that I suggest can be broken down into two stages, which I will outline below.

3.5 Encounter

The first stage involves a self-reflexive awareness of ourselves in place. To do this, I suggest that first we anthropomorphise place: that we literally regard it as having the human ability to 'do': to live, to grow and to remember. I propose, then, that we observe how it 'behaves' in the present time of viewing by bodily inhabiting the place and by being fully present in it.[13] This allows us to engage in a close, hushed and stilled observation of the place's details. In other words, if the visitor in a place is still and quiet enough, and pays close enough attention, she can become aware of what (and indeed how) the place is 'doing' around her. She can also become aware of her own response. We see the place with intelligence. It is a method of encounter that cannot be rushed. That is not to say that to engage with place in a meaningful way always has to involve a slow process, but that, as visitors, we concentrate on the quality of attention that we bring to the place. As Basso suggests, relationships to places are 'most richly lived and surely felt' when people make them the object of awareness and reflection, when they self-consciously attend to them, pausing to 'actively sense them' (1996: 54). It is then that we 'become sharply aware of the complex attachments that link [us] to features of the physical world' (ibid.: 55).

The second stage of the method involves a processing of or responding to our engagement with place. This can involve a thinking-through and remembering of the encounter, a documentation of it (in the broadest sense), but also, perhaps, the production of work that invites new encounters, that encourages new dialogues between the people visiting that place and the place itself. So the ethical relationship fostered in stage one, becomes, in turn, the ground upon which creative action might be attempted.

The possibility is opened up, then, for making other work, inventing new critical and/or artistic projects developed from the initial encounter. In this way, places can be animated as sites for reflection, creativity and change. But it is important, when responding to place in this way, that we are conscious of ourselves as rememberers and imaginers, that we are alert to the fact that we bring our own preconceptions (cultural, social and historical) to the context of the place, and will inevitably project our own fears and desires on the surfaces that it offers. And that these, in turn, will leave their own traces.

Artistic works that I particularly feel embody ethical responses to place (or places) are therefore quiet, open-ended and transitory. Importantly, while drawing the visitor's attention to the place in question, they also invite him or her to imagine further. These conditions tie in closely with Lippard's definition of a place-specific art (1997). Indeed, place-specific art for Lippard is an art governed by a place ethic. It is a form of art that illuminates and accentuates its location, rather than just occupying it. It is temporal and ephemeral, 'produced in partnership with the imagination and responses of its viewers or users' (Lippard 1997: 290). She suggests that perhaps the place-specific work she is proposing is something small and subtle that highlights the place, that makes the place the art itself. As much as a place-specific art, I feel that she is equally promoting, simply, a way of appreciating place. Lippard's place-specific artwork, which 'offers tantalizing glimpses of new ways to enter everyday life' (ibid.: 286), becomes, therefore, a tool to facilitate this way of appreciating.

Examples of contemporary works which I feel are place-specific in Lippard's sense, and invite the type of encounter I put forward here, include John Newling's 2010 *Root Zone* and *Local History* projects. For *Root Zone*, he first cultivated an area of land under a tree outside his house to grow herbs and strawberries which he encouraged local residents to harvest and take cuttings from. For *Local History*, he collected and pressed leaves and flowers from that site and placed them into books in the local history section of his local library, so that readers might come across them by chance, as delicate, evocative and strangely personal markers. According to his website, his projects all review 'the tacit agreements of place', and I think offer fresh ways of encountering the places in which we all find ourselves day to day.[14]

In a slightly different vein, there is the work of Lucy Harrison, who often combines photographs, observations and chance encounters with discarded historical material (such as old and obsolete tourist guides, discarded letters and postcards or found images), to explore specific places and examine the subjective nature of how we experience place, memory and location. For part of her 2009 *Remains* project, for example, she investigated the Arts Barn at the Institute of Contemporary Interdisciplinary Arts (ICIA) at Bath University (where she was in residence) in its last months before demolition.[15] By gathering written and oral histories, found materials and her own documentation, she provided a novel and multi-faceted memorial for the building. This was displayed alongside a series of photographs of other places (demolition sites in particular) and writings relating to the buildings that have been there previously and to other coincidences that she remembered from those locations.

A different example of a place-specific work in this context might be Roger Hiorns' 2008–9 *Seizure* installation in London, where he filled a condemned council flat in Elephant and Castle with copper sulphate solution and then drained it, which resulted in vibrant blue crystals growing to cover all the interior surfaces. Visitors were allowed to walk around inside the small rooms free of charge and for as long as they liked after donning a pair of wellington boots. The silent and unexpectedly beautiful work was both spectacular and understated, and invited the viewer to pay attention to the details of the building, the place, in new and imaginative ways.

There is also Wrights and Sites' recent contribution to the *Wonders of Weston* 2010 programme of artworks, *Everything You Need to Build a Town is Here*.[16] For this project they created a series of 41 signs scattered across a variety of locations in Weston-super-Mare, from public gardens, to the museum, car parks, restaurants and allotments. The brief and carefully-worded metal plaques appear without explanation and offer instructions, observations or comments, which are designed to encourage the reader to somehow engage with their immediate vicinity by way of real or imagined actions. At the Old Town Quarry, which the artists describe as the keystone site for the series, there is a

Figure 3.1 Lucy Harrison, images from *Remains*, 2009: (top) University of Bath Arts Barn, 2009; (bottom) Olympic Construction site, 2007. Reproduced by kind permission of the artist.

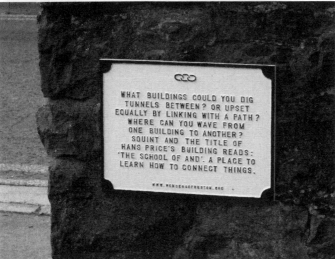

WHAT BUILDINGS COULD YOU DIG
TUNNELS BETWEEN? OR UPSET
EQUALLY BY LINKING WITH A PATH?
WHERE CAN YOU WAVE FROM
ONE BUILDING TO ANOTHER?
SQUINT AND THE TITLE OF
HANS PRICE'S BUILDING READS:
'THE SCHOOL OF AND'. A PLACE TO
LEARN HOW TO CONNECT THINGS.

Figure 3.2 Wrights and Sites, images from *Everything You Need to Build a Town is Here*, 2010. Hans Price's 'School of Art and Science' at Weston-super-Mare with plaque by Wrights and Sites. Reproduced by kind permission of Phil Smith.

map and a description of the project in its entirety. Not only does the work lead the visitor (tourist and resident alike) to unexpected places, but it also highlights the layering of historical and contemporary stories and associations that surround us everywhere.

The final example of a place-specific work that I would like to offer here, which also operates as both art object and tool for facilitating new ways to enter everyday life (Lippard 1997: 286), is one of Jane Rendell's site-writings[17]: her 2002 text-based installation, *Confessional Construction*. Rendell was invited to write a page that would be pasted to an outside wall of BookArtBookShop in London for a month as part of a project curated by Brigid McLeer called LLAW. The page or poster presented three voices: an autobiographical statement which was interwoven with more critical reflections on what it means to confess, both of which were placed alongside a column of footnotes, numbered from top to bottom (as one would build a wall) containing specifications on how to build a wall. It referenced the site in which it was installed (the wall and the bookshop) while also suggesting that a confession is a construction rather than a revelation of the self (Rendell 2010: 53). As with the other artworks that I have discussed here, it formed a compelling call to public imagination, drawing on the specifics of a place, as far as one can be specific about place, given its ever-shifting, liminal make-up.

To summarise, the mode of encounter that I suggest here has two stages, or rather I suggest an encounter and then a creative and ethical response to that encounter. Massey describes these two stages succinctly when she writes 'We come to each place with the necessity, the responsibility, to examine anew *and* to invent' (2005: 169, emphasis added). In *The Lure of the Local*, Lippard elaborates: 'If places are stories waiting to be unearthed, artists could be the storytellers who can relate the local to the grander, more familiar and perhaps more insidious narratives. Every story told suggests those that remain buried and untold' (1997: 287). Stories beget stories, of course. Not only do the works I have discussed here invite their spectators to examine specific places anew, but by unearthing particular stories, they encourage the invention of more. And the more stories that are created in relation to a place, the more that place remains 'multiple and unfixed'. Whether we encounter place directly (by passing through it for example) or through an artwork, if our response to it can be creative, it is also ethical.

3.6 What now? (Or: conclusion)

I would like to think that any place can be engaged with in the way that I set out here. This includes the places that we take for granted (where we sleep, where we work), places of transit (for example, the station we rush through each morning on the way to work, the garage where we refuel the car). It includes places we do or do not want to let go of (where we grew up perhaps), places that are forgotten and neglected (underneath, behind, and of course between) and smaller places still: table-tops, pages in books, folded-down corners, margins.

Joyce scribbled the words 'places remember events' in the margin of his notes for *Ulysses*. The margin on that particular page, as a place in its own right, remembered him. This place, here and now (where you are) might remember you. You are implicated. You are responsible.

Notes

1 James Joyce, 1919 Ulysses notesheet for 'Cyclops'. See P.F. Herring (1972: 119).
2 Environmentalist James Lovelock originally renamed the earth 'Gaia' (which is ancient Greek for 'earth' and also refers to the primal goddess and original mother of all beings) and put forward the Gaia hypothesis (1979/2000).
3 See also Richard Sennett (1994), where he examines the history of the development of the city in terms of the human body's function and perception, describing the city's activities in the terminology of physiology, in terms of veins and arteries for example.
4 He refers specifically to Heidegger's 1951 essay 'Building Dwelling Thinking' (Farrell Krell 1993: 347–63) and Cumming's writings on Sartre (1965: 87–91).
5 Two recent and useful resources on memory and memory studies include Rossington and Whitehead (2007) and Misztal (2003).
6 Kansteiner echoes the discussion in Klein (2000).
7 See her website: http://traumatourism.net (accessed 28 August 2008). Other interesting works on trauma, memory and place include Jordan (2006) and Till (2005).
8 Environmental historians have also developed ways of talking about place that tie in closely with Massey's progressive sense of place. See, for example, Cronon (1991) and Cronon *et al.* (1992: 28–51).
9 Relevant in this context are also Gandy (2002) and Clayton (2000). These deal with the way in which places (New York and British Columbia respectively) have been constructed through relationships with the outside.
10 For an in-depth discussion of how Levinas' ideas can be read in conjunction with environmental ethics, see Llewelyn (1991). He presents the possibility that the concept of the Other may be extended in an environmental sense to embrace all living organisms and the non-living components of environments. Indeed, he develops an 'eco-ethics' by cross-reading Levinas and Heidegger among others.
11 See Næss (1973), reprinted in Sessions (1995: 151–5). For a historical survey and commentary on the development of deep ecology, see Witoszek and Brennan (1999). See also Warwick Fox's 'Deep Ecology: A New Philosophy of Our Time?' in Light and Rolston (2003: 252–61). For a useful overview of environmental ethics more generally by Clare Palmer, see Light and Rolston (2003: 15–37).
12 For example, eco-feminists such as Val Plumwood (1993) argue that deep ecology provides no space for difference, and environmental historian Ramachandra Guha (Witoszek and Brennan 1999: 473–9) condemns it as being elitist and imperialist, taking away from the usefulness of 'shallow ecology', which deals with concrete and particular environmental issues that might be more pressing in poorer developing countries.
13 I borrow Marc Augé's term here (1995: 85). I read his definition of the 'non-place', as an attitude or feeling on behalf of the individual rather than a physical, feature-less location. Non-place is a travelling-through of place, a momentary dissolving or blurring of place.
14 See www.john-newling.com (accessed 17 February 2011).
15 See www.lucy-harrison.co.uk (accessed 18 February 2011).
16 See www.wondersofweston.org/ (accessed 22 February 2011).
17 Rendell's practice of site-writing is at once a form of art criticism and a form of situated practice. It does not always respond directly to physical locations but often responds to the 'material, emotional, political and conceptual' sites of pre-existing artworks (Rendell 2010: 2).

References

Augé, M. (1995) *Non-Places: Introduction to an Anthropology of Supermodernity*, trans. J. Howe, London: Verso.

Basso, K. (1996) 'Wisdom Sits in Places: Notes on a Western Apache Landscape' in K. Basso and S. Feld (eds) *Senses of Place*, Santa Fe: School of American Research Press.

Clark, L.B. (2006) 'Placed and Displaced: Trauma Memorials' in L. Hill and H. Paris (eds) *Performance and Place*, Hampshire; New York: Palgrave Macmillan.

Clayton, D. (2000) *Islands of Truth: the Imperial Fashioning of Vancouver Island*, Vancouver: UBC Press.

Cronon, W. (1991) *Nature's Metropolis*, New York: Norton.

Cronon, W., Miles, G. and Gitline, J. (eds) (1992) *Under an Open Sky*, New York: Norton.

Cumming, R. (ed.) (1965) *The Philosophy of Jean-Paul Sartre*, New York: Vintage Books.

Eade, J. (2001) *Placing London: From Imperial Capital to Global City*, Oxford: Berghahn Press.

Farell Krell, D. (ed.) (1993) *Martin Heidegger: Basic Writings*, 2nd edn, London: Routledge.

Gandy, M. (2002) *Concrete and Clay: Reworking Nature in New York City*, Cambridge, MA: MIT Press.

Gottlieb, R.S. (1994) 'Ethics and Trauma: Levinas, Feminism, and Deep Ecology', *Cross Currents*, 44: 2.

Herring, P.F. (ed.) (1972) *Joyce's Ulysses Notesheets in the British Museum*, Charlottesville, VA: University Press of Virginia Press.

Jordan, J.A. (2006) *Structures of Memory: Understanding Urban Change in Berlin and Beyond*, California: Stanford University Press.

Kansteiner, W. (2002) 'Finding Meaning in Memory: A Methodological Critique of Collective Memory Studies', *History and Theory*, 41: 2: 179–97.

Klein, K.L. (2000) 'On the Emergence of "Memory" in Historical Discourse', *Representations*, 69: 127–50.

Lennon, J. and Foley, M. (2000) *Dark Tourism*, London: Continuum.

Levinas, E. (1985) *Ethics and Infinity*, trans. R.A. Cohen, Pittsuburgh, PA: Duquesne University Press.

Levinas, E. (1989) *The Levinas Reader*, edited by Seán Hand, Oxford: Blackwell.

Levinas, E. (1996) 'Transcendence and Height' in A.T. Peperzak, S.Critchley and R. Bernasconi (eds) *Emmanuel Levinas: Basic Philosophical Writings*, Bloomington, IN: Indiana University Press, pp. 11–31.

Levinas, E. (2001) *Totality and Infinity: An Essay on Exteriority*, trans. A. Lingis, Pittsburgh, PA: Duquesne University Press.

Light, A. and Rolston, H. (eds) (2003) *Environmental Ethics: An Anthology*, Oxford: Blackwell.

Lippard, L. (1997) *The Lure of the Local: Senses of Place in a Multicentered Society*, New York: The New York Press.

Llewelyn, J. (1991) *The Middle Voice of Ecological Conscience: A Chiasmatic Reading of Responsibility in the Neighborhood of Levinas, Heidegger and Others*, New York: St Martin's Press.

Lovelock, J. (1979/2000) *Gaia: A New Look at Life on Earth*, Oxford: Oxford University Press.

Massey, D. (1994) *Space, Place and Gender*, Cambridge: Polity Press.

Massey, D. (2005) *For Space*, London: SAGE Publications.

Misztal, B.A. (2003) *Theories of Social Remembering*, Berkshire: McGraw-Hill Education.

Næss, A. (1973) 'The Shallow and the Deep, Long-Range Ecology Movement', *Inquiry*, 16: 1, pp. 95–100.

Plumwood, V. (1993) *Feminism and the Mastery of Nature*, London: Routledge.

Rendell, J. (2010) *Site-Writing: The Architecture of Art Criticism*, London: I.B.Taurus.

Rossington, M. and Whitehead, A. (eds) (2007) *Theories of Memory: a Reader*, Edinburgh: Edinburgh University Press.

Sennett, R. (1994) *Flesh and Stone: The Body and the City in Western Civilization*, London: Faber & Faber.

Sessions, G. (ed.) (1995) *Deep Ecology for the 21st Century*, Boston: Shambhala.

Sutton, J. (2003) 'Memory: Philosophical issues' in Lynn Nadel (ed.) *Encyclopaedia of Cognitive Science*, London: Nature Publishing Group.

Till, K.E. (2005) *The New Berlin: Memory, Politics, Place*, University of Minnesota Press.

Tumarkin, M. (2005) *Traumascapes: The Power and Fate of Places Transformed by Tragedy*, Carlton: Melbourne University Press.

Witoszek, N. and Brennan, A. (eds) (1999) *Philosophical Dialogues: Arne Næss and the Progress of Eco-Philosophy*, New York: Rowan and Littlefield.

4 Border crossings

Practices for beating the bounds

Emma Cocker

Located at the interstice where art practice and social anthropology meet and begin to share vocabulary, this chapter explores the project *BorderXing* by artists Heath Bunting and Kayle Brandon through the prism of ideas and concepts of liminality, drawing on the writing of Arnold van Gennep and Victor Turner. *BorderXing* is an ongoing project (2002 onwards) where Brandon and Bunting endeavour to illegally cross the national borders of various European countries, without interruption from customs, immigration or border police. Approached through the frame of liminality it becomes possible to argue that within this project, the border is not so much crossed in resistance to its specific law and logic, as activated as a critical site of resistance, wherein to practise or rehearse a set of tactics through which wider structures of capture and control might also be challenged. Here, inhabiting the specificity of one liminal landscape – the border – provokes the production of new ways of operating, which in turn, might contribute to a more critical approach to the navigation or negotiation of the wider cultural landscape.

As the chapter develops it will become necessary to further differentiate *BorderXing* from the liminal experience described in both van Gennep and Turner's writing. Unlike an actual rite of passage – involving a tripartite structure of separation, transition and re-aggregation (Turner 2009/1969: 94) – Brandon and Bunting's intent seems towards harnessing the disruptive, unsettling or destabilizing potential of both the liminal landscape and liminality, using questions generated through this experience to ask further questions, purposefully leaving the situation open. *BorderXing* is performed within the context of an art practice; it is an appropriation rather than actualization of a rite of passage. The artists' border crossing is performed in the subjunctive mode of 'as if' where the structure of a transitional rite is approached optionally and with certain mischief, a degree of play. Within Brandon and Bunting's *BorderXing* project, a model of territorial passage and its liminal associations are purposefully adopted, borrowed or even played with as part of a critical practice, where the dominant structure becomes questioned and subjected to scrutiny rather than endorsed and reinforced. Turner uses the term 'liminoid' to describe secular situations where a liminal structure is adopted voluntarily without the attendant transition in – or augmentation of – social status (Turner 1982: 32).[1] Whilst the liminoid experience is not typically considered to facilitate social transition *within* the terms of the dominant social structure, within the context of an art project such as *BorderXing*, a form of productive knowledge (*techné*) is generated which supports a transition *away* from social norms.

Brandon and Bunting are two UK-based artists whose collaboration extends from their joint involvement in the collective, irational.org.[2] Initiated by Bunting working with Brandon, *BorderXing* deals with the navigation and negotiation of a physical landscape where the desire to cut across or breach a territorial boundary witnessed in earlier work becomes extended to the borders of Europe.[3] Since Brandon and Bunting are European citizens, it would be easy for them to cross the border between one European country and another by the official channels. However, within this sustained performance – where they have already crossed 24 European borders – the artists refuse to take the authorized and endorsed routes (or indeed their passports), but instead find ways of crossing the territorial line via alternative paths, through forests, across rivers, over mountains, even underground. The artists purposefully navigate the wilderness routes and no-man's lands, the physical margins and liminal spaces of a geographical terrain.

In one sense, the project could be conceived as an act of resistance, a refusal to accept the authority of a territorial border, an attempt to render its logic and law porous. By illegally crossing the border between one country and another, Brandon and Bunting challenge the rule and reach of various national boundaries, in turn commenting on how mobility and movement within the European Union – for non-EU travellers in particular – is increasingly controlled and monitored, restricted by governments and associated bureaucracies. *BorderXing* tests the efficacy of political constraints on human mobility by revealing the physical border markers – such as posts and fences – to be precarious or makeshift, traversable or porous.

Van Gennep's chapter on 'The Territorial Passage' in *The Rites of Passage* (2004/1960) provides a useful coordinate against which to plot Brandon and Bunting's *BorderXing*, not least for gauging how attitudes towards mobility have changed since the early 1900s.[4] Van Gennep situates the idea of 'territorial passage' – as a specific category within his classification of rites of passage – in contrast to contemporary experiences and perceptions of travel, stating that:

> Except in the few countries where a passport is still in use, a person in these days may pass freely from one civilized region to another. The frontier, an imaginary line connecting milestones or stakes, is visible – in an exaggerated fashion – only on maps. But not so long ago the passage from one country to another ... was accompanied by various formalities.
>
> (van Gennep 2004/1960: 15)

Van Gennep differentiates the contemporary moment – of the early *twentieth* century – from earlier periods (and 'less civilized' places), where 'territorial passage' was often accompanied by 'formalities' that ranged from the political, legal and economic to those of a more 'magico-religious nature' (van Gennep

Figures 4.1–4.2 Images from *BorderXing* slideshow, Heath Bunting and Kayle Brandon, 2004. Images courtesy of the artists.

2004/1960: 15). Yet, in the twenty-first century, travel has increasingly become *re*-accompanied by 'various formalities', national borders tightened rather than dissolved. The neoliberal landscape is not borderless, nor is contemporary mobility unimpeded. Mobility is an uneven privilege to which not all are granted access. For Zygmunt Bauman, the smooth routes of international flight paths are largely for those who 'circulate close to the top of the global power pyramid, to whom space matters little and distance is not a bother; people at home in many places but in no one in particular' (Bauman 2005: 4). Bauman argues that 'freedom to move' and 'freedom to choose' is unevenly distributed, since for many 'there are neither unguarded exits nor hospitable open entry gates' (Bauman 2005: 5). Political, legal and economic 'formalities' are now as likely to be used to prevent the free passage of a person from one place to another, where they have become used as impediments or obstacles through which to thwart mobility or block the way. Brandon and Bunting's project can be considered a refusal of the 'various formalities' – whether political, legal or economic – that *now* accompany territorial passage, in turn discrediting the promise of unimpeded mobility championed within neoliberal rhetoric. However, the project can also be considered as an attempt to resurrect or re-activate something of the 'magico-religious nature' of territorial passage, harnessing the potency of the border or threshold (as a liminal landscape) and of the event of border crossing (as a liminal act).

Brandon and Bunting's *BorderXing* – like many of their projects – is located purposefully between one kind of practice and another, where it can be contextualized against the politics of activist practice, as well as various forms of radical or tactical cartography.[5] Brandon and Bunting can also be considered in relation to other artists whose nomadic practices use travel as their medium in order to interrogate a particular border terrain or contested landscape.[6] Critics such as Marcus Verhagen have challenged the unquestioned romanticism surrounding the rhetoric of the nomadic artist, by arguing that they are little more than re-worked versions of global itinerancy (Verhagen 2006: 7–10).[7] Rather than simply replicating those forms of travel symptomatic of the fluid conditions of late capitalism, Verhagen argues that there are also other – potentially more critical or resistant – models of nomadic practice, that picture 'travel as fraught and communication across cultures as halting and eventful rather than fluid' (Verhagen 2006: 10). Certainly, in refusing the smooth routes of the contemporary (neoliberal) nomad, *BorderXing* exposes the presence of actual barriers within the supposedly borderless neoliberal landscape, which thwart the mobility of those who lack the correct papers or passports. Yet, by illegally crossing European borders, the artists refuse to accept the authority of national boundaries, demonstrating how even the most impervious barrier can be rendered porous, with the knowledge of how to navigate a way through. Curator Kit Hammonds notes how *BorderXing* tests 'the idea of freedom of movement between the conglomerate of countries known as the European Union' (Hammonds 2010: 29). The project reveals different levels of fortification between one country and another; documentation from

Figures 4.3–4.4 Images from *BorderXing* slideshow, Heath Bunting and Kayle Brandon, 2004. Images courtesy of the artists.

the artists' crossings reveals inconsistencies in how the national border is marked and monitored. Hammonds observes,

> 'Fortress Britain' is shown to be just that, with razor wire and high fences preventing any attempts to enter the country. In contrast, Nordic landscapes and frozen lakes provide idyllic backdrops as well as pathways to navigate between countries, and eastern frontiers appear relatively simple to traverse.
>
> (Hammonds 2010: 30)

BorderXing tests the impermeability of each border, as the artists devise ways through which to pass, cross, traverse, circumvent or jump over the boundary separating one European country from another. The various forms of *Border-Xing* 'guide' produced by the artists operate (playfully and indeed provocatively) as a set of instructions or a toolkit for other would-be border-crossers.[8]

BorderXing implicitly critiques the authority of national borders and the ideology of national identity to which they attest, resisting the territorial implications of the border – and its attendant structures of capture and control – by wilfully and illegally crossing the line. However, rather than operating solely as a form of negation or refusal, *BorderXing* can be explored in more affirmative terms. Whilst border crossing is typically considered in teleological terms – seemingly motivated by the desire to get to the other side – for Brandon and Bunting the performative navigation or negotiation of the border itself (as obstacle, limit or constraint) seems to function as critically as the actual crossing itself. For the artists, a spatial or social obstacle emerges as a site of critical leverage or pressure against which to work.[9] Within their practice, obstacles operate as productive constraints that necessitate unexpected ways of being or behaving, forcing the emergence of new tactical ways of operating.[10] Here, the critical potential of the *BorderXing* project is not so much in the literal crossing of the border, but rather in how the artists activate the liminal space of the border itself as a productive site of resistant and dissident inhabitation. Brandon and Bunting's practice makes explicit the connection between spatial *and* social manifestations of liminality. Their projects present strategies for how the spatial and social landscape might be performed differently from dominant ideological expectations, where their navigation and inhabitation of indeterminate geographies or border terrains is considered synchronous to the conception of other, less acquiescent, ways of living and performing a life. For Brandon and Bunting, the liminal landscape provides germinal conditions wherein to test and expand their critical capabilities, where the crossing of a border is undertaken as part of the wider process of 'producing themselves' (differently) as resistant and critical subjects. In this sense perhaps, their border crossings perform analogously to van Gennep's category of territorial passage where the navigation of a given landscape is accompanied by an attendant change or transformation in the life – or capacity – of the person undertaking the crossing.

BorderXing functions as part of Brandon and Bunting's ongoing endeavour to develop critical or tactical ways of operating differently from those models of citizenship perpetuated by the dominant neoliberal model. The notion of attempting to 'produce oneself differently' emerges as a philosophical enquiry, echoing the work of various theorists and philosophers who have advocated the necessity of viewing life as a kind of project or mode of invention, a material to be worked. For Michel Foucault the 'elaboration of one's own life as a personal work of art' can be understood as the search for a 'personal ethics' or 'ethics of existence' (Foucault 1990: 49). Patrick ffrench explores the shift in Foucault's work from an earlier interest in 'panoptic modes of surveillance and control' (for example in *Discipline and Punish*, 1975) towards the seemingly more affirmative direction developed as part of his conceptualization of 'life as a work of art' or 'life as project' (ffrench 2005: 205). Similarly, Brandon and Bunting's interrogation of the border as a site of surveillance and social control can be seen as orienting away from critique, towards possibilities of a more constitutive kind. Their work can be considered in relation to Foucault's notion of life as 'project'; theirs is a self-constituting practice wherein they attempt to develop new 'possibilities for life' or rehearse a form of 'self-stylisation in ethical life' (ffrench 2005: 208). For Foucault, such a project is necessarily an experimental pursuit practiced 'at the limit of ourselves' (Foucault 1997: 316), which rests, as ffrench notes, 'on knowledge of practical systems that will enable individuals to know the rules of the rationalities determining what and how they are, think and do, and thereby to modify the rules of the game' (ffrench 2005: 212). Certainly, in *BorderXing* Brandon and Bunting develop a particular kind of border knowledge specifically for the purposes of modifying its rules, for changing how the logic of the border is apprehended.

Within *BorderXing*, the border is not just a line to be crossed, but rather emerges as a germinal or transformative site wherein to rehearse or test one's capacity as a resistant subject, for practising how to navigate limits or constraints. Systems of capture and control are apprehended as obstacles to be worked around, not as limits to be passively obeyed. Whilst not of the kind of social transition generally supported by a liminal rite of passage (where the individual moves from one level of the social hierarchy to another), Brandon and Bunting's *BorderXing* nonetheless involves a potential augmentation or increase in their capacity for functioning as critical, rather than acquiescent, subjects. Within their work, the practice of attempting to transform oneself requires its own rite of passage, involving the cultivation of constitutive or self-initiated 'trials' that encourage transition away from or in resistance to social norms. Additionally, the specificity of Brandon and Bunting's own territorial passage operates in propositional or instructional terms, where it is used to encourage – even recruit – further 'initiates' to the practice of border crossing. The *BorderXing Guide* is a web-based resource that contains information about routes for crossing between various pairs of countries, and documentation of the artists' border crossing including hiking maps, lists of necessary tools and directions. The *BorderXing Guide* is limited through a database of authorized online clients only; to access the guide a potential user must either apply directly to the artists or travel to one of the designated locations granted web access.[11] In this sense, access to the detailed information of the *BorderXing* project requires the under-taking of a preliminary journey or a process of initiation for the would-be traveller.

BorderXing also evokes or inverts other ceremonial practices, operating as a ritual *reversal* of 'beating the bounds'. Beating the bounds is an ancient custom, involving a communal walk around the boundary of a parish on Ascension Day. Brandon and Bunting attempt to 'beat the bounds' in dual terms: they identify the various lines of division and classification that separate one territory from another, whilst simultaneously trying to beat or defeat their authority. They 'beat the bounds' by proposing potential ways out or around, by devising potential exit strategies from their logic. However, the scoring of a territorial line is not always established through the imposition of a fence or wall. As van Gennep states,

> More often the boundary is marked by an object – a stake, portal, or upright rock (milestone or landmark) – whose installation at that particular spot had been accompanied by rites of consecration. ... The prohibition against enter-ing a given territory is therefore intrinsically magico-religious.
>
> (van Gennep 2004/1960: 15–16)

Borders are not always signalled by a continuous line on land but can exist as much in an imaginary or even *narrative* sense, where the boundary is often drawn in contractual rather than physical terms. Irit Rogoff asserts that the border is an imaginary concept, 'far removed from geological formation and pat-terns of settlement, a fantasy of division projected on to the terrain from afar' (Rogoff 2000: 115). For Michel de Certeau, it is stories that 'found spaces'; he states '(t)he story's first function is to authorize, or more exactly, to *found*' (de Certeau 1984: 123).[12] Certainly, some of the borders encountered by Brandon and Bunting as part of their *BorderXing* project would have already been physi-cally porous, permeable. The symbolic signification of a border is often less easy to define, its power less easy to cross or counter. *BorderXing* is thus not just the breach of a physical border but rather it could be considered a ritual deterritori-alization performed to defuse or deflate the authority that the imaginary line on a map upholds.

Brandon and Bunting not only diffuse the authority of the border by crossing it, but also affect a shift in its classificatory status, transforming it from an authoritative line into an interstitial zone of playful or subversive inhabitation. The inhabitation of a no-man's land operates as a refusal of the border's binary logic of separation and division – by effectively sitting on the fence – or else a desire to become located beyond the bounds of societal rule, where (proposition-ally at least) one might become exempt from the authority that exists to either side. Rogoff argues that,

> While a national geographical entity produces and polices identity, the notion of a 'zone' is one suspended between various identities – a site of

evacuation in which the 'law' of each identity does not apply, having been supplanted by a set of contingent 'rules'.

(Rogoff 2000: 120)

BorderXing can thus be understood as an attempt to temporarily *unbelong*, to inhabit the gap or no-man's land that exists between one country and another. For Rogoff, ' "to unbelong" and to "not be at home" is the very condition of critical theoretical activity' (2000: 18). She argues that 'unbelonging' is not the condition of, 'being at a loss, of inhabiting a lack, of not having anything, but rather an active, daily disassociation in the attempt to clear the ground for something else to emerge' (Rogoff: 2001). She makes the call for a:

> (N)ecessary evolution of an active category of 'unbelonging' – not as marginality and not as defiant opposition and certainly not as a mode of 'dropping out', but as a critical refusal of the terms – and of the implication of those terms – which come to be naturalized within the parameters of any given debate. All this by working from within those parameters rather than outside of them.

(Rogoff 2000: 5)

Thus to 'unbelong' does not involve an attempt to become spatially located beyond the bounds of various systems of capture – for one side of the border is just as territorialized as the other – but rather the challenge is one of learning how to inhabit the gaps or loopholes between one system of rule and another. The task is not one of crossing a territorial line but of changing it, renaming it, of inhabiting it differently.

Within *BorderXing*, the borders between countries operate as blindspots where it is possible to momentarily escape or exist between the terms of either side of the line. The artists inhabit the border zone itself, as an interregnum site of suspended identity or of momentary lawlessness. Georges Teyssot reflects on this classificatory shift where, '(t)he frontier loses the meaning of pure obstacle and becomes voidal and interstitial, a space where things can happen, a happening, a performance, an event or a narrative, for instance – an in-cident' (Teysott 2005: 107). Drawing on the writing of de Certeau, Teyssot elaborates that,

> 'spaces between' have the power to become symbols of exchanges and encounters. As such, they offer the ability to gather events that occur 'there'. The frontier, as it were, belongs to a logic of ambiguity, or ambivalence: the void of the border can turn the limit into a crossing, a passage; or the river into a bridge.

(Teysott 2005: 107)

Brandon and Bunting inhabit rivers as bridges, limits as crossings; effectively changing the terms of how the landscape is navigated. They attempt to reclaim the possibility of neutrality within even the most territorialized zones, proposing a return of 'free' areas within the landscape. Whilst in contemporary times one European country 'touches' another (leaving little, if any, zone between), van Gennep notes that in earlier historical periods, 'Each country was surrounded by a strip of neutral ground which in practice was divided into sections of marches' (van Gennep 2004/1960: 17). He goes on to reflect that whilst these 'marches' have all but disappeared, 'the term 'letter of marquee' retains the meaning of a permit to pass from one territory to another through a neutral zone' (van Gennep 2004/1960: 18). Van Gennep notes that the 'neutral zones' were often located in deserts or marshes, 'and most frequently virgin forests where everyone has full rights to travel and hunt' (van Gennep 2004/1960: 18). These 'zones' were often considered sacred since, as van Gennep remarks, 'Whoever passes from one to the other finds himself physically and magico-religiously in a special situation for a certain length of time: he wavers between two worlds' (van Gennep 2004/1960: 18). Thus by inhabiting a 'neutral zone' between one country and another Brandon and Bunting hope to re-activate the 'marches' and perhaps even the 'magico-religious' potency therein; they endeavour to occupy the space 'between two worlds'.

Inhabiting the neutral zone between one territorialized state and another, Brandon and Bunting's position can be considered in analogous terms to the interregnum condition experienced by initiates within rituals or rites of passage, pilgrimage or sacred journeys. Following van Gennep, Turner describes the structure of a rite of passage in tripartite terms involving three phases: '*separation, transition, and incorporation*' (Turner 1982: 24) or 'separation, margin (or *limen*, signifying "threshold" in Latin), and aggregation' (Turner 2009/1969: 94). Turner states that the first phase involves the 'detachment of the individual or group either from an earlier fixed point in the social structure, from a set of cultural conditions (a "state") or both', whilst 'in the third phase (reaggregation or reincorporation), the passage is consummated' and the ritual subject returned to a 'relatively stable state' (Turner 2009/1969: 95). Between these two phases (which operate as exit and re-entry points between the normative social structure and the 'anti-structural' realm of ritual) the subject passes through an intervening transitional or liminal phase.[13] Turner describes how during the liminal phase of ritual performance the characteristics of the social structure are no longer and not yet applicable as ritual subjects 'pass through a period and area of ambiguity' (Turner 1982: 24). During this phase, it becomes possible for the initiate to momentarily escape the rules and regulations of a given society, the terms of the ritual providing a kind of exemption from habitual logic; they are 'no longer classified and not yet classified' (Turner 1967: 96). Here, the initiate or novice remains 'temporarily undefined, beyond the normative social structure' (Turner 1982: 27). Turner asserts that:

> The attributes of liminality or of liminal *personae* ('threshold people') are necessarily ambiguous, since this condition and these persons elude or slip through the network of classifications that normally locate states and positions in cultural space. Liminal entities are neither here nor there; they are

betwixt and between the positions assigned and arrayed by law, custom, conventions, and ceremonial.

(Turner 2009/1969: 95)

BorderXing evokes a form of liminal or transitional rite (that of territorial passage), where Brandon and Bunting seem intent on activating the specific 'permissions' or 'exemptions' commonly associated with liminality. They attempt to momentarily 'unbelong' by locating the spatial threshold between territorialized zones, 'betwixt and between' the law of one state and another. However, the project also serves to reflect on other more insidious forms of control and restriction, for physical barriers have increasingly become supplanted by an invisible infrastructure of surveillance and monitoring. Communication networks and pervasive technologies have created new borderlands or margins between physical and virtual realms that are patrolled increasingly by newly emerging systems of control. Unlike the physical border whose terms of confinement and capture remain relatively fixed and static, the reach and influence of these immaterial systems of control is less easy to discern.[14] During their border crossings Brandon and Bunting are as likely to be identified by their mobile phone signal as by their physical presence. Their inhabitation of wilderness routes within the physical landscape is necessarily echoed by a quest for blindspots or 'seams' within the virtual realm, 'neutral spaces' wherein to slip beneath the radar of network connectivity, fall out of range.

For Brandon and Bunting, the desire to unbelong or fall out of range does not signal a passive or romantic longing for some uninhabited wilderness beyond the limits of societal reach, but rather operates as a way of actively creating a productive gap into which other ways of operating can be called or conjured. Their confrontative event of illegally crossing a national border is used to create a breach, not only of the border but also of 'structure' itself, providing momentary access to what Turner would call 'anti-structure', the 'subjunctive world' of the liminal phase. The 'subjunctive' mood of a verb is used to express supposition, desire, hypothesis, or possibility. Turner notes that the subjunctive 'is a world of "as if" … It is "if it *were* so," not "it *is* so"' (Turner 1982: 82–83). So too, the subjunctive nature of liminality encourages the conception of things as otherwise. It invites towards a process of thinking differently and of seeing things differently. In his foreword to Turner's *The Ritual Process*, Roger D. Abrahams remarks that, 'through acts of turning the world upside down the very possibility of openness and change emerges' (Abrahams 1995: x). The liminal phase of a ritual is a space of questioning and critique of the dominant social structure, a subversion or inversion of its rules. As Turner notes, 'if liminality is regarded as a time and place of withdrawal from normal modes of social action, it can be seen as potentially a period of scrutinization of the central values and axioms of the culture in which it occurs' (Turner 1995: 167). Here, he argues, 'Ambiguity reigns; people and public policies may be judged skeptically in relation to deep values; the vices, follies, stupidities, and abuses of contemporary holders of high political, economic, or religious status may be satirized, ridiculed, or condemned'

(Turner 1987: 102). However, the disruptive dimension of liminality is carefully managed within the context of a ritual or rite of passage, where for Turner, it can 'never be much more than a subversive flicker ... put into the service of normativeness almost as soon as it appears' (Turner 1982: 44–45).[15] Alternatively, within Brandon and Bunting's work these critical forces are positively unleashed; the artists harness the disruptive, questioning or critical dimensions of liminality without then returning a sense of order.

Brandon and Bunting appropriate the structure of a territorial passage, where emphasis is placed on the initial phases of separation and transition. However, the artists seem to stall or suspend the process of territorial passage in its liminal phase; their quest seems less motivated by eventual re-aggregation and increased social status, as by the will to unbelong or become unbound by the terms of the dominant structure. Within their project, liminality becomes an endpoint rather than an intermediary phase. Their border crossings are performed at the limit of legality and have the capacity to diminish or weaken the artists' position further. Unlike the liminal rite of a territorial passage they do not result in an increase in social status. Moreover, their crossings are repeated, resolution is not accomplished. The ritual passage does not come to an identifiable end. *BorderXing* resembles a liminal rite, without sharing its intent. Furthermore, within *Border-Xing*, the liminal experience is entered into voluntarily, out of choice. In this sense, it is closer to what Turner would denote as a form of ludic liminality or liminoid experience, since '(o)ptation pervades the liminoid phenomenon, obligation the liminal' (Turner 1982: 43). Whilst the liminal experience often reinforces and works *with* existing social hierarchies, Turner argues that, 'liminoid phenomena ... are often parts of social critiques or even revolutionary manifestos ... exposing the injustices, inefficiencies, and immoralities of the mainstream economic and political structure' (Turner 1982: 54–55). Rather than being easily – unquestionably – assimilated back into the existing social order then, the critical subject produced through the liminoid experience has the capacity to conceive of things differently or invite change; they have a transformative potential. For Turner, liminoid experiences are closer to play or even 'playing at', where a form of pseudo-liminality is entered voluntarily as a form of leisure pursuit or entertainment. Whilst *BorderXing* appears liminoid in its optionality and mode of critique, it is less easy to categorize in other terms. Turner asserts that, 'One *works* at the liminal, one *plays* with the liminoid' (Turner 1982: 55). Art practice disturbs these categorical demarcations by being *both*. The liminoid nature of *BorderXing* is not so much 'play-separated-from-work' as 'play-as-work'; the artists *work* hard to produce their conditions of 'freedom-from' and 'freedom-to', rather than simply 'enjoying' the illusory liberation that leisure time (and the liminoid experience) typically affords.[16]

Within Brandon and Bunting's practice a ritual space is opened up where optional rules apply. For Turner, the liminal phase of a rite of passage opens up, 'an interval, however brief, of margin or *limen*, when the past is momentarily negated, suspended, or abrogated and the future has not yet begun, an instant of pure potentiality where everything, as it were trembles in the balance' (Turner

1982: 44). Liminality – and the liminal landscape of the border zone – operates beyond the limits of normative laws and logic, where habitual forms of knowledge no longer suffice. The liminal landscape of the border creates the critical conditions of urgency or emergency. It forces the taking of a different tack, provoking the cultivation of other ways of operating. For Brandon and Bunting, the border operates as a critical context for activating a form of productive or tactical knowledge, which in turn has the capacity to harness the potential indeterminacy – or indeterminate potential – afforded by both their liminal position and the liminal landscape they inhabit. Through the process of *BorderXing*, Brandon and Bunting cultivate a resistant or dissident knowledge (a liminal knowledge of liminal spaces), through which they are able to devise 'ways out' of structural control or create moments of porosity within the system, without ever fully leaving its frame. Their specific form of tactical knowledge can be conceived as a manifestation of *techné* – a particular mode of 'knowing' and of navigating the world – which is activated through the interrogation of a particular limit or constraint and through an attempt to render this limit porous or malleable. Tracing the origins of *techné* within Ancient Greek culture, Janet Atwill reflects on how it is the form of knowledge 'persistently implicated in the transgression of boundaries, its story is tied to the construction of limits at a number of points – limits of knowledge and subjectivity, as well as social, political and economic limits' (Atwill 2009: 2–3). Atwill states, 'A techné deforms limits into new paths in order to reach – or better yet, to produce – an alternative destination' (Atwill 2009: 69). She argues that 'Techné challenges … forces and limits with its power to discover (*heuriskein*) and invent new paths (*poroi*)' (Atwill 2009: 48). In some senses, it is possible to conceive of techné as a liminal knowledge, that of liminal personae. For Atwill, techné is a form of knowledge that refuses to be identified with a stable or normative subject, where akin to the ritual subject of a rite of passage, 'the subjects identified with techné are often in a state of flux or transformation' (Atwill 2009: 48). Furthermore, techné is often associated with those with little structural power; its force is activated from a position of perceived weakness where a 'way through' or 'way out' *(poros)* of a situation is created through wily means rather than through force. Here, the 'power of the weak' is not one of magico-religious import (as it is within liminality), but rather it emerges as a set of tactics that are both activated by and capable of working with the indeterminacy of a situation in flux.

Techné is associated with an attendant form of cunning intelligence (*mêtis*) and a mode of time characterized by opportunism, the 'right time' (*kairos*). Writing on the specific subject of *mêtis*, Marcel Detienne and Jean-Pierre Vernant describe it as, 'a type of intelligence and of thought, a way of knowing … it is applied to situations which are transient, shifting, disconcerting, and ambiguous, situations which do not lend themselves to precise measurement, exact calculation or rigorous logic' (Detienne and Vernant 1991/1978: 3–4). Harnessing the properties of dexterity, sureness of eye and sharp-wittedness, *mêtis* 'attempts to reach its desired goal by feeling its way and guessing'; it is a 'type of cognition which is alien to truth and quite separate from *episteme*, knowledge' (Detienne and Vernant 1991/1978: 4). For Detienne and Vernant, *mêtis* is the art of preparing for what cannot or could not have been anticipated or planned, 'where every new trial demands the invention of new ploys, the discovery of a way out (*poros*) that is hidden' (Detienne and Vernant 1991/1978: 21). The knowledge(s) developed by Brandon and Bunting as part of their *BorderXing* project can be considered as a form of techné. Theirs is a way of operating capable of setting up the conditions wherein *kairos* (the time of opportunity) might arise and in knowing (through a form of *mêtis* or intuitive intelligence) how and when to act in response. The 'transient, shifting, disconcerting, and ambiguous' nature of a particular liminal landscape (the border between one country and another) is approached as a productive constraint or limit wherein to cultivate and practice techné, wherein to rehearse ways of rendering the limit porous.

Whilst the border operates as a specific kind of liminal landscape, the contemporary landscape – as it is increasingly shaped or indeed unshaped by the processes of global capital – might be considered as a liminal landscape in itself, a space of transience, transition and perpetual flux. The new world order is no longer considered in stable categories, for now everywhere appears to be constantly shifting; everything seemingly a little liquid, precarious. Contemporary times are now often characterized by their liminal properties – ambiguity, openness, and indeterminacy – however unlike traditional conceptualizations of liminality such experiences are perpetual rather than passing. The individual is never re-aggregated back into a stable societal landscape (for this has all but disappeared), but instead remains interminably disoriented, in limbo. Bauman describes contemporary life as *liquid modernity* or *liquid life*, a state of things where all is at once disposable and constantly shifting. He states that,

> Liquid modern is a society in which the conditions under which its members act change faster than it takes the ways of acting to consolidate into habits and routines. ... Liquid life is a precarious life, lived under the conditions of constant uncertainty.
>
> (Bauman 2005: 1–2)

The properties of liminality now seemingly describe the structurally normative rather than its subjunctive anti-structure. Rather than a state of exception or indeterminacy that – like the border – exists between one territorialized zone and another, it could be argued that the destabilized and destabilizing aspects of the liminal condition have become the rule. By practising how to navigate the discrete liminal landscape of the border, Brandon and Bunting cultivate the skills and knowledge(s) necessary for critically negotiating the indeterminacies of neoliberal landscape at large.

Nicolas Bourriaud argues that the way to confront the increasingly precarious terms of contemporary times is to know how to beat neoliberal precarity at its own game, by being *more than* (Bourriaud 2009: 53).[17] His comments echo those of Detienne and Vernant, for whom the indeterminacy of a shifting situation requires the cultivation of similarly slippery skills. They suggest that in order for the individual to confront the 'multiple, changing reality whose limitless polymorphic powers render it almost impossible to seize', he should become 'even more multiple, more mobile, more polyvalent than his adversary' (Detienne and Vernant 1991/1978: 5). They argue that, 'Victory over a shifting reality whose continuous metamorphoses make it almost impossible to grasp, can only be won through an even greater degree of mobility, an even greater power of transformation' (Detienne and Vernant 1991/1978: 20). The experiential knowledge (*techné*) that Brandon and Bunting glean from their encounter with the particular liminal landscape of the border has the capacity to be applied elsewhere. Atwill suggests that techné, 'may be described as a dynamis (or power), transferable guides and strategies, a cunningly conceived plan – even a trick or trap. This knowledge is stable enough to be taught and transferred but flexible enough to be adapted to particular situations and purposes' (Atwill 2009: 48). In this sense, the techné and attendant intelligence (*mêtis*) cultivated within the liminal context of Brandon and Bunting's border crossing might be adapted to other situations that are 'transient, shifting, disconcerting, and ambiguous'. Their *BorderXing* project thus operates as both a guide and point of provocation through which to further interrogate the increasingly liminal landscapes of the contemporary neoliberal world.

Notes

1 Turner differentiates between 'liminal' and 'liminoid' experiences, where ' "liminoid" *resembles* without being identical to "liminal" ', with '– oid' having its origins in the Greek — *eidos*, meaning both a form, shape or 'like, resembling' (Turner 1982: 32).
2 Available at www.irational.org/ (accessed 3 April 2011).
3 An earlier project *D'fence Cuts* (2002) involved the strategic targeting and cutting of all fences between two points on a selected route.
4 *The Rites of Passage* was originally written in 1908.
5 The cartographical imperative of Brandon and Bunting's *BorderXing* project is discussed further in Emma Cocker, 'Exit Strategies – Looking for Loopholes' in Karen Bishop (ed.) *The Cartographical Necessity of Exile*, forthcoming.
6 For example, in *The Loop* (1997), artist Francis Alÿs spent 29 days travelling between the neighbouring border locations Tijuana (Baja California, Mexico) and San Diego (California, United States), electing to take a roundabout route around the world, crossing through 16 different cities in order to avoid the Mexico/United States border itself. *BorderXing* more specifically recalls the project *Green Border* (1993) by Christian Philipp Müller in which the artist attempted to illegally cross Austria's green borders on foot, breaching the often invisible territorial line between Austria and the former Eastern-block countries of the Czech Republic, Slovakia, Hungary, and Slovenia and the western countries of Italy, Switzerland, Liechtenstein, and Germany.
7 Verhagen specifically comments on the form of 'smooth' nomadism – within the work of artists such as Rirkrit Tiravanija – often championed by Nicolas Bourriaud, for example, in publications such as *Relational Aesthetics* (1998), *Postproduction* (2002) and *Altermodernism* (2009).
8 See Brandon and Bunting, *Botanical Guide to BorderXing*, available at http://duo.irational.org/botanical_guide_to_borderxing/; the *BorderXing* slideshow, available at http://duo.irational.org/borderxing_slide_show/borderxing_slide_show001.html; and *BorderXing Guide*, available at http://irational.org/cgi-bin/border/clients/deny.pl (all accessed 3 April 2011).

9 See also Brandon and Bunting's *Tour d'fence* (2002) where urban structures and street furniture shifted from obstacle to impromptu obstacle course, operating as challenges against which to practice nascent skills of *parkour.*

10 Architectural theorists Arakawa and Gins further elaborate how the navigation of obstacles involves a critical engagement with one's environment and thus one's own life (Gins and Arakawa, 2002).

11 Authorization to the *BorderXing Guide* is granted to clients with a static IP (Internet Protocol) address and includes *any* client from a list of countries including Bahrain, Qatar, Antarctica, Liberia, Japan, Saint Lucia, Haiti, Poland, Slovenia, Malaysia or the Ukraine, and then a specific named list of clients (including individuals and arts organizations or those who have gained the artists' trust). See the *BorderXing* client request site, available at http://irational.org/cgi-bin/border/clients/deny.pl (accessed 3 April 2011).

12 For de Certeau, the 'operations of marking out boundaries' consist of 'narrative contracts and complications of stories,... composed of fragments drawn from earlier stories and fitted together in makeshift fashion (*bricolés*). In this sense, they shed light on the formation of myths, since they also have the function of founding and articulating spaces' (de Certeau 1984: 122–123).

13 Van Gennep further differentiates between different kinds of rites, which he categorizes as 'preliminal rites (rites of separation), liminal rites (rites of transition), and postliminal rites (rites of incorporation)', each of which might in turn involve the three distinct phases of passage (van Gennep 2004/1960: 11).

14 Deleuze sketches the terms of contemporary life as a totally administered system or control society. He locates the shift towards total administration in terms of a societal paradigm shift, from a *disciplinary society* (as defined by Michel Foucault) where the individual moved between various named sites of confinement or *molds*, towards the conditions of a *control society*, a 'new system of domination' (Deleuze 1995a: 182). Within a control society, Deleuze asserts, 'the various forms of control ... are inseparable variations ... continually changing from one moment to the next, or like a sieve whose mesh varies from one point to another' (Deleuze 1995a: 178–179).

15 In fact, Turner notes how the turbulence and 'topsy-turvy-dom' of liminality was often used to reinforce stability in the post-liminal phase, where 'reversal underlines to the members of a community that chaos is the alternative to cosmos, so they'd better stick to cosmos' (Turner 1982: 41).

16 Furthermore, optionality requires an ethical rather than obedient engagement; for Deleuze, 'it's a matter of optional rules that make existence a work of art, rules at once ethical and aesthetic that constitute ways of existing or styles of life' (Deleuze 1995b: 98).

17 Bourriaud states, 'Let's invent new meanings for flexibility. ... Let us confront the increasing precariousness of our experience with a resolutely precarious mode of thought that infiltrates and invades the very networks that stifle and smother us' (Bourriaud 2009: 53).

References

Abrahams, R.D. (1995) 'Foreword', in V. Turner, *The Ritual Process, Structure and Anti-Structure*, New Brunswick and London: Aldine Transaction.

Atwill, J.M. (2009) *Rhetoric Reclaimed: Aristotle and the Liberal Arts Tradition*, Ithaca and London: Cornell University Press.

Bauman, Z. (2005) *Liquid Life*, Cambridge: Polity Press.

Brandon, K. and Bunting, H. (n.d.) irational.org. Available at www.irational.org/ (accessed 3 April 2011).

Brandon, K and Bunting, H. (n.d.) *BorderXing slideshow*. Available at: http://duo.ira-tional.org/borderxing_slide_show/borderxing_slide_show001.html (accessed 3 April 2011).

Brandon, K and Bunting, H. (n.d.) *Botanical Guide to BorderXing.* Available at: http://duo.irational.org/botanical_guide_to_borderxing/ (accessed 3 April 2011).

Brandon, K and Bunting, H. (n.d.) *BorderXing Guide*. Available at: http://irational.org/cgi-bin/border/clients/deny.pl (accessed 3 April 2011).

Bourriaud, N. (2009) *The Radicant*, New York: Lukas & Sternberg.

Cocker, E. (forthcoming) 'Exit Strategies – Looking for Loopholes', in K. Bishop (ed.), *The Cartographical Necessity of Exile*.

de Certeau, M. (1984) *The Practice of Everyday Life*, trans. Steven Rendall, Berkeley, Los Angeles and London: University of California Press.

Deleuze, G. (1995a) 'Postscript on Control Societies', *Negotiations: 1972–1990*, New York: Columbia University Press.

Deleuze, G. (1995b) 'Life as a Work of Art', *Negotiations: 1972–1990*, New York: Columbia University Press.

Detienne, M and Vernant, J.-P. (1991/1978) *Cunning Intelligence in Greek Culture and Society*, trans. Janet Lloyd, Chicago: University of Chicago Press.

ffrench, P. (2005), 'Michel Foucault, Life as Work of Art', in Johnnie Gratton and Michael Sherringham (eds) *The Art of the Project: Projects and Experiments in Modern French Culture*, New York and Oxford: Berghahn Books.

Foucault, M. (1990) 'An Aesthetics of Existence', in L. Kritzman (ed.) *Politics, Philosophy, Culture*, London: Routledge.

Foucault, M. (1997) *The Essential Works of Michel Foucault* Vol. 1: Ethics: Subjectivity and Truth, edited by Paul Rabinov, trans. Robert Hurley *et al.*, Harmonsworth: Penguin.

Gins, M. and Arakawa, S. (2002) S. *Architectural Body*, The University of Alabama Press.

Hammonds, K. (2010) *Ground Level*, London: Hayward Publishing.

Rogoff, I. (2000) *Terra Infirma, Geography's Visual Culture*, London and New York: Routledge.

Rogoff, I. (2001) 'Without: A conversation Interview', *Art Journal*, 60 (3), pp. 34–41.

Teysott, G. (2005) 'A Topology of Thresholds', *Home Cultures*, 2 (1), pp. 89–116.

Turner, V. (1967) *The Forest of Symbols: Aspects of Ndembu Ritual*, Ithaca: Cornell University Press.

Turner, V. (1982) *From Ritual to Theatre: The Human Seriousness of Play*, New York: PAJ Publications.

Turner, V. (1987) *The Anthropology of Performance*, New York: PAJ Publications.

Turner, V. (2009/1969) *The Ritual Process, Structure and Anti-Structure*, New Brunswick and London: Aldine Transaction.

van Gennep, A. (2004/1960) *The Rites of Passage*, trans. M.B. Vizedom and G.L. Caffee, Routledge Editions – Anthropology and Ethnography.

Verhagen, M. (2006) 'Nomadism', *Art Monthly*, October, pp. 7–10.

Part II
Gleaning and liminality
Edgelands, wetlands, estuaries

5   Walking the edges

Towards a visual ethnography of beachscapes

Kevin Meethan

Introduction: spaces of liminality

Language constantly shifts and changes, words and phrases come into fashion, are adopted by others, subjected to scrutiny and take on new meanings, perhaps changing over time into something quite removed from its original usage. This is certainly the case with liminality, which I first encountered as an undergraduate reading the work of Victor Turner for the first time. Turner (1967), reworking van Gennep's original coining of the term saw liminality was a temporary state, typically involving separation from day-to-day society and the placing of the individual in a socially ambiguous category that was also demarcated spatially and temporally, a separation from one social role with the deliberate intention of future reintegration in a new social role. As such the state of liminality while ambiguous, a state of betwixt and between, was also conscious and intentional, part of a wider framework which functioned (in the broadest sense of the word) to maintain social order through ritual processes, many of which we recognise in our own lives.

Just as Turner reworked van Gennep's concept, others have reworked Turner's and liminality has been adopted and adapted in a number of academic disciplines beyond anthropology, and the concept can be found in fields as diverse as management studies (Sturdy *et al.* 2006), health studies (Iedema *et al.* 2005; Mahon-Daly and Andrews 2003), education (Starr-Glass and Schwartzbaum 2003), as well as studies of cyber space (Madge and O'Connor 2005), governance (Ilcan *et al.* 2003), sexuality (Wilson 2002) and of course tourism (Preston-Whyte 2004).

Most importantly though is the way in which liminality is applied to the spatial aspects of our lives. Turner's original three-fold model of separation, liminality and reintegration has now broadened to signify more general states of ambiguity, liminal spaces as 'in-between' places of transit such as airports, railway stations, motorway service stations (Augé 1995), the spaces of mobility that characterise our restless and mobile contemporary world. For Iedema *et al.* (2005) they are spaces of perfomativity, places of intersection and interaction where roles and identities can be negotiated, and embodied (Mahon-Daly and Andrews 2003). While such definitions point to the importance of agency and the negotiation of roles and meanings, liminality can also refer to places that are neither – nor such as allotments which are not quite urban, not quite rural spaces, or the abandoned industrial sites that Edensor (2005) describes.

These liminal spaces, writes Preston-Whyte, exist in a metaphorical way beyond '…normal social and cultural states' (2004: 350) and tourism spaces, I would argue are also places of inbetweenness, they are ludic spaces that also involves the work of others and are occupied by the tourists on a temporary basis. Tourist behaviour is different from the usual established routines of daily life and involves separation, the crossing of a threshold, a limited time spent as a tourist, and a crossing back into the accepted routines and spaces of daily life. Tourist spaces are places set apart, and marked both physically and metaphorically as such, and beaches are the most inbetween of all; in many ways we can see that tourist space and tourism exhibits many of the characteristics of liminality.

Beaches are the interface between dry land and the sea, and as such are both land and water, subject to a daily and seasonal rhythm of tidal movements. At low tides the beach changes and extends, another world is revealed, while at times of high tide the beach may disappear completely. Beaches are also ludic spaces that in the UK at least were central to the growth and development of tourism, and also acted as the national boundary that marked 'us' off from 'them'. Beaches are rarely inhabited but often used, and while a space of play to some, the beach and the sea is also the place of work to others, not just those who work directly in the tourist industry but also fishermen and the entire maritime sector. As well as being a place of recreation beaches can also be places of hazards and dangers; as someone who lives in the southwest of the UK, where coastal tourism still draws in the visitors, every summer I hear reports of holidaymakers being rescued from the sea having been carried out by tides or wind, or caught out by an incoming tide, and the occasional case where someone is not so lucky. In the winter a combination of high tides and high winds can quickly turn a benign environment into a dangerous and chaotic one. A beach can be a place of loneliness and solitude, or it can be a rowdy place of fun and amusement.

Beaches are 'edge spaces' both physically and metaphorically, and feature significantly in British culture and public memory (for example see Payne 2007; Quilley 2000). In history as well as folklore and popular fiction, the beach has been a place of transgression, the place where smugglers and pirates land their booty, where wreckers lure unsuspecting ships to their doom, in more modern times a place to escape to, in more than one way as the beach is also the place where inhibitions can be shed, and not just in the form of naturist beaches, many resorts were – and still are – associated with carnivalesque, risqué behaviour (Shields 1991) and a lax sexual morality. In the UK the beaches are regarded as public spaces, open to all, and while landowners may control access, it is the Crown who owns the foreshore between the low and high water marks.

Beaches are then, I would argue, a perfect example of marginal, inbetween spaces, zones of liminality that hold a fascination for many that few other landscape forms do, as can be seen by their continued popularity as tourist destinations.

Of course, there are many kinds of beaches, the ones discussed here are in Devon are a popular destination that has long been a tourist resort, and they are different from other beaches found nearby in Devon and Cornwall, such as the surfing beaches at Newquay, and different again from those you find on the east coast of England, or in the Western Isles of Scotland, and very different again from the mythical place of escape depicted in the film *The Beach* (2000).

The significance of place, whether liminal or not, is created by the interplay between people and place, the way that people move through and occupy space as much as the meanings they impose and derive from that space, but above all else, such spatiality is not static or fixed. This latter aspect has been recently and usefully described by Edensor as one of rhythmical interactions between people, time and space which combine in an overall '...ensemble of rhythms that interweave in and across place to produce a mix of events of varying regularity. Such multiple rhythms are dynamic, producing an ever changing time-space' (Edensor 2010: 69). I will return to the notion of rhythms later in this chapter, but for now the question is how we can determine what these rhythms are, how can we best record activities in a way that will allow us to reveal the interweaving of space/time in relation to liminal beachscapes, and my suggestion is photography, or perhaps more accurately, participant observation through a lens.

Photography as method

We live in a culture that is awash with visual representations which are an integral part of our lives (Knoblaugh *et al.* 2008; Knowles and Sweetman 2004). Advances in digital technology (Parmeggiani 2009) also means that image making, manipulation and dissemination are within the means of millions of people, even if only through the ubiquitous camera phone, a situation comparable in many ways to the invention of roll film and the Kodak box camera which democratised photography in the 1890s (Tagg 1988: 66).

The first point we need to consider here is that there is no unified field of photography, rather there are different sets of practices that produce different kinds of images for different purposes (Tagg 1988). In everyday use photographs remind us of special events/people as in the holiday snapshot, while we also have the conventions of portraiture and wedding photographs. There is also a division between professional and amateur photographers. Photographs are used for reporting current events, as evidence in courts, as propaganda, and in advertising, textbooks, websites and so on. Photographs also play a significant role in '...constituting and sustaining both individual and collective notions of landscape and identity' (Schwarz and Ryan 2003: 6) and have also figured in the social sciences. As Becker points out, in the early days of sociological development, photographs were used to provide 'objective evidence' of social conditions, a concern that was later overshadowed when sociology moved towards 'scientific generalization' (2004: 193–194).

In other words, we are dealing with a number of social conventions and practices which shape both the production and consumption of photographs;

Bohnsack also notes that image interpretation in our daily lives is both habitual and structured by tacit knowledge (2008: para 11) involving what Baetens (2009) describes as visual literacy or visual competence, that is the extent to which the viewer understands '...the conventions through which the meanings of visual images are created' (Messaris and Moriarty 2005: 481, cited in Müller 2008: 103) and such meanings are defined by context and the discourse in which they are framed (Pink 2001). One of the most widespread of these conventions – that the camera does not lie – is that it gives us an accurate, unbiased and objective recording of things as they *really* are, that photographs provide a (more or less) realistic analogical representation of the material world is simply wrong, all of which adds up to what I term the fallacy of naive realism. Now while it cannot be denied that photographs do have the capability of capturing data in a form that suggests they are entirely realistic and therefore objective, this is not the case, and is an argument that is as old as photography itself (Christmann 2008; Goldstein 2007; Grady 2008; Kember 2003; Lister 2003; Tagg 1988). This fallacy of naive realism is simply accepted, or as Lister puts it, has a deep 'appeal to commonsense' (2003: 220) and is also related to the widespread assumption within mainstream filmmaking, television and more recently gaming, that the illusion of realism is the overriding principle for pictorial representational forms, even when fantasy worlds are involved. I would suggest that these related ideas are linked to the assumption that the technology of photography somehow bypasses human agency, and therefore removes subjectivity because it is a mechanical process (Lister 2003; Wagner 2007).

However, the assumptions of naive realism do not hold up to any real scrutiny. At a simple level, photography requires human agency: if a camera is pointing in one direction it is not pointing in another, the act of framing a picture is both inclusive and exclusive, or as Grady puts it, a photograph is '...a record of that to which attention has been paid' (2004: 21). However, it is also important to note that any form of recording – and by this I would include notetaking as well – is a partial and limited view in one way or another, but this is an issue I will return to later. On a more technical note, photographs are projections of three dimensional objects on to a two-dimensional flat plane: we do not perceive the world through an oblong frame with a specified width–height ratio, and the optics of camera lenses do not mimic the optics of the human eye (Christmann 2008; Goldstein 2007; Grady 2008). All in all, '...photographs do not create "visual copies" of objects' writes Christmann, '...but "imagined pictures"' (2008: para 6).

There are two points I would like to make here. The first is to agree with Goldstein's (2007) blunt assertion that all photographs 'lie', and second to add the caveat that this is not a problem as long as we are aware of the ways in which they do, the ways in which the pictures have been framed and taken, and the intention behind them. Goldstein sums up the issues quite neatly as follows:

> Every image is manipulated, thus no image represents reality. Content depends on a large number of technical and aesthetic choices made by the

photographer, based on his or her intent. The response of the viewer to the image will be based on content, perception of intent and context.

(Goldstein 2007: 79)

Photographs do have a number of unique attributes, the most important being the capacity to freeze a moment in time and space, to extract an almost permanent record of appearances (albeit partial and selective) from the flux of daily life. The capacity of photographs to frame time and space, to select a moment as being of particular importance – the snapshot – also creates problems relating to the lack of narrative and context of that such framing presents. To take a photograph is to decontextaulise it, any meaning which is not inherent in the image itself, nor in the actions or objects it portrays is lost as meanings are defined by context and the discourse in which they are framed (Pink 2001), and as Grady puts it, a photograph is '…a record of that to which attention has been paid' (2004: 21).

In turn this decontextualisation has been a long standing criticism of photography and indeed other fixed images, as Baetens (2009: 143) writes, they are '…considered to be good at 'showing' but not very good at "telling"', or in other words the act of isolation from the temporal flow also removes the possibility of narrative. However, this presupposes that the photograph is only concerned with what is termed the 'decisive moment' that supposedly reveals the essence of the subject in question (see for example Goldstein 2007: 71–72). A single photograph may lack a narrative before and after, but this lifting out has some advantages; it allows us to scrutinise the particular over an extended period – in research terms the isolation from daily rhythms can be a distinct advantage, not a disadvantage.

Participant observation through a lens

As noted above there are many forms of photographic practice, the one I adopted in this instance was based on the longstanding tradition of the documentary (Banks 2001, 2007; Becker 2004; Knowles and Sweetman 2004; Moore *et al.* 2008; Pink 2001) that is a collection of images that would act – given all the caveats outlined above – as a record of what was seen as I walked a particular route. Taking photographs I would argue is a form of participant observation, and the practice of walking has also been part of the ethnographic tradition (Edensor 2000, 2010; Ingold and Vergunst 2008; Pink *et al.* 2010). Walking, watching and listening are integral parts of participant observation, a means to get to know the research setting. Walking is also part of sightseeing or indeed is a recreational pastime itself, indeed parts of the route were very busy with people walking, whether with dogs, as couples, alone or in groups.

Earlier I mentioned that one of the problems of photographs is the way in which they decontextualise the image, in this instance what I found was that the linear narrative framework of each walk provided the context and the metadata embedded in each image recorded the time and date so the exact sequence can be reconstructed through a series of specific moments in space/time. This was a deliberate attempt to build up a large set of visual data in the same way that a set of oral or written data would be compiled whilst undertaking ethnographic research and writing fieldnotes. In effect this was participant observation through a camera lens, a different kind of photographic approach say to one more rooted in aesthetic concerns, or one where the use of photographs is primarily the recording of family, friends and their activities. However, practice is something to be worked at, while undertaking the research, I became conscious early on that I was beginning to be too selective about what I photographed, and found myself wondering if yet another shot of the seawall looking towards Langstone Rock, or another of trains rattling along the tracks would actually add anything to the overall project. However, I decided to take the pictures even if I knew I already had four or five of the same location and did not presume familiarity with the route.

Each sequence was scrutinised and as themes emerged they were then followed up, in effect this was a form of purposive sampling. For example on my first visit to Dawlish Warren for this project I was struck by the number of signs that were present and on subsequent visits made a specific point of recording all of them, and by doing so I then became aware of the other signage that existed along the route and recorded that. In turn, paying close attention to that made me notice the graffiti that had been scratched onto the bricks of a footbridge and written in the cement repairs of the sea wall.

I am very aware that atmospheric conditions not only affect the rhythms and flows of tourists through space but also the impressions of a place that can be conveyed in a photograph, a place seen in summer sunshine is very different from when it rains, or when seen through a low misty haze, or at sunset. So I attempted, with some success, to walk the route under different weather conditions on different days of the week, and also at times of low and high tide. With repeated visits over the period of a year, from the start of one tourist season to another, I began to notice things very differently and became more concerned with details that had previously gone unnoticed, as with the graffiti, or that I had not really considered such as the flora of the warren. When I found old photographs of the holiday homes that had once been built there in the first half of the twentieth century I deliberately searched for evidence of them, without success. Having looked at old pictures of Dawlish I found myself working out where they had been taken and taking a photograph myself from the same spot. There is then a comparative historical element to this project, deeper rhythms to be uncovered, but for reasons of space that cannot be dealt with here.

Walking

The route I walked from Starcross to Dawlish in Devon is also part of the South West Coast Path (www.southwestcoastpath.com, see also Wylie 2005) and comprises of three distinct sections: the west side of the River Exe estuary, the sand spit of Dawlish Warren at the mouth of the Exe, and the beach from Langstone

Rock to Dawlish (see Figure 5.1).The direct route from Starcross to Dawlish is approximately six kilometres (km), if the distance to the eastern end of Dawlish Warren and back is added in, that comes to approximately 10 km in total. Between April 2010 and April 2011 I walked the route and visited specific sites along it 18 times, taking a total of 2151 photographs which were then analysed using Nvivo 8. As with field notes I found this was an iterative process: each set of pictures recorded a specific route, and I also wanted the pictures to record each walk and the banal details such as what was on sale in the shops and what the cafe menus were offering. Tourism in the area is predominantly characterised by holiday park units (static caravans and holiday chalets) and touring caravan pitches (Corporate Consultation Service, Devon County Council 2008), as well as some small hotels and bed and breakfast accommodation, and is what can be regarded as traditional family oriented seaside holidays, but the route also

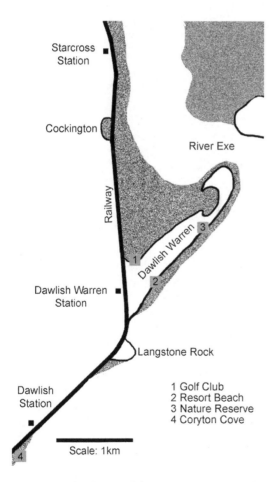

Figure 5.1 Sketch map of the route, scale is approximate.

takes in some important wildlife habitats, and because of the railway, industrial heritage.

The walks began at Starcross, a small village that has been a ferry crossing over the River Exe for many years. The more recent story of this stretch of river and coast, like many other resorts and tourist sites in the UK, is intimately connected with the arrival of the railway, which is one of the most notable physical features of this stretch of coast and is part of the mainline that runs from Penzance in Cornwall to London and via Bristol to the midlands, north and Scotland. Constructed in the 1840s by the engineer Brunel, it is unclear why he or the railway company chose to build the line so close to the river's edge, in some places actually beyond the then high water mark, as that involved the construction of a massive embankment that acts as a seawall, and between Starcross and Dawlish Warren defines the edge of the Exe estuary.

Access to the river is either through small narrow underpasses, known locally as 'creeps' or over the lines at pedestrian crossings. At the small village of Cockington, the railway cuts across the mouth of the small harbour; the low bridge has two access channels that allow the harbour to remain tidal and provide access to the river beyond. At low tide the estuary reveals extensive mud flats, and there is little human activity on the estuarine shore. This is marginal land in more than one sense: poor access and the fact that it is river mud rather than beach sand means it is not suitable for anything other than fishing, cockling and mooring some leisure craft. As the line reaches Dawlish Warren, a 2.4 km long sand spit of dunes that protects the mouth of the Exe, it turns along the coast to run south west at the foot of the red sandstone cliffs from Langstone Rock to Dawlish. Here, the stone seawall that carries the railway is at places 6–8 metres above the level of the beach, and has a small walkway along the top, separated from the railway lines by a low wall. As with the estuary, at high tide the beach is completely submerged except for a short stretch of sand at Langstone Rock, and another at Dawlish, at low tide the remains of other sea defences are uncovered.

Even in the days of brash, self-confident Victorian engineering, the decision to take the coastal route west from Exeter rather than an inland one seemed reckless, as it involved not only building on the soft estuary mud, but also the cutting back of the cliffs and after Dawlish, the construction of several tunnels and another massive seawall that takes the line to Teignmouth and beyond. At times and especially during the winter, high seas often break over the tracks making it impassable, and the wall needs constant and costly maintenance; cliff falls and breaches of the sea wall caused by sea erosion have been problems ever since the line was first constructed. However, the legacy is one of the more scenic stretches of railway in the UK. As Wylie (2005: 235) points out, walking inevitably '…involves at least some attunement with the various sensibilities still distilling from sublime and romantic figurations of self, travel, landscape and nature.' In this case we can also add the industrial heritage of Brunel.

The railway is also of historic interest as it was originally an atmospheric railway which used a novel means of propulsion that required a series of coal fired pumping stations alongside the line creating a vacuum in a pipe laid between the rails, which pulled along a piston attached to the train. Due to a number of technical problems this system was only in use for a short period of time, and the only surviving remains of this rather eccentric footnote to engineering history are the pumping stations at Starcross and Totnes. A series of signboards, called the 'Brunel Way' have been placed at strategic points along the route from Dawlish Warren to Dawlish, and narrate the story of the railway and town, providing another way to interpret place. While the route itself is a defined linear pathway it also passes through a number of distinct zones, especially when Dawlish Warren is taken into account. From Starcross to the warren the path runs along the road where it is still possible in places to see the original estuary shoreline. There are a few houses along this stretch of the road, but the character of the landscape suddenly changes on arrival at Dawlish Warren. On both sides of the road are extensive caravan parks with both static and touring pitches and also a number of holiday chalet/bungalow parks that also contain paddling pools and children's playgrounds. Associated with these sites are a number of small shops and cafes selling souvenirs, beach goods, ice cream, fish and chips, pizzas and burgers.

As the road turns away from the estuary to climb the hill over to Dawlish the path continues alongside the railway to the station, which was built in 1902 to cater for and encourage the number of day trippers who were visiting from Exeter.

Figure 5.2 The resort area beach at Dawlish Warren in June. Most visitors stay within a short distance of this section of beach and its associated shops.

There is a large car park near to Dawlish Warren station, access to the warren is via a narrow 'creep' under the railway, just wide enough for a single file of cars and of pedestrians. On the other side of the tunnel is another extensive car park, a cafe, a small funfair, go kart rides and crazy golf, and the path leads on to a pub, several fast food outlets, amusement arcades and shops selling beach goods, before climbing to the sea wall. This part of the warren in called the resort area, and is where most of the visitors congregate. The warren is also home to a private golf club on the northern side.

The warren has had a complicated history (Barber 2001; Sims 1998) and in the first half of the twentieth century was the site of many summer holiday homes, all of which had disappeared by the 1960s due to erosion. Early maps and photographs reveal that the warren has changed shape significantly and within short periods of time, it has always been a place at risk from the sea. Over the years there have been many attempts to buttress the dunes as well as the installation of wooden groynes and towards Langstone Rock extensive engineering work has been undertaken, large boulders or rip-rap, some of which were imported from Norway, have been placed along the western edge of the warren by the seawall to absorb the power of the waves (see www.geograph.org.uk/gridref/SX9878).

Zones of control

Dawlish Warren is also a Blue Flag beach, that is, it meets certain criteria for water quality, and is one of the many designations that are applied to the Warren and surrounding areas. The Exe estuary itself is subject to five different conservation designations, and is a recognised internationally important wetland site, in particular for its wildfowl, while Dawlish Warren itself encompasses a National Nature Reserve on its northern side that includes part of the estuary (access to this area is forbidden), a Local Nature Reserve and also a Special Area of Conservation. In addition to the seaside elements, the warren also has a nature reserve office with a small exhibition detailing the natural history of the warren.

This is not one single place, rather it encompasses several zones of control with varying degrees of access. Walking east along the warren towards the mouth of the River Exe at Warren Point the different uses of space become apparent. As noted, most tourists tend to congregate near to the shops, funfair and pub, and clearly thin out the further eastwards one goes. What the pictures also reveal is the way that people dressed was rather uniform, for both men and women wear shorts, flip-flops or trainers with casual T shirts, all of which signify leisure and are also very practical beachwear. Away from the beach the inner warren is much quieter, the walkers and visitors here tend not to be family groups with small children, and are often bird watching or fishing. Those who were seen on the nature reserve tended to wear walking boots and long trousers; bird watchers were identifiable by the binoculars, telescopes and long lensed cameras that they carried. During the summer small groups of people had landed from boats, or were walking their dogs when restrictions allowed, and in some

Figure 5.3 Impromptu beach sculpture at the eastern end of the warren, this one looked like the framework of a small shelter and had disappeared by my next visit.

Figure 5.4 Entrance to the nature reserve, the dunes here have been fenced off to prevent erosion.

cases where they were not. Occasionally people would be picnicking, although this was more common towards the tourist beach. At times, even during the height of the tourist season the eastern end of the warren would be almost empty of people. I came across evidence that small fires had been lit, despite the ban on them and barbecues, debris such as beer cans and empty bottles of alcohol next to the ashes indicated impromptu night-time parties, on a few occasions I came across examples of 'beach sculpture' where drift wood had clearly been gathered and arranged in a playful manner.

During the spring, parts of the eastern end are cordoned off to protect the nesting wildfowl and dogs are not allowed on the eastern end of the beach either though some people clearly disregarded this. It is impossible to enter the warren or any of the zones without being confronted by signs informing you of the restrictions in force: no cycling; no camping; no fires; no barbecues; no access; golf club members only. Other areas have been fenced off to help prevent erosion especially along the dune crest that faces the sea, the nature reserve that is evident today is the result of a complex set of historical factors that are both environmental and social, without the sea defences the warren would probably have eroded and disappeared many years ago.

From the warren the path runs along the railway embankment and at Langstone Rock along the top of the seawall. When the tide is fully in most of the beach is covered apart from a small stretch of sand by Langstone Rock, and also at Dawlish. This stretch of the route is more like a corridor between the warren

Figure 5.5 Looking seaward from Dawlish, access to the beach is under the rail bridge that cuts across the natural valley mouth and the outfall of Dawlish Water. The station is just out of shot to the left of the picture.

and Dawlish, and, as it is less regulated than the beaches on the warren, is also popular for dog walkers. Few people – those fishing aside – sit on this stretch of the beach, and if they do it tends to be at either end.

At Dawlish, as at Cockington, the railway makes no concession to the topography of the small town. Set in a shallow valley, most of the town is aligned along the banks of a small stream, Dawlish Water, stretching inland. Early prints also show that some large terraced houses had been constructed on the seafront facing the sea, and the town had already become established as a tourist resort before the arrival of the railway. Brunel's railway hugs the cliffs and simply straddles the valley, effectively cutting the town off from the beach which can only be accessed under a rather low viaduct or by two footbridges, both some distance from the station.

At Dawlish the kinds of tourists also change. Families still predominated but added to these were coachloads of more elderly people and while some ventured under the railway and onto the beach, most strolled around the town along the landscaped banks of Dawlish water, a linear park that extends about half a kilometre inland. There are a number of shops like those at the warren that sell beach goods and souvenirs, a number of cafes, pubs and an amusement arcade, all of which fill up quickly when the rain begins. The seawall itself continues a short distance from Dawlish station until the track enters the first of several tunnels. From here, the path passes around a small headland to Coryton Cove, the last accessible beach for several kilometres. This is a different space again; unlike the other beaches, at low tides rockpools are exposed and searching them for crabs and other marine life is a popular activity for both adults and children.

Figure 5.6 Low tide at Coryton Cove, searching the rock pools.

One aspect of behaviour that was common to all the beaches along this route is that a great deal of time seems to be spent by people simply looking at the sea or in the better weather, sunbathing, children play at the water's edge, following the tideline as it come is or goes out, others dig in the sand. Sometimes there are people body boarding or surfing but these are not good surfing beaches. The space is occupied for brief, transitory periods, although some groups may spend a whole day there, or even a succession of days but even in the height of the summer season it is unusual to see people on the beaches before 10 am and after 5 pm. On the controlled space of the warren the number of visitors was much lower than on the resort and other beaches.

Conclusions

There are two main themes to this chapter, one relating to liminality and the rhythms of the beaches, and the other to methodology. As I mentioned at the start, beaches of the kind described here are liminal, in-between spaces in both physical and metaphorical senses, they are always (leaving aside those who work on them and the sea) places apart, places to escape to, to occupy temporarily while away from home. In this instance the specific locations of the beaches are affected and in part determined by the way the railway imposes itself on the landscape, defining the edge between land and sea, while also acting as a transitory corridor through the spaces described here, as well a route in and a route out.

Earlier I mentioned that the uses of space could be thought of as complex interplays of different rhythms and patterns, and in turn these can be both long and short term: like other seaside resorts in the UK the occupation of the beaches follows a long-term seasonal rhythm and within that a weekly rhythm, both of which are partly dictated by the seasons and partly by the necessity of work. There was, as I noted, also a daily rhythm of occupancy in the more populated areas of the beaches that also in part related to the shifting tidal patterns, and also the particular designations that were evident on Dawlish Warren. Compared to the resort area the eastern end of the warren was underused; the majority of beach users tended to cluster close to the amenities of shops, cafes and pubs, a socially accepted zone of compliance. The beaches are also spaces of performance, where being a tourist is signalled by a number of routine activities and mode of dress, all of which mark the conspicuous use of leisure time. However, we also have to bear in mind that beaches, and the ways they are used, reveal both general and place specific behaviour and while I have not undertaken sustained observational work of this kind in other places, I know for example that behaviour on the surfing beaches of Cornwall and Devon is of a different order from that written about here.

The kinds of activities described here will be familiar to many, yet we should not presume that familiarity is a substitute for close observation, there was an order, an overall rhythm to the use of the beaches that was only revealed by repeated observations, which brings me to a final few words on methods. While the use of photography has both a history and precedents within the social sciences it has tended to remain a minority pursuit; however, with digital technology possibilities are opened up for the development of methods in new ways. In particular I would argue that photography – and by implication video – has the ability to broaden the scope of ethnography: with a camera I was able to gather data that was far richer in detail than field notes would allow. Of course that in turn raises a number of epistemological as well as practical issues, but they are for another time and place.

References

Augé, M. (1995) *Non-Places: Introduction to an anthropology of supermodernity.* Verso: London.

Baetens, J. (2009) 'Is a Photograph Worth a Thousand Films?' *Visual Studies*, 24 (2): 143–148.

Banks, M. (2001) *Visual Methods in Social Research.* Sage: London.

Banks, M. (2007) *Using Visual Data in Qualitative Research.* Sage: London.

Barber, C. (2001) *The Story of Dawlish Warren.* Obelisk Publications: Exeter.

Becker, H. (2004) 'Afterword: Photography as evidence, photographs as exposition.' In Knowles, C. and Sweetman, P. (eds) (2004) *Picturing the Social Landscape: Visual methods and the sociological imagination.* Routledge: London.

Bohnsack, R. (2008) 'The Interpretation of Pictures and the Documentary Method', *Forum Qualitative Sozialforschung/Forum: Qualitative Research*, 9 (3), available at http://www.qualitative-research.net/index.php/fqs/article/view/1171 (accessed 23 December 2011).

Christmann, G. (2008) 'The Power of Photographs of Buildings in the Dresden Urban Discourse: Towards a visual discourse analysis', *Forum Qualitative Sozialforschung/ Forum: Qualitative Research* 9 (3), available at http://www.qualitative-research.net/ index.php/fqs/article/view/1163 (accessed 23 December 2011).

Corporate Consultation Service, Devon County Council (2008) *Tourism Trends in Devon 2007.* Devon County Council: Exeter, available at www.devon.gov.uk/tourismtrends07. pdf (accessed 23 December 2011).

Edensor, T. (2000) 'Walking in the British Countryside: Reflexivity, embodied practices and ways to escape', *Body and Society*, 63 (3–4): 81–106.

Edensor, T. (2005) *Industrial Ruins: Space, Aesthetics and Materiality.* Oxford: Berg.

Edensor, T. (2010) 'Walking in Rhythm: Place, regulation, style and the flow of experience', *Visual Studies*, 25 (1): 69–79.

Goldstein, B. (2007) 'All Photographs Lie: Images as data.' In Stanczak, G.C. (ed.) *Visual Research Methods: Image, society and representation.* Sage: Thousand Oaks.

Grady, J. (2004) 'Working with Visible Evidence: An invitation and some practical advice.' In Knowles, C. and Sweetman, P. (eds) *Picturing the Social Landscape: Visual methods and the sociological imagination.* Routledge: London.

Grady, J. (2008) 'Visual Research at the Crossroads', *Forum Qualitative Sozialforschung/ Forum: Qualitative Research*, 9 (3), available at http://www.qualitative-research.net/ index.php/fqs/article/view/1173 (accessed 23 December 2011).

Iedema, R., Long, D., Carroll, K., Stenglin, M. and Braithwaite, J. (2005) 'Corridor Work: How Liminal Space becomes a Resource for Handling Complexities of Multi-disciplinary Health Care.' Asia-Pacific Researchers in Organization Studies: 11th

International Colloquium (APROS 11), Melbourne, Australia, 4–7 December 2005. Available at http://search.informit.com.au/documentSummary;dn=305691933675194;r es=IELHSS (accessed 23 December 2011).

Ilcan, S.M, O'Connor, D.M, and Oliver, M.L. (2003) 'Contract Governance and the Canadian Public Sector', *Relations industrielles/Industrial Relations*, 58 (4): 620–643.

Ingold, T. and Vergunst, J.L. (eds) (2008) *Ways of Walking: Ethnography and practice on foot*. Ashgate: Aldershot.

Kember.S. (2003) ' "The Shadow of the Object": Photography and realism.' In Wells, L. (ed.) *The Photography Reader*. Routledge: London.

Knoblaugh, H., Bear, A., Laurier, E., Petschke, S. and Schnettler, B. (2008) 'Visual Analysis: New Developments in the interpretive analysis of video and photography', *Forum Qualitative Sozialforschung/Forum: Qualitative Research*, 9 (3), available at http://www.qualitative-research.net/index.php/fqs/article/view/1170 (accessed 23 December 2011).

Knowles, C. and Sweetman, P. (eds) (2004) *Picturing the Social Landscape: Visual methods and the sociological imagination*. Routledge: London.

Lister, M. (2003) 'Extracts from Introduction to the Photographic Image in Digital Culture.' In Wells, L. (ed.) *The Photography Reader*. Routledge: London.

Madge. C. and O'Connor, H. (2005) 'Mothers in the making? Exploring liminality in cyber/space.' *Transactions of the Institute of British Geographers*, 30 (1): 83–97.

Mahon-Daly, P. and Andrews, G.J. (2003) 'Liminality and breastfeeding: women negotiating space and two bodies.' *Health & Place*, 8 (2): 61–76.

Messaris, P. and Moriarty, S. (2005) 'Visual Literacy Theory.' In Smith, K., Moriarty, S., Barbatsis, G. and Kenny, K. (eds) *Handbook of Visual Communication: Theory, methods and media*. Lawrence Erlbaum: Mahwah, NJ.

Moore, G., Croxford, B., Adams, M., Rafaee, M., Cox, T. and Sharples, S. (2008) 'The Photo-Survey Research Method: Capturing life in the city', *Visual Studies*, 23 (1): 50–62.

Müller, M.G. (2008) 'Visual Competence: A new paradigm for studying visuals in the social sciences?' *Visual Studies,* 23 (2): 101–112.

Parmeggiani, P. (2009) 'Going Digital: Using new technologies in visual sociology', *Visual Studies*, 24 (1): 71–81.

Payne, C. (2007) *Where the Sea Meets the Land: Artists on the coast in nineteenth century Britain.* Sansom & Co: Bristol.

Pink, S. (2001) *Doing Visual Ethnography*. Sage: London.

Pink, S., Hubbard, P., O'Neill, M. and Radley, A. (2010) 'Walking Across Disciplines: From ethnography to arts practice', *Visual Studies*, 25 (1): 1–7.

Preston-Whyte, R. (2004) 'The Beach as a Liminal Space.' In Lew, A., Hall, C.M. and Williams, A.M. (eds) *A Companion to Tourism*. Oxford: Blackwell.

Quilley, G. (2000) 'Missing the Boat: The place of the maritime in British visual culture', *Visual Culture in Britain*, 1 (2): 69–79.

Schwarz, J.M. and Ryan, J.R. (2003) 'Introduction: Photography and the Geographical Imagination.' In Schwarz, J.M. and Ryan, J.R. (eds) *Picturing Place: Photography and the Geographical Imagination.* I.B. Taurus: London.

Shields, R. (1991) *Places on the Margin: Alternative geographies of modernity*. London: Routledge.

Sims, P. (1998) *Dawlish Warren and the Sea.* Oxford: Thematic Trails.

Starr-Glass, D and Schwartzbaum, A. (2003) 'A Liminal Space: Challenges and opportunities in accreditation of prior learning in Judaic Studies', *Assessment & Evaluation in Higher Education*, 28 (2): 179–192.

Sturdy, A. Schwarz, M. and Spicer. A. (2006) 'Guess who's coming to dinner? Structures and uses of liminality in strategic management consultancy', *Human Relations*, 59 (7): 929–960.

Tagg, J. (1988) *The Burden of Representation: Essays on Photographies and Histories.* Macmillan: Basingstoke.

Turner, V.W. (1967) *The Forest of Symbols: Aspects of Ndembu Ritual.* Cornell University Press: Ithica, NY.

Wagner, J. (2007) 'Observing Culture and Social Life: Documentary photography, fieldwork and social research', in Stanczak, G.C. (ed.) *Visual Research Methods: Image, society and representation.* Sage: Thousand Oaks.

Wilson, M. (2002) ' "I am the Prince of Pain, for I am a Princess in the Brain": Liminal Transgender Identities, Narratives and the Elimination of Ambiguities', *Sexualities*, 5 (4): 425–448.

Wylie, J. (2005) 'A Single Day's Walking: Narrating self and landscape on the South West Coast Path', *Transactions of the Institute of British Geographers*, 30 (2): 234–247.

6   The dynamics of liminality in Estonian mires

Piret Pungas and Ester Võsu

Introduction: a theoretical perspective on the liminality of mires

From the socio-cultural perspective, humans have always been in need of boundaries – either between individuals, groups and cultures, or more generally
between culture and its 'other' (e.g. 'nature'). In cultural semiotics boundaries
are not rigid barriers but more akin to membranes that selectively allow the
exchange between 'inside' and 'outside' realms, and therefore become zones
rich in distinct significant phenomena (Lotman 2001: 131–142). Boundaries are
also crucial in biological systems, where they enable evolution and growth from
the micro level of cells up to the macro level of ecosystems (cf. Hoffmeyer and
Faverau 2009). Boundaries and edges also characterize the dynamics of landscapes (Olwig 2005; van de Noort and O'Sullivan 2005: 83).

One way to conceptualize boundaries in culture is through liminality, which
is etymologically (from Latin *limen*) a spatial term referring to a 'threshold'. A
liminal place is situated in between two (or more) distinct environments, yet
cannot be identified with either of them.[1] A threshold may be a place with more
or less distinguishable borders, but it may likewise be an imaginary in-between
place that unites different social statuses, which, from the historical perspective,
are created through human practice, often in the form of rituals. In this chapter
we approach the mire as a place related to both ecological and social liminality,
an in-between environment for multiple biological reasons that are mutually
related to different cultural practices, beliefs and values.

From the anthropological viewpoint, liminality means 'being-on-a-threshold', it
is 'a state which is betwixt-and-between the normal, day to day cultural and social
states and processes of getting and spending, preserving law and order, and registering structural status' (Turner 1979 (1977): 465). According to this view, a liminal
place exists only inasmuch as it is related to particular cultural practices (e.g. different kinds of initiation rituals or 'rites of passage', as introduced by Arnold van
Gennep). These practices, norms and values are related to liminal places; they are
considered to be clearly distinct from the routines and rules of everyday life.

Liminality can be revealed not only from the spatial, but also from the temporal perspective. Since liminal time is not controlled by the clock, it is a time of

enchantment when anything might, even should, happen (Turner 1979 (1977): 465). Although Victor Turner describes liminality primarily as a state of temporary change, a transition that is characteristic of certain phases in the ritual process, it is also possible to consider liminality in space or in the social status of human beings as 'the state of more-or-less permanent "outsider-hood"' (Trubshaw 1995) (examples of which are various marginal persons such as witches, healers, shamans, diviners, mediums, priests, etc.).

Furthermore, 'through liminality anthropology has found it possible to focus conceptually upon such phenomena as marginality, alterity, rebellion, ostracism, subalternity, pollution, eccentricity and deviance' (Rapport and Overing 2000: 229). Thus liminality as a social phenomenon is rather rich in examples and the multiplicity of ways in which someone may be considered to belong to cultural 'borderlines' remind us, in turn, of the importance of the distinction between centre and periphery of social space. Although the distinction and the dynamics between the two have been interpreted in various different ways, one almost universal rule may be recognized – those cultural groups or individuals who are significantly different from the ones belonging to the centre were settled on the periphery and were thereby marginalized. In different periods, the accepted norms of behaviour for moving from the boundary to centre have been different (Lotman 2001: 140–141), although it should be remembered that not all liminal places (especially those created in certain rituals) are socially marginal and not all socially marginal places are liminal (cf. van de Noort and O'Sullivan 2007).

However, in this chapter we want to conceptualize liminality not just as a social phenomenon; we also wish to shed light on Estonian mires as a particular kind of liminal or hybrid environment that is neither mineral land nor water, 'a continuum between terra and aqua' (Howarth 2001: 65). The mire is a liminal ecosystem due to excessive water and because of this it lacks nutrients, the ground is soft and the landscape may disorient the visitor. However, for human beings liminality may seasonally diminish in the mire (at least in the temperate zone). During winter and early spring mires form a useful bridge that made the distances to be travelled shorter. During warmer seasons mires may be very difficult to cross, but different species of berries still attract people to visit them. This leads us to the various cultural practices and beliefs that may appear because of the liminality of the environment.

The particular ecological conditions and the abundance of mires in Estonia have influenced local life and cultural beliefs. Examples of this are provided by heritage that refers to mires (proverbs, folktales, etc.), the consideration of mires in Estonian literature, and many mire-related activities that have transformed them and human beings too, to a larger or smaller extent over the centuries. Thus a study of mires as liminal environments allows for a simultaneous study of different social liminalities and the variegated borders within culture. Our study is based on different empirical sources. We have used the archives of the Estonian National Museum (ERM) for the correspondents' responses to questionnaires on gathering (Sion 1947; Pärdi 1983) and on winter roads (Loosalu and Konsin

1982).[2] The answers to the inquiry carried out by Piret Pungas in 2006–2007[3] are also used. This data is supplemented by several references to examples derived from the folklore archives[4] of the Estonian Literary Museum and examples from Estonian literature.

For our analysis we proceeded from the expanded treatment of liminality, introduced above, as the general theoretical framework – this covers ecological and social, spatial and temporal dimensions. These different aspects of liminality are juxtaposed in our research to embodied practices and knowledges that constitute places for human beings (Ingold 2000; 2009). It is through the examination of changes in the various mire-related practices and knowledges that we come to understand the shifting meanings of liminality of wetlands in Estonian culture.

We argue that the Estonian mire is a liminal landscape, and that the dynamics of this liminality depend on social and economic formations, changing value judgments, knowledges and practices. The purposes of the paper are to (1) analyse both ecological and cultural reasons that turn mires into liminal places; (2) study the natural factors and human practices and beliefs that are conductive of this liminality, and (3) survey some of the more relevant cultural practices that have transformed the liminality of mires.

Mire as a borderland in nature and society

In general, due to its geographical location and characteristic ecosystems, Estonia may be considered a borderland in the sense that 'here there are many transitional regions of different types of natures and cultures, for which reason the concentration of different borders (geological, geographical, biological and cultural) is larger in Estonia than in many other places in the world' (Kull 2001). Due to the flat topography, a variety of glacial formations and humid temperate climate, Estonia is rich in inland wetlands – mires, wet forests and grasslands. According to the Ramsar Convention Secretariat (2006), 'wetlands are areas of marsh, fen, peatland or water, whether natural or artificial, permanent or temporary, with water that is static or flowing, fresh, brackish, or salt including areas of marine water, the depth of which at low tide does not exceed six meters'. This same source defines mire as a peatland where peat is constantly forming and accumulating. According to Masing *et al.* (2000) almost 21.5 per cent of Estonian territory (45,000 km[2]) is covered with mires.

Translating the term mire into Estonian, the general term *soo* appears to be the best interpretation, as well as the Finnish peat-based soils, called *suo* (cf. Tanskanen 2011). The Merriam-Webster Dictionary defines mire as wet spongy earth (as of a bog or marsh); heavy, often deep mud or slush; or a troublesome or intractable situation ('found themselves in a mire of debt').[5] There are, of course, other words in English (such as bog, swamp, fen, marsh) that refer more precisely to different types of mires.

The general development of mires in Estonia can be divided into three main stages (Valk 1988). The first stage is a fen. Fen peat is usually black or black-brown and the remains of plants are highly decomposed. Mire birches, willows, sedges and reed are species characteristic to groundwater-fed fens. The fen then evolves into transitional mire as the peat layer thickens. Both fen and bog species are present in transitional mires. The bog is the final stage of mire development, in which all nutrients are derived from precipitation. The peat layer is so thick at the bog stage that the mire surface is usually higher than the surrounding areas, forming domes or raised plateaus. Characteristic plant species in bogs are sphagnum mosses (*Sphagnum*), pine (*Pinus sylvestris*), cotton-grass (*Eriophorum vaginatum*) and cranberry (*Oxycoccus palustris*). Distinct ecological boundaries exist inside the mire itself, and between its different stages of development, in which the most notable indicators of the transfer are different plant species. In addition, borders can be noticed in the micro-relief as well, where the concentration of water or peat leads into different and specific places – to bog pools, lakes in the mire, hollows, mire hills, edges of the bog, mire turfs, etc.

From the human perspective, the more specific borders within the mire are perceivable by those who enter the mire. However, without a specific reason, Estonians have avoided mires and have only gone there for hunting, berry-picking or have used them as winter roads. As an unfamiliar environment, mires infused people with greater feelings of uncertainty than the more frequently visited forest, and the former was often associated with supernatural forces (Hiiemäe 1988: 223).

An unfamiliar environment that is not treated as one's own is frequently a basis for hearsay and myth. In general, one can assume that mire-related folklore has been quite widespread in Estonia, but until today, very little of it has been preserved and recorded. Thus the amount of mire-related data in the folklore archives of the RKM and ERM, recorded during the Soviet era, is scant. On the one hand, mires were considered to be relatively useless at the time, worth something only when drained. The second reason was the emphasis placed in folkloristics on genres (e.g. folk tales, local myths) that relegated the social aspect of the subject matter (such as when, to whom and how folk tales were told) to the background. The most characteristic tales about mires to be found in the Estonian Folklore Archives (ERA) are tales about the creation of mires (e.g. RKM II 4, 530/1 (11)), mythic creatures (ERA II 242, 209/11 (1)) and folktale-style measuring of the depth of bog pools (ERA II 38, 502 (102)). The archives of ERM also include replies from correspondents on gathering and on winter roads established in mires.

Although it was possible to pick berries and hunt for prey in mires, it was perceived as relatively unproductive land that occupied extensive territories. Thus there developed a firm ambition (and a need, since the population had increased) to push the boundaries of usable lands on the expense of the unusable, that is, mires. This culminated with the development of artificial drainage systems in mires. According to Paal and Leibak (2011), nearly 70 per cent of mires in Estonia are currently affected by drainage (approximately one million hectares) that was established for agriculture, forestry and mining.

Today, mires are appreciated in the ecological context – they are recognized as an important habitat for many globally endangered plant and animal species, such as eagles and large carnivores. 'As a remnant of fast-receding wildness, wetlands are the landscape equivalent of extinct or endangered species' (Howarth 2001: 66). In addition to their ecological value, natural mires are known to accumulate carbon (Salm, *et al.* 2009), balance river and flood systems (Masing, *et al.* 2010), and provide a remarkable area for hiking and walking. Arguably, mires have been discovered to represent ecological values and their wilderness has been turned into a tourist attraction, spiced with cultural phenomena due to its ecological liminality.

Factors contributing to the ecological and social liminality of mires

From the ecological point of view, the mire is a complicated area for human beings to live in, in which the central role for human activities and attitudes is determined by the abundance of water. Rules that are in effect on mineral land are no longer valid in mires, yet the rules of water are not yet valid, either. This marginal status and a certain ambiguity for the outside perspective has influenced people's perception: 'for thousands of years, the human attitude toward wetlands was consistently negative: they were read as dangerous, useless, fearful, filthy, diseased, noxious' (Howarth 2001: 58). In what follows, we present the ecological factors of mires that have turned them into both ecologically and socially liminal landscapes.

Vegetative growth in mires loses its connection with groundwater as the fen turns into a bog, the plants can no longer acquire minerals except from dust and precipitation; bog water becomes increasingly acidic. The poverty of nutrients in raised bogs leads to an impoverished and undersized vegetation. The latter, in its turn, opens up the landscape (comparable to moorlands of Scotland and Ireland, the subarctic region in the Northern Hemisphere, etc.). Thus raised bogs are, due to their poor nutrient value, ecologically more liminal than fens, which are still relatively rich in nutrients, since plant life can acquire minerals from the ground water; at the same time, however, for human beings fens are much more difficult to traverse due to their thick scrubs and carrs, and their sods.

In Estonian folktales, the poor nutrient value of mires is reflected in proverbs in which the analogy of mires in a description of something cultural usually has negative connotations, since the fertility of the land was the primary source of sustenance. One of the more common expressions related to mires, '*omadega rappa minema*' ('to get mired in') primarily means that an activity has ended up somewhere from which one can no longer proceed further (i.e., a dead end). Poor nutrient value is also characterized by the following proverbs: *maasikas ei kasva rabasoos* – ('strawberries do not grow in swamps') – since strawberries require nutritious soil, this proverb says that as long as the environment is infertile one should not expect much to grow in it. The saying '*kus mägi, seal mõis, kus küngas, seal kõrts, talud soo ja raba sees*' ('a manor on top of a mountain, a tavern on top of a hill, but farmsteads in bogs and swamps') refers to living places divided according to economic wealth. The proverb '*lage soo – lagund regi, joobnud naene – nutja laps*' ('bare swamp – broken sledge, drunken woman – crying child') indicates that since not even trees grow in mires, there is no money to repair the sledge, and that a woman who drinks is bad for the well-being of children. '*Rikkal hea raba pealgi elada*' ('Rich people live well even in bogs') means that those who have money can survive even in the harshest of conditions. The saying '*ega palk soo pääl ei kasva*' ('salaries/tree trunks do not grow in bogs', a play on the homonym of *palk*) refers to a poor growth environment where neither income nor timber grows.

The softness, the threat of sinking in – due to low oxygen content, peat forms from incompletely decomposed and sedimented plant remains, soaked in water, and it is springy and oozy under the soles. Legs sink into the ground to a greater or lesser extent, and this (occasionally entirely justifiably) could pose the risk of drowning. For this reason, walking in a mire requires certain skills that must be acquired through immediate bodily experience – one must know the mire and how to move around in it, the techniques for moving on the springy and unstable surface do not feel the same as moving on solid ground, and there is a continuous search for balance through an active interaction between the body and the environment (cf. Ingold 2008).

In Estonian literary history, there are numerous references to the frightening nature of mires; one of the more representative ones is the following:

> *I am lost in a bog. It's evening. … There are blinking lights. … Swaying … the swamp sways already several footsteps ahead. You can't stay in the same spot for more than a minute, otherwise the thin layer of grass will rip apart under the feet and I will fall – into hell. … Confounds! How firm the footing in the Luxembourg gardens in Paris is right at this very moment. Do they over there have any inkling that there are bogs in the world?*
>
> (Luts 1914: 16)

Disorienting – for someone unfamiliar with the mire, it may look monotonous. Bare bogs have almost no landmarks, whereas the scrubs in fens block all visual objects from sight; in addition, the trees growing there are usually too slender for someone who has become lost to climb up and try and find a landmark connected to human habitats. For centuries, people have become lost in mires; people tell different stories about getting lost, and some of these stories are still published in the media.

In order to avoid getting lost, signs created in the natural environment were used as navigation aids, for instance: '…some tree-branches were broken, or some other signs were made on trees or ground, in order to come back with their aid. In case of separation, people hooted at each other' (KV 77, 127–130). In addition, people sometimes brought their own cultural signs to the mire, often associated with various beliefs: 'When somebody got lost, they would spit into their palm and then strike the spit with the other hand's finger; whatever direction the spit jumped, there you would go' (KV 77, 85–89) or 'But when people got lost, a woman must put the skirt on inside-out and a man must put the hat on inside-out. This way you could get back to your own people' (KV 77, 25–29).

Because of these disorienting factors, mires could also become refuges for social outcasts and others from local communities. In Estonian culture, mires traditionally have negative connotations, but for those marginal in a society it is precisely the mire environment that could turn into a safe refuge because of the ecological characteristics described above. In earlier times, serfs escaped into mires to get away from hostile landlords, young men escaped from conscription (in the nineteenth century, Russian military service lasted for 25 years), and from wars; people who were special in some respect – healers, witches, hermits – found their residence in mires. Refugees who knew the layout of the surrounding mires used the danger of sinking and of getting lost for escaping from enemies, since enemies were usually foreign and hence unfamiliar with the terrain. Mires thus became 'transitional zones' (Howarth 2001: 63–64) for refugees, a temporary hideout that occasionally turned into a permanent abode, in which a suitable place for living was found, such as swamp islands.

In Estonia, even fortifications were built onto mires, such as the castrum Soontagana, approachable only by a single secret road, built on top of poles rammed into the bog. 'The one who failed to notice the signs would step off the track and sink' (Saal 1921). Hanso (1977: 670) describes the origin of the ancient settlement in the mire in the following story:

More than 300 years ago, the Sindi baron flogged a slave girl. The swain of the lass lost his self-control, grabbed an axe and knocked the baron unconscious. The consequences of the deed would have been dire. Axe in hand, the lad ran into the forest and no-one saw him ever since. ... It was believed that the young man killed himself or perished in the depths of the forest. Yet he was not made of soft timber. After becoming lost for a time in the dense thickets between mires ... he finally reached a larger and higher hillock. ... Over time, the man built himself an abode on that hill ... secretly, he brought his sweetheart back with him from Sindi, and somehow managed to acquire some grain seeds and some livestock. Thus did the new life begin.

The more liminal the landscape, the more one traversing it must know local circumstances in order to survive; one needs to be skilled in reading topographic and other signs. The most important mire-dwellers of the past century were partisans, for whom mires provided political refuge after the Second World War. For example, in the Alam-Pedja bog near the River Emajõgi, several partisans hid themselves in 1949–1955, as has been recalled by Linda Reinhold, the wife of one of the partisans (Püttsepp 2003).

People capable of reading the local landscape may be termed existential insiders (Relph 1974). For example, there is validity in the knowledge that particularly soft spots, into which one can sink, are covered with bright green sphagnum moss. It is of course relevant whether someone who has ended up in the mire by accident notices this or is capable of distinguishing between the colours of mosses. The responses to research conducted by Pungas (2006–2007, see note 3) made it clear that as an emotion, fear of sinking and getting lost in mires is still prevalent, but the boardwalks now built into mires that make moving easier have alleviated these fears considerably.

Liminality is often accompanied by the supernatural, with many strange creatures living in mires. In the ERA the following mire-related phenomena and creatures are to be found: nixies (ERA II 230, 421/2 (4)), will-o'-the-wisps (ERA II 293, 18/9/ (11)), skeletons (ERA II 220, 82/3 (29)), souls of the dead (*koll* or *bogey* originally referred to the soul of a dead person in ancient Fenno-Baltic languages) (ERA II 240, 58/9 (27)), revenants (ERA II 241, 324/5 (5)), snake kings, spooks, and others.

In the Estonian folk tradition mires were bewitched places where weird things could happen. 'The didactic of folk traditions used its modes of description for considering threats that in fact lay in wait for the inexperienced swamp-visitor' (Hiiemäe 1988: 223). According to folk beliefs, a supernatural experience had a central role in descriptions of mires, meaning that fairies and tricksters were not only discussed abstractly, but the beliefs were supplemented with descriptions of personal experiences (cf. Valk 1999: 486–487). For example: 'woodcutters had to cross a bog located between Tõruvere and Kuningvere. Returning home, one man became hungry, found a slice of bread in the bog, ate half of it and dropped the other half. The next day, there was half of the neighbour's dead cat where the bread had been. The man fell ill and died.' (ERA II 250, 311 (3)). Another strategy for avoiding mythical creatures or for staying on their good side is the tradition of bringing a piece of 'fairy bread' with you if you entered an unfamiliar forest or mire (KV 77, 31–38).

Unlike other mythical phenomena, there are several scientific explanations for the existence of will-o'-the wisps, one of the more frequently mentioned 'creatures' in folk stories. According to one theory, the blue or greenish light seen in swamps is caused by the burning of swamp gases that seep to the ground as a result of decaying, fermenting or rotting organic matter. Faint and stationary pockets of fire in the darkness of nature may also be bioluminescent algae or fungi. Glow-worms have also sometimes been regarded as will-o'-the-wisps. It has also been opined that will-o'-the wisps that move about and are similar to globes of light are in fact natural phenomena, such as ball lightning.

Today, traditional tales from Estonian folklore about tricksters and other supernatural creatures are used to encourage mire visitation, rather than to warn about the dangers of swamps. The media has turned the former mythical swamp-dwelling creatures into bugbears whose purpose in mires is to teach and instruct children through edutainment. Research conducted in 2006–2007 indicates that for contemporary respondents these stories and beliefs still exist in their collective memory; they affirmed that one can end up in a vicious circle in a mire (that is, one keeps going around in circles, unable to get out of the swamp) or meet fairies, nixies, ogres, trolls, will-o'-the-wisps and souls of the dead.

Liminality in mires and changing cultural practices

Although mires in general have had a liminal status in the history of Estonian national culture, each particular mire has its own distinctive features both in its geography and in mire-related practices, which can occasionally reduce its liminal character. In what follows, we wish to present a brief overview of five practices (gathering, navigating through bogs, draining, peat mining and recreation) that, to a greater or lesser extent, have influenced the natural and cultural functioning of the mire. Hunting and herb-gathering have been left out of the practices to be considered, since berry-picking already presents an example of an ancient practice that has had a relatively low impact on mire landscapes.

The abundance of mires and forests in Estonia has preserved the role of gathering as providing additional food for centuries. Yet

> more widespread berry-picking only began during the late nineteenth, early twentieth century, when merchants started to take forest produce to St. Petersburg and to other cities in the Baltic region. Cranberries, cowberries and blackberries were the main items to be transported.
>
> (Luts 1998: 158)

According to the replies provided by the correspondents of the ERM, there were some noteworthy rules associated with berry-picking. The respondents referred to manor lands as the grounds for gathering berries, and to strict prohibitions associated with it. For example, gathered berries must be shared with the landlord. For this reason, trips to the forests and mires were often done in secret. Evading the prohibition was widespread – people stole from manor lands, but not from farmstead woods. If one was caught by the forester while stealing from the manor woods, the fate of the mushroomer or berry-picker depended on the whims of the particular landlord and forester. The most common punishment was to give away the pickings. In worse cases, secret berry-picking could be punished by flogging. Manor lands were nationalized in 1920 and were divided up among the farmers. Farmers went berry-picking on their own lands, asked permission from others or went in secret.

During the Soviet regime, after the nationalization of the land in 1940s, picking forest berries – especially cranberries – became a widespread collective activity. For this purpose, organized transportation was often provided by larger institutions and during the season there were special trains and buses, and even ferries subsidized by the state that took people to mires and forests. It was both a subsistence-economy addition to the table during the conditions of Soviet deficit economy, and an opportunity to spend leisure time (Piiri 2006: 63–64). In the early 1990s, after Estonia had regained independence, gathering wild berries diminished due to decreasing purchase prices, the deficiency of sugar, and later also because of the improvement in people's living standards and the establishment of consumer society (cf. Paal 1999: 131–140). According to a survey conducted by the Estonian Institute of Economic Research (2010), gathering wild berries and preserving them for private use was still a significant activity of alternative food consumption in Estonian households in 2009. Today, gathering also provides a possibility for active recreation for urban inhabitants.

In addition to gathering and hunting, mires have provided seasonal opportunities for navigating through otherwise inaccessible landscapes and establishing temporary infrastructure. For centuries, the abundance of mires has hindered the construction of roads, yet up until the middle of the last century there was a curious network of roads in landscapes that were otherwise inaccessible and impenetrable. The network of winter roads and its accompanying infrastructure (such as taverns) shortened the distances to be travelled, made an otherwise 'passive period' of a year (Pungas *et al.* 2005) more 'active', and for a long time created a unique travelling culture. Winter roads are a characteristic example of the changing seasonal liminality of the landscape and temporary practices related to mires that block human ways of transportation during other seasons (cf. Ingold 1993; Olwig 2005).

Winter landscape could act both as an obstacle or as support for the movement of people or animals (Palang *et al.* 2007: 11); the frost builds natural 'bridges' in otherwise impassable and dangerous lands (Lehari 2005: 124). Winter roads can only be located at places where the soil is frozen over, where the snow endures yet where snowdrift does not usually cover the tracks. For the local inhabitants, choosing the right places for winter roads and being able to navigate through them presumed a specialized knowledge that was inherited from generation to generation (Kask 1992).

Today, all that remains of former winter roads are trails perceivable from aerial photographs, tavern ruins and data from historical archives that 'translate' this history for visitors on educational trails. Former winter roads have been used for creating educational trails, and some former tavern buildings have been restored and modernized for the purposes of nature education. Hikers are taken into mires and, as an exotic means of transportation, snow shoes are often provided.

While the above mire practices have had a limited impact on transforming mires, mire draining, peat mining and many other amelioration works of the past century have entirely altered the appearance of many Estonian mires. The main reason for digging drainage systems was to drain off excessive water in order to expand the amount of arable land and to increase its fertility. In 1908, the Baltic Mire Improvement Society (Tartu Balti Sooparanduse Selts) was founded in Tartu for the purpose of providing scientific assistance on drainage methods and systems to farmers and landlords (Sepp 2001: 9). Human labour was gradually replaced by machines and the extent of the drainage systems increased rapidly during the twentieth century, especially after the Second World War.

In addition to intensive economic pressure, the nature protection movement became active with respect to mires. The environmentalists started an information campaign about the importance of mires by publishing articles in the magazine *Eesti Loodus* (e.g. Masing 1968; 1970). Thirty mire reserves were founded in 1981, covering 122,189 hectares in total. The activities of this movement were later referred to as the 'mire wars'. As Valk (1988: 5) put it: 'due to generations of human activity, the time is now past when mires were seen as nothing but terrifying wetlands where bugbears roam'.

In addition the natural importance of mires, peat mining and gathering, a new branch of economy – nature tourism – has appeared, commodifying the recreational value of mires. Due to their varied liminal characteristics, mires are landscapes that stimulate all of the senses and provide bodily engaging and even challenging experiences, especially for urban inhabitants. During the past 30 years, the importance of mires for hiking routes and educational trips has increased. For example, the Soomaa National Park is present on the website of the European Destination of Excellence (EDEN).[6]

A new infrastructure has been designed to replace former winter roads – boardwalks that aid in designating courses and reduce the softness and dangerousness of the soil, making trips into mires more secure and less liminal. Boardwalks built on public lands are accessible to all, as long as proper rules of conduct are followed. In order for visitors to experience a closer connection to mire landscapes, official and independent berry-picking and year-round snow shoe trips are organized.

In general, the information provided during organized trips is predominantly educational in nature (e.g. the development of mires, descriptions of plant and animal species) (Pungas *et al.* n.d.). During the past decade, however, the number of tales and myths drawn from the cultural heritage of mires has increased, from textbooks to talks by guides and plaques on educational trails. Some of the mire-related tales are drawn from different archives in Estonia or have been heard from elderly locals, some of the stories are also made up, and thus rely on the imaginary and invented cultural heritage. The heritage and tales that are passed on usually serve several purposes – through stories, they try to turn the swamps as liminal landscapes into more familiar ones, and to provide the unknown mire landscape with places that the stories refer to; to simplify geographical information and to make it easier to acquire; to make mires more exciting, more mysterious, so that the liminal status of mires can be preserved at least in tales.

Thus contemporary nature tourism and nature protection makes the liminality of mires antithetic – people go to the mires more frequently, yet at the same time their contact with the mire is not particularly immediate, since most mire visitors (with the exception of berry-pickers) use boardwalks. The liminality of mires is thereby reduced. The stories that are now told about mires attempt to preserve this liminality, with some tales trying to make them even more liminal than they really are.

Conclusion

This chapter has examined different ecological and cultural reasons that turn Estonian mires into liminal landscapes, and the workings of the different interactive dynamics of these reasons during the past few hundred years. The dynamics of liminality are most fruitfully revealed by focusing on folk traditions, remembrances, stories derived from literature and replies provided by respondents about mires, all of which brought out people's value judgments, knowledges and practices.

Changes in the meaning of mires over time have been related to different conceptions of their value. Until the mid-twentieth century, mires were thought to be useless and frightening places that lack fertile lands and where people may lose their way or drown; one had to carefully survey their surroundings and be prepared to meet supernatural beings. No one entered the mire without reason (which included gathering, hunting, and use of winter roads). The terrifying tales that made mires into even more alien places in the eyes of the people were often probably invented by the adults and told to children to prevent them from wandering into the mire alone, since one can indeed become lost or drown there.

At the same time, marginal social groups – slaves, partisans, war refugees – turned mires into places for their own use and saw the liminal characteristics of mires as a refuge. Their fear of alien, negative experiences overcame their fear and contempt of mires. They learned to read the signs of mires and with this the apparent chaos (i.e. neither land nor water) for the outsiders (such as enemies) became, for the people living in the mire, order and regularity, in which one could move and even live. Thus mires as generally peripheral places for a society became for socially marginal and rejected people a natural part of everyday life, used as a shelter of social freedom.

From the mid-nineteenth century, attempts have been made to reduce the area of mires as landscape unsuitable for agriculture and turn it into mineral land – mires were drained and peat was used for fuel and as bedding for animals. Mire draining continued until the second half of the twentieth century, when scientists began to emphasize the great importance of mires for nature preservation, and the former wasteland turned into an ecologically valuable landscape that required protection. The liminal properties of mires and their heterogeneous multisensory experience today allow the mires to be used as attractive destinations for recreation.

At the same time, the popularization of mires and their easy access to everyone alters the liminality of this landscape. Mires are advertised by the organizers of nature tourism as some of the few remaining examples of pristine wilderness, and there is frequent desire to experience mires as this kind of wild and singular place. At the same time, one must guarantee a safe passage through the mire for people unfamiliar with it – for this purpose, boardwalks have been built in mires, which allow for a better planning of mire usage and protection. As a result, the liminal and mysterious characteristics of mires have been reduced, and in order to preserve this, people have again turned to the cultural heritage, adding to it, if needed, contemporary fictions and imaginations.

Acknowledgements

This paper has been supported by the European Union through the European Regional Development Fund (Centre of Excellence in Cultural Theory, CECT);

the Estonian Ministry of Education target-financed projects No SF0130033s07 Landscape Practice and Heritage, SF0180049s09 Landscape changes in Estonia related to global climate warming and human activity and SF0180157s08 Dynamic Perspectives of Identity Politics – Analysis of Dialogue and Conflict; and the Estonian Science Foundation grant No 8040 Impact of urbanization to landscape pattern and changes in the settlement structure of Estonia. We would also like to thank Riste Keskpaik and Riin Magnus for valuable suggestions and comments and Silver Rattasepp for revising the language.

Notes

1 Our usage of the concept of place and the distinction between place and environment is derived from the works of the anthropologist Tim Ingold (2000; 2009). From the human perspective, a place is always actively experienced, and human activities are inseparable from the natural environment. The concept of environment refers to the natural conditions in which humans and other organisms live.

2 In 1931, the Estonian National Museum (ERM) established a network of correspondents. The mission of the correspondents is to provide replies to the questionnaires sent out by the ERM. The present paper makes use of the replies to questionnaire no. 43. (*On the gathering of mushrooms, berries, nuts and other vegetative foods*), composed by V. Sion in 1947, questionnaire no. 168 (*Gathering of berries, mushrooms and nuts*) composed by H. Pärdi in 1983 and questionnaire no. 167 (*Winter roads*) composed by J. Loosalu and K. Konsin in 1982.

3 Inquiry 'What do you think about mires' among the Estonian population ($n=676$) is a part of Piret Pungas' doctoral dissertation. The purpose of the inquiry was to study the knowledge of contemporary Estonians about mires as natural habitats, its usages, value judgments and beliefs associated with mires. The inquiry covered all of the counties in Estonia; respondents were between ages seven and 75. Of the respondents, 64.9 per cent were female, 26.2 per cent were male, while 8.9 per cent chose not to indicate gender. The written inquiry was carried out in different public places (e.g. trains, libraries, etc.).

4 The manuscripts in the Estonian Literary Museum are divided into several collections, named after the person or institution that organized the given collection. The reference accompanying each piece of folklore indicates its location in the folklore collection and its origin. Acronyms are used in this paper to refer to the following sources:

ERA – folklore collection of the Estonian Folklore Archives (1927–1944)
RKM – folklore collection of the Department of Folklore in the Estonian Literary Museum
ERM – Estonian National Museum Archives
KV – written thematic narratives in the Correspondents Archives' in the Estonian National Museum

5 Merriam-Webster Online: www.merriam-webster.com/dictionary/mire (accessed 12 May 2011).

6 European Destination of Excellence (EDEN). Soomaa National Park (Estonia): http://ec.europa.eu/enterprise/sectors/tourism/eden/themes-destinations/countries/estonia/soomaa/index_et.htm (accessed 12 May 2011).

References

Sources

ERA II 38, 502 (102) < Viru-Jaagupi, Roela v – R. Põldmäe 1931.
ERA II 220, 82/3 (29) < Järva-Jaani, Vajangu v – M. Lokk 1939.
ERA II 230, 421/2 (4) < Kihelkonna, Rootsi k – Kihelkonna algkool 1939.
ERA II 240, 58/9 (27).
ERA II 241, 324/5 (5) < Otepää, Pangodi v, Laguja k, Jõeharu t – E. Martin 1939.
ERA II 242, 209/11 (1) < Rõngu, Aakre v, Põhu k – J. Vaher 1924.
ERA II 250, 311 (3) < Kodavere, Alatskivi.
ERA II 293, 18/9/ (11) < Jüri, Kurna v, Sausti k – E. Rootsna 1941.
RKM II 4, 530/1 (11) < Püha, Suure-Rootsi k – A. Sepp 1946.
KV 77, 25–29, Torma, P. Ariste.
KV 77, 31–38, Viru-Nigula, A. Krikmann.
KV 77, 85–89, Märjamaa, E. Poom.
KV 77, 127–130, Suure-Jaani, Vastsemõisa parish, E. Vingissaar.

Literature

Estonian Institute of Economic Research (2010) 'Elanike toitumisharjumused ja ostueelis-tused' (The inhabitants' eating habits and purchase preferences), www.ki.ee/publikatsioo-nid/Elanike_toitumisharjumused_ja_toidukaupade_ostueelistused_2009.pdf (accessed 18 May 2011).

Hanso, E. (1977) 'Kivinina muistne asundus laante ja rabade varjul' (The ancient settle-ment of Kivinina in the shade of woods and mires), *Eesti Loodus* (Estonian Nature), 10: 670–671.

Hiiemäe, M. (1988) 'Sood rahvapärimuses' (Mires in folk traditions), in: U. Valk (ed.) *Eesti sood* (Estonian Mires), Tallinn: Valgus.

Hoffmeyer, J. and Faverau, D. (2009) *Biosemiotics: an examination into the signs of life and the life of signs*, Scranton, PA: University of Scranton Press.

Howarth, W. (2001) 'Reading the wetlands', in P.C. Adams, S. Hoelscher and K.E. Till (eds) *Place in context. Rethinking Humanist Geographies*, London, Minneapolis: Uni-versity of Minnesota Press.

Ingold, T. (2008) 'Introduction', in T. Ingold and J.L. Vergunst (eds) *Ways of Walking. Ethnography and Practice of Foot*, Aldershot: Ashgate Publishing Ltd.

Ingold, T. (1993) 'The temporality of the landscape', *World Archaeology*, 25–2: 152–174.

Ingold, T. (2009) 'Against Space: Place, Movement, Knowledge', in: P.W. Kirby (ed.) *Boundless Words: An Anthropological Approach to Movement*, Berghahn Books.

Ingold, T. (2000) *The Perception of the Environment: Essays in Livelihood, Dwelling and Skill*, London, New York: Routledge.

Kask, I. (1992) 'Miks Pärnusse otse ei saa?' (Why can't one get directly to Pärnu?) *Eesti Loodus* (Estonian Nature), 4: 254–256.

Kull, K. (2001) 'Mida tähendab metsarahvas: looduse loodud eestlasest ja tema maastike keelest' (On the meaning of 'forest people': of Estonians created by nature, and the language of its landscapes), in: H. Palang and H, Sooväli (eds) *Maastik: loodus ja kultuur. maas-tikukäsitlusi Eestis* (Landscape: Nature and Culture, Approaches to Landscapes in Estonia). Publicationes Instituti Geographici Universitatis Tartuensis, Tartu: Tartu Ülikooli Kirjastus.

Lehari, K. (2005) 'Talvelooded' (Winter Tales), in T. Maran and K. Tüür (eds) *Eesti looduskultuur* (Estonian Nature-Culture), Tartu: Bookmill.

Lotman, Y. (2001) *Universe of the mind: a semiotic theory of culture.* London, New York: I.B. Tauris.

Luts, O. (1914) *Soo* (Mire). Tartu: Noor-Eesti.

Luts, A. (1998) 'Loodusvarud majandamises' (Natural resources in management), in A. Viires and E. Vunder (eds) *Eesti rahvakultuur* (Estonian Folk Culture), Tallinn: Eesti Entsüklopeediakirjastus.

Masing, V. (1968) 'Rabadest, nende arengust ja uurimisest' (On mires, their development and study), *Eesti Loodus* (Estonian Nature) 8: 451–458.

Masing, V. (1970) 'Mida teha rabadega I-II' (What to do with mires I-II), *Eesti Loodus* (Estonian Nature), 8/9: 515–520.

Masing, V., Paal, J., Kuresoo, A. (2000) 'Biodiversity of Estonian wetlands', in B. Gopal, W.J. Junk and J.A. Davis (eds) *Biodiversity in wetlands: assessment, function and conservation 1*, Leiden, The Netherlands: Backhuys Publishers.

Masing, V., Botch, M. and Läänelaid, A. (2010) 'Mires of the former Soviet Union', *Wetlands Ecological Management*, 18: 397–433.

Olwig, K.R. (2005) 'Liminality, seasonality and landscape', *Landscape Research*, 30–2: 259–271.

Paal, T. (1999) 'Metsamarjade ja seente varud ning kasutamine Eestis' (The supplies and use of forest berries and mushrooms in Estonia). *Metsanduslikud Uurimused* (Forestry Studies), 31: 131–140, http://mivana.emu.ee/orb.aw/class=file/action=preview/id =269075/mets_31-15.pdf (accessed 17 May 2011).

Paal, J. and Leibak, E. (2011) 'Estonian mires: Inventory habitats', Tartu: Estonian Nature Fund, http://issuu.com/elfond/docs/estonian_mires_inventory (accessed 5 January 2012).

Palang, H., Printsmann, A. and Sooväli, H. (2007) 'Seasonality and landscapes', in H. Palang, A. Printsmann and H. Sooväli (eds) *Seasonal landscapes*, 7, Springer: Verlaq.

Piiri, R. (2006) 'See varumise harjumus – toidukultuurist nõukogude Eestis' (That habit of gathering – on food culture in Soviet Estonia), *Eesti Rahva Muuseumi Aastaraamat* (Yearbook of the Estonian National Museum), *XLIX*, Tartu.

Pungas, P., Oja, T. and Palang, H. (2005) 'Seasonality in Estonian traditional landscape: the example of large village swings', *Landscape Research*, 30–2: 241–257.

Pungas, P., Oja, T., Kohv, M. and Palang, H. (n.d.) 'Meaning of mires: between the personal and the institutional level'. Forthcoming.

Püttsepp, J. (2003) '91-aastane põdrakütt Linda' (Linda, the 91-year old elk-hunter), *Eesti Ekspress* (Estonian Express), 26 November.

Ramsar Convention Secretariat (2006) *The Ramsar Convention Manual: a guide to the Convention on Wetlands (Ramsar, Iran, 1971)*, 4th edn Ramsar Convention Secretariat, Gland, Switzerland, www.ramsar.org/pdf/lib/lib_manual2006e.pdf (accessed 12 April 2011).

Rapport, N. and Overing, J. (2000) *Social and Cultural Anthropology: The Key Concepts.* London, New York: Routledge.

Relph, E. (1974) *Place and placelessness.* London: Page Bros (Norwich) Limited.

Saal, A. (1921) *Wambola. Jutustus wanast Eesti ajaloost (1209–1212)* (Wambola. A tale of ancient Estonian History (1209–1212)), Tartu: Hermann.

Salm, J.O., Kimmel, K., Uri, V. and Mander, Ü. (2009) 'Global warming potential of drained and undrained peatlands in Estonia: a synthesis', *Wetlands*, 29, 4: 1081–1092.

Sepp, M. (2001) 'Sookultuuri vanemast ajaloost Eestis' (On the earlier history of mire culture in Estonia), *Toimetised* (Proceedings), 5, Tallinn: Eesti Maaparandajate Selts.

Tanskanen, M. (2011) 'The cultivated mire landscape as a mirror of Finnish society', in Z. Roca, P. Claval and J. Agnew (eds) *Landscapes, identities and development: Europe and beyond.* Aldershot: Ashgate.

Trubshaw, B. (1995) 'The metaphors and rituals of place and time – an introduction to liminality or Why Christopher Robin wouldn't walk on the cracks', *At the Edge No. 1,* www.indigogroup.co.uk/edge/liminal.htm (accessed 12 April 2011) (originally published in *Mercian Mysteries,* No. 22, February 1995).

Turner, V. 1979 (1977) 'Frame, Flow and Reflection: Ritual and Drama as Public Liminality', *Japanese Journal of Religious Studies,* 614, December: 465–499 (Originally published in *Performance in postmodern culture,* Madison, Wisconsin: Coda Press, Inc., 1977).

Valk, U. (1988) *Eesti sood* (Estonian mires), Tallinn: Valgus.

Valk, Ü. (1999) 'Inimene ja teispoolsus eesti rahvausundis' (Humans and the otherness in Estonian folk religion), in A. Viires and E. Vunder (eds) *Eesti rahvakultuur* (Estonian Folk Culture), Tallinn: Eesti Entsüklopeediakirjastus.

Van de Noort, R. and O'Sullivan, A. (2005) 'Places, perceptions, boundaries and tasks: rethinking landscapes in wetland archaeology', in: J. Barber and A. Sheridan (eds) *Archaeology from the wetlands: recent perspectives.* Edinburgh: Historic Scotland, pp. 79–89.

7 The Sands of Dee

Estuarine excursions in liminal space

Les Roberts

Come friendly bombs…
(John Betjeman)

Decoys, oblivion, modern nature

During the Second World War the port city of Liverpool on the Mersey Estuary was the target of frequent bombing raids by the Luftwaffe. The city's strategic importance meant that Liverpool and nearby locations such as Bootle and Birkenhead suffered some of the heaviest bombing in the UK, second only to London in the scale of its devastation and human toll. As part of military efforts to mitigate the impact of the bombing, decoys were established on and around the Wirral peninsula, including several at locations on the Dee Estuary. The most northerly of these was situated on Hilbre, one of the three rocky islands at the mouth of the estuary. Others included Heswall decoy, designed to trick the Luftwaffe pilots into thinking they were bombing the north docklands area of Liverpool, and, further south along the Wirral side of the estuary, Burton Marsh decoy, which was a decoy for Garston Docks in the south of Liverpool. During the hours of darkness this flat expanse of marshland, stretching out towards the mud flats and river on the far side of the estuary in North Wales, was transformed into a littoral space of performance. Rigged up with poles, wires, electric lights and bonfires the marshland terrain, with its tangle of gullies and ponds, reflected the dance of illumination up into the night sky, creating the smoke and mirrors illusion of a populous industrial landscape plunged into incendiary chaos.[1]

If the aerial perspective framed an ostensibly cartographic space of illusion, views of the marshland decoy obtainable at ground level were of a landscape reconstructed (re-staged) as *mise-en-scène*. Indeed, in the absence of photographic evidence it is as a film set that this historical spectacle offers itself up to the imagination: a space of artifice that could just as well have been presided over by Michael Powell and Emeric Pressburger (of whom more later) as by a military strategist. The allusion to cinema in relation to the bomb decoys is rendered all the more persuasive by the fact that these 'fields of deception' were developed with the help of technicians from the film industry (Dobinson 2000: 25–8). Decoy sites such as Burton Marsh have attracted the interests of military archaeologists, who, picking over any surviving structures and relics help map a hitherto little known geography of Britain's wartime heritage. Yet it is precisely the performative attributes of these landscapes – their material and symbolic architectures of oblivion and memory; the heterotopic invocation of other worlds: other spaces and times – that makes them so compelling. In this regard the decoy may be looked upon as a metonym for the Dee Estuary more generally. Accordingly, it is as a space of performance – a liminal zone of myth, ritual and practice – that I have set out to navigate this landscape (textually, historically and geographically); selected tracings of which form the basis of this chapter.

The example of the Burton Marsh and other estuary bomb decoys is also instructive insofar as it draws attention to another defining characteristic of the estuarine landscape: its inherent marginality. Perched on the edge of the land, away from populated urban areas and straddling built and natural environments (and sea and land), the impact of bombing raids on the Dee Estuary (unlike the Mersey Estuary) would, of course, have been comparatively minimal. More pointedly, the example brings with it the observation that the capacity of a landscape to invite and *accommodate* oblivion – whether in terms of aerial bombardment, military testing, landfill and waste management sites, or environmentally high-risk industries, such as nuclear and other power generating plants, for example – represents one of the measures by which to gauge its status as *liminal* in the terms elaborated here. The perceived or actual threat of danger, contagion or what Mary Douglas (1966) described as 'matter out of place' powerfully underscores the sense of an unstable and precarious landscape. Navigation or (in an inversion of the transitory properties of liminal spaces) *habitation* carries with it the elemental risk of injury or death. In the case of the Dee Estuary, this zonal uncertainty is further reinforced by the instability of a hazardous 'natural' topography comprised of marshland and intertidal mud and sand flats.

Given that much of the estuarine landscape is the product of human intervention on a grand scale (particularly that of Nathaniel Kinderley's River Dee Company – see below), the extent to which it can indeed be described as natural is a moot point. As a partly reclaimed landscape, a product of industrial engineering, it is more instructive to look upon the Dee Estuary (or at least those elements that are of concern here) as an exemplar of what artist and filmmaker Derek Jarman (after Maggi Hambling) describes as 'modern nature' (1992: 8). Jarman is referring to the quintessential liminal landscape that is Dungeness: a huge shingle bank (the largest in Europe) on the south east coast of England where Jarman lived until his death in 1994. Dominated by the brooding presence of the nuclear power station, with large stretches of the beach and adjoining marshland (marked 'Danger Area' on the map) used for military training, and a vast canvas of sky bearing down on the land, topologically Dungeness bears some resemblance to the sprawling estuarine landscapes of the Dee: the 'empty' spaces in-between the coastlines of Wirral (in England) and Flintshire (in North

Wales). Take a walk around Burton Marsh today and, while it is unlikely that you would be exposing yourself to the threat of aerial bombardment, you might unwittingly find yourself dodging stray bullets from the nearby Ministry of Defence Rifle Range at Sealand (a place that toponymically references its liminal status). Trudge a circuitous path across the marsh in the direction of the river and sooner or later you'll discover the contingent geography that governs this space: linearity has little or no application here; in this environment wayfinding defines a temporality not a geography: routes (such as there are) are as tangible as the footprints (and accompanying squelches) that dissolve into the marshland almost as soon as the next one is made. Look south towards Flintshire Bridge, the vertical landmark that lays totemic claim to the Deeside region, and it is an industrial landscape that dominates: Connah's Quay Power Station on the south side of the River Dee, and Deeside Power Station and Corus Steelworks to the north. If you make it across the marsh to the main road that serves the industrial zone you will find yourself gravitated towards the cable-stayed crossing over the Dee, only to find that this too is something of a non-place as pedestrians are prohibited to cross.

In short, this is a landscape that inhibits dwelling, lingering, or even navigation. If its transformative energies translate to, on the one hand, the abstract mobilities of the river crossing (the bridge was described by one local resident as a 'road to nowhere'[2]), and, on the other, the threat (or allure) of danger, death

Figure 7.1 'Wayfinding': Burton Marsh looking south-west towards Connah's Quay Power Station, showing GPS tracks (in white) of walk by the author, November 2010.

and oblivion (the 'off-road' excursions through marshland terrain), then to what extent can we meaningfully describe the estuary as a liminal space?

Exploring more closely the social, cultural and historical geography of the Dee Estuary we can see how structures of liminality have remained deeply embedded in the topography of the region. First, it is a borderzone between England and Wales, and politics of identity and territoriality have played a form-ative role in shaping the landscape, as indeed have the many routes and connec-tions that have defined and *refined* its relational geographies. Second, much of the physical landscape may be described as liminal insofar as it is land reclaimed from the river and marshland by canal engineers in the eighteenth century, some parts of which are under threat of re-reclamation by the Dee as the estuarine ecology changes and the wetlands reassert their authority over the dry. A further liminal characteristic of this landscape, one that interlaces the borderzone and 'sea-land' liminalities, is the interstitial zone that marks the limen or threshold between the living and the dead. Oblivion, as Marc Augé reminds us, is the negation of memory: '[r]emembering or forgetting is doing gardener's work, selecting, pruning' (2004: 17). In order to remember it is necessary at the same time to forget. Liminal rites of transition – and by extension the spaces in which they are practised – provide the possibilities of a *strategic amnesia* by which, paradoxically, an archaeology of deep memory may be performed. Cultivating a (spatial) dialogue between the living and the dead – between the estuarine way-farers of the past and those of the present – the place or *topos* of the liminal is explored here through topoanalytic (Bachelard 1994) reflection on the act and trope of *drowning*.

The Sands of Dee

> *O Mary, go and call the cattle home*
> *And call the cattle home,*
> *And call the cattle home*
> *Across the sands of Dee*
> *The western wind was wild and dank with foam,*
> *And all alone went she.*
>   (Charles Kingsley, 'The Sands of Dee', 1849)

Working on ideas for a music video for the Manchester band New Order, in 1988 the American film producer Michael Shamberg approached the legendary British director Michael Powell – by then well into his eighties – to see if he would be interested in directing the video. Powell expressed interest in the project, and proposed the idea of a short film based around Charles Kingsley's poem 'The Sands of Dee'. The poem tells the tragic tale of a cattle girl called Mary who ventures out onto the sands of the estuary and is overtaken by the tides and drowned, her body later found caught amongst the fishing nets. In preparation for the film Powell and his wife, the film editor Thelma Schoon-maker, went on a location scout to the Dee Estuary, but, due to delays in the production and Powell's subsequent death, the film was never made. Powell's preference for casting the actress Tilda Swinton in the role of the cattle girl Mary – he described the close up of Swinton dead in the salmon nets as being 'box office'[3] – provides an indication that, had it been completed, the film would have owed some debt to the work of one of British film's heirs to Powell's legacy, Derek Jarman. Whether the brownfield sites and edgelands of the River Thames in 1988's *The Last of England* (in which Swinton performs an apocalyptic dance against the burning backdrop of a city doomed by Thatcherism) or the vast shingle expanse of Dungeness in *The Garden* (1990) – the setting for a contemporary retelling of the Passion – Jarman's films often inhabit liminal landscapes in which the performative presence of Tilda Swinton is a recurrent element.

In *Blue*, Jarman's final feature released shortly before his death in 1994, the metaphor of drowning – of dwelling for eternity in '*submarine gardens*' – is woven into a poetic meditation on the imminence (and immanence) of death, the final breaching of the limen between presence and oblivion: *Deep waters/ Washing the isle of the dead/In coral harbours.../Across the still seabed/We lie there/Fanned by the billowing/Sails of forgotten ships/Tossed by the mournful winds/Of the deep.* While Powell's interest in Kingsley's poem and the landscape that inspired it may have been similarly bound up with a growing sense of mortality, it is more instructive to attribute it to the director's long-standing fascination with the Old Testament story of Moses and the parting of the Red Sea.[4] As a visual motif, the image of the sea as an epic, portentous force that at any moment might engulf an otherwise insignificant humanity appears in several of Powell and Pressburger's films: in *The Red Shoes*, for example, the centrepiece performance of 'The Ballet of the Red Shoes' is at one point flooded with crashing waves (Conrad 1992); in *I Know Where I'm Going* 'the epic drama of the Corryvreckan whirlpool' was inspired, as Ian Christie (2001) notes, by Cecil B. DeMille's 1923 portrayal of the parting of the Red Sea in *The Ten Commandments*. But perhaps the most striking example can be found in *The Elusive Pimpernel*, made in 1950. Temporarily holed up in the abbey at the island of Mont St Michel in Normandy, the Pimpernel/Sir Percy Blakeney (played by David Niven) is planning his escape back across the Channel with his latest consignment of aristocratic asylum seekers. Strategically deploying the forces of nature, he tricks his arch nemesis Chauvelin (Cyril Cusack) and the advancing forces of the French Republic by timing his escape just as the tide is coming in, cutting off Mont St Michel from the mainland and engulfing the army as they attempt to apprehend the Pimpernel before he makes his escape.

From a contemporary perspective, the association between asylum seekers and metaphors of water and the sea is more likely to connote negative attitudes surrounding immigration policy. The fear of being 'swamped' or 'flooded', rhetoric frequently deployed in right-wing British newspapers such as the *Daily Mail* and the *Sun*, draws on these metaphorical associations to present a view of the nation as a bastion community struggling to maintain the sanctity of its borders from forces beyond its immediate power to control. The strengthening of

Figure 7.2 'Welcome to Poland': the River Dee at Saltney on the England/Wales border.

national frontiers of identity (a logic which 'goes against the tide' of trans-national mobility and increased global flows), as with environmental efforts to prevent coastal erosion and the encroachment of the sea, becomes essentially a reactive and defensive exercise, predicated on the management or containment of 'otherness'. It is not the spirit of the Pimpernel that pervades the liminal land-scapes of millennial Britain, but a Canute-like denial of the borderzone as a porous space of flows and 'radical openness' (hooks 1990).

Viewed in the aftermath of the death of 23 Chinese migrant workers in More-cambe Bay in February 2004, Powell and Pressburger's magnificent set-piece of Mont St Michel mnemonically evokes a more tragic *mise-en-scène*, where the confluent themes of migrancy and drowning have soberingly literal connotations. Located on the north west coast of England in Lancashire, Morecambe Bay is notorious for its fast moving tides and treacherous quicksand, as well as its lucrative cockle beds. Despite the dangers posed by this stretch of coastline the Bay has long attracted itinerant workers, many of whom, as with the Chinese cockle pickers, were (until the introduction of the 2004 Gangmasters Act[5]) at the mercy of exploitative and illegal gangmasters. While the Morecambe Bay inci-dent brought to light the appalling conditions faced by these migrant workers, it also forced an awareness of the extent to which such groups are an invisible but immutable presence, occupying a ghostly liminal zone on the social and geo-graphic margins of the nation; caught in the interstices of transnational space.

Prior to 2004 hundreds of cockle pickers were drawn to the sandbanks of the Dee Estuary, which, like Morecambe Bay also boasts a thriving cockling industry. Working in similarly hazardous conditions, the pickers now harvest the banks in more sustainable numbers, although there are still tensions between local cocklers and those from outside the area, and unlicensed cockling remains rife. In an effort to control cockle picking in the estuary, the Environment Agency use so-called 'Cockle Cams' to monitor cockling teams. Heat-sensor searches by police helicopter have also been used to locate unlicensed pickers working the cockle beds at night (Butler 2008; Wainwright 2010).

> *The western tide crept up along the sand,*
> *And o'er and o'er the sand,*
> *And round and round the sand,*
> *As far as eye could see.*
> *The rolling mist came down and hid the land:*
> *And never home came she.*

Had it been written today, Kingsley's poem 'The Sands of Dee' might well have recounted the tale of a cockle picker rather than a cattle girl. Either way, as a lyrical reflection on a landscape in which poor and marginal groups have for centuries eked out a precarious living, and through which individuals of all classes once travelled along the many fords that snaked across the sands, the poem sketches the outlines of a deep topography that has long been shaped by the omnipresent threat of drowning.

Cestrian Book of the Dead

Straddling the England–Wales border near the Roman city of Chester, the town of Saltney takes its name from the former salt marshes that occupied the area prior to the canalisation of the Dee in 1732 and subsequent reclamation of land either side of the river. As with other areas of marshland in the estuary, Saltney Marshes were renowned for being a dangerous landscape to attempt passage through, partly on account of the wild and waterlogged terrain, but also because it provided refuge for criminals and other undesirables to whom travellers ran the risk of falling victim. Church Registers between 1585 and 1750 record many instances of deaths by drowning or murder on Saltney Marsh (Anon. 1989: 2). Known by the Welsh as '*Morfa Caer Leon*', or 'marsh of the fort of the legions' (Owen 1994: 125), the route westward into Wales from Roman Chester was barred by this wild expanse of *morfa*, which Gee Williams in her short story of the same name describes as 'two thousand acres of legion-defying swamp' (2008: 186; Mason 1987: 153). It was not until the reclamation of the marshland in the eighteenth century that safe and direct passage westward through Saltney to the Welsh district of Broughton became possible (on what is now the A5104 Chester Road).

Saltney today turns its back on the river. Even along River Lane – the former industrial hub of the town – the canalised stretch of Dee to which Saltney owes its existence tries its level best to conceal itself from view. De-industrialisation and modern transport communications have rendered it an industrial ruin: a silted relic of modern nature. This is not to suggest that it is a forgotten or desolate landscape – dog walkers, cyclists and joggers move leisurely along the embankments or linger for a moment atop the footbridge at Saltney Ferry (named after the river crossing it replaced). Even death still has its place here. But, as with the case of a local man found hanging from the bridge early one morning in 2009, the river becomes a sacred and intimately private place of death where final acts of ritual oblivion are silently observed. Although the river has for centuries been a place where people have chosen to end their life – the Dee Bridge in Chester was a particularly popular suicide spot (see below) – what distinguishes the types of death that occur on or around the Dee today from those of earlier times is the extent to which they are detached from the everyday and mundane. Separation – whether from life, society, loved ones, habitat (and habitus), environment, and so on – is the prerequisite for transition: the *liminal phase*. The margins, edgelands and in-between spaces of the river become, in turn, its spatial correlate: the *liminal zone* where the living are ushered from this world into the next. Whereas, before the estuarine landscape was drained and tamed (and its inhabitants displaced from the newly reclaimed land), the liminality that defined this space was more firmly embedded in the social practices of everyday life. By examining coroners' records of deaths by drowning that occurred at Chester and at various locations on the Dee Estuary we can get a clear sense of a landscape that was geographically but by no means socially or culturally marginal, and whose transitional properties were intrinsically bound up with the 'mesh-works' (Ingold 2007: 80) of mobility, wayfinding and everyday habitus by which, as a social space, it was constituted.

Dating back to the early 1500s the Chester Quarter Sessions Coroners' Inquest records[6] provide a fascinating insight into the ways different social actors engaged with the Dee, whether in and around Chester or further out along the estuary in ports such as Parkgate, at one time a major departure point for Ireland. The records include details of the names and locations (where known) of over 300 deaths by drowning from Chester to the mouth of the river at Liverpool Bay. For example:

- *Ales Rutter, drowned while washing clothes at 'the cage', a common washing place. June 11th 1630*
- *William Cowpack, fell into the Dee while gathering daisys and was drowned. April 2nd 1775*
- *Boniventrus Hanky, drowned while bathing at 'Le Posterne'. Aug. 6th 1586*
- *Edward Davenport, drowned when he rode his horse, while under the influence of drink, into the Dee at the bottom of Sandy Lane. Dec. 3rd 1700*
- *John Blundell drowned when he fell overboard in a drunken stupor from a certain sloop near the Crane. Aug. 24th 1734*
- *Unknown girl, fell off cart with a drunken driver while crossing the ford to Hawarden and was drowned. May 4th 1730*

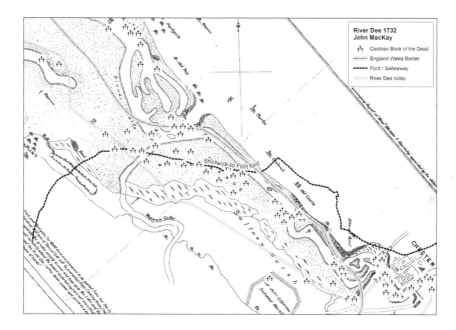

Figure 7.3 'Cestrian Book of the Dead': GIS map of sites of death by drowning on the Dee Estuary, 1524–1871. Topographic map made in 1732 by John Mackay.

As nearly half of the entries record the exact (or approximate) location of death it is possible to geo-reference the sites of drowning, and from this attempt to formulate a clearer understanding of the social geography of the estuary's pre-reclamation landscapes. The Cestrian Book of the Dead – a digital necrogeographic map of Dee drowning locations – traces the performative spaces of the living (public laundry areas, recreation sites, fords, pathways, etc.) by spatialising the patterns and clusters where drowning fatalities were recorded.

Most of the drownings occurred in three main locations: the Dee Bridge in Chester, the port of Parkgate, and the Shotwick to Flint ford. The Dee Bridge, overlooking the weir and salmon leap, is where the medieval mills were sited and where, at the nearby 'cage' (salmon cages), people congregated to wash their clothes. The majority of deaths by suicide on the Dee are recorded here. Records also show that attempts were made to cross the river via the weir, which, as with the nearby ford, offered a toll-free, but dangerous alternative to the bridge. Downriver at Parkgate, many of those who drowned were mariners falling overboard (often as a result of inebriation) when transferring to and from ships moored at the port. By the early eighteenth century Parkgate had become the main anchorage serving Chester, whose fortunes as a trading port had declined due to silting which had made river navigation increasingly difficult. From the sixteenth century ports had been established at successive locations downriver at Shotwick, Burton, Neston and Parkgate, but each in turn would also fall into decline due to the build up of silt, a situation which would eventually contribute to the rise of Liverpool as a major port city.

Another notorious place of drowning was on and around the ford at Shotwick which was part of an ancient salt traders' route called 'Saltesway', an important line of communication between North Wales, Cheshire and Lancashire. A description of the ford is contained in the travel memoirs of Celia Fiennes who passed through Cheshire in 1698:

> I forded over the Dee when the tide was out, all upon the sands at least a mile, which was as smooth as a die, being a few hours left of the flood. ... When the tide is fully out they frequently ford in many places which they mark as the sands fall, and go near nine or ten miles over the sands from Chester to Burton on to Flint town almost.
>
> (quoted in Young 1926: 154)

As those travelling into Wales via the Dee Bridge in Chester would have faced a long detour to avoid Saltney Marshes (as well as pay tolls to cross the bridge), the fords downriver at Blacon and Shotwick were widely used, despite the hazardous and constantly shifting sands, which claimed many lives (Thacker *et al.* 2005):

- *Unknown man, drowned while attempting to cross the ford at Shotwick. May 26th 1681*
- *Arthur Carr, apprentice to John Lovett, merchant of Dublin, mistakenly forded the Dee near Shotwick while riding to Parkgate to embark for Ireland and was drowned trying to return. April 23rd 1698*
- *Anne Blackburn, widow, drowned while crossing the sands from Flint. June 24th 1718*
- *Thomas Pearson, labourer, drowned while attempting to ford the Dee from the Welsh side. Aug. 18th 1725*
- *Alice, wife of Thomas Harrison, drowned while crossing Shotwick ford. Jan. 9th 1753*
- *Thomas Harrison, drowned while crossing Shotwick ford. Jan. 12th 1753*

The latter two are consecutive entries on the page: husband and wife drown crossing the ford in January 1753, three days apart. Did Thomas Harrison already know that his wife Alice had died when he set out across the sands? Was he attempting to complete the journey where she had failed? Perhaps he had gone to look for her or retrieve her body? Or, possessed by grief, he had resolved to join her in her watery grave? And where were they headed anyway? These and other fragmentary tales of life and death on the Dee have no resolution other than that of their documented fate. That much we know. Clipped narratives, they haunt the palimpsestic spaces of the estuary and, in so doing, reinscribe their presence on a landscape savaged by oblivion. As topographic features the fords are as intangible as the memories they evoke. The route of Shotwick to Flint ford appears on John Boydell's 1771 map of the estuary, but in actuality its location would have changed over time, rendering it all but unmappable. Nonetheless, provisionally at least Boydell's ford remains a line that can be drawn in the sands, whether as GIS polyline data overlaid on a present day map of the estuary, or by attempting to navigate its deep topographies on foot. The latter strategy – a psycho-topographic mode of intervention 'in the field' – draws the layered geographies of past and present into oblique confrontation. Through this process the shapes, vectors and affective geometries of today's estuary are brought into relief, revealing a physical landscape that bears little resemblance to that through which the wayfarers of the past once travelled. By the late eighteenth century, the fords, along with Parkgate's brief status as a port, had become early casualties of modern nature.

Sealand empire: taming the land

Always shifting, the sands of Dee not only posed challenges for those navigating the estuary on foot, horse or cart, they also impeded safe river navigation to Chester, a problem that had been the bane of city officials since the fourteenth century (Pritchard 2002: 168). In an ill-fated attempt to address the problems of silting and to reverse Chester's decline, in the early 1700s the city authorities began to consider the option of implementing a canalisation scheme, called the New Cut or Navigation Cut. The aim was to re-route the river from its old course along the Wirral side of the estuary through a deeper channel on the Welsh side so as to improve navigation along the estuary to Chester. One of the criteria that prospective engineers were required to address when constructing the channel was to ensure the prevention of future silting or at least reduce it to sustainable levels. In 1733 an Act of Parliament 'to recover and preserve the Navigation of the River' was passed which granted exclusive rights to Nathanial Kinderley and the newly formed River Dee Company (ibid.). Completed in 1740, the New Cut runs for five miles through the former Saltney Marshes to Connah's Quay where it joins the estuary.

In what seems to have been a monumentally bad negotiation on the part of the city authorities (Armour 1956: 109–10), Chester relinquished all rights to the estuary and in exchange for undertaking and completing the canalisation scheme, Kinderley received all the lands reclaimed by the drainage of the former marshes, as well as the levying of tolls on shipping tonnage. Kinderley ignored completely the requirements for the project to prevent silting. One of the consequences of the reclamation of Saltney Marshes was the eviction of poorer classes who used the area as common land and grazing land for cattle. The rich soil of the reclaimed land was perfect for arable farming and was thus extremely profitable to the River Dee Company. Meanwhile the river continued to silt up and Chester's fortunes continued to decline. Less than a century later in 1826 the *Chester Chronicle* reported the minutes of a meeting of the River Dee Commissioners in which it was acknowledged that 'The Port of Chester is gone', putting the blame squarely on Kinderley and the River Dee Company (Herson 1996: 75; see also Armour 1956: 78–110). As John Young, writing in 1926, concludes:

the indiscriminate reclaiming of land in the upper estuary [the area now called Sealand] … did more, perhaps, than anything else to bring about the great increase of silting … *Dee Estuary simply stands out as one great tragedy* – one which might not have been so great had it not been for Man's selfish desire for immediate wealth, as illustrated by the policy of the River Dee company.

(1926: 194, 4, emphasis added)

The sheer scale of the folly and impact of the canalisation scheme on the landscape and ecology of the estuary has been immense. Looking north westward from Saltney Ferry footbridge the geometric precision of the New Cut leads the eye towards a vanishing point that converges at Flintshire Bridge. Old and new, horizontal and vertical, these abstract formations hold their sway over a landscape tamed. The rational uniformity of Kinderley's navigation has ironed out the contingent and uncertain; and with it much of the vitality, sociality and history that had formerly defined this liminal zone. Boats are rarely seen on this stretch of the Dee, with the exception of the Afon Dyfrdwy,[7] the barge that carries the Airbus A380 wings from the nearby Broughton factory where they are made to Mostyn Docks further up the Flintshire coastline.

The marshland reclaimed either side of the New Cut is now largely characterised by low-lying farmland, retail parks and industrial sites. The settlements of Saltney, Saltney Ferry (Mold Junction), Sealand, and Sandycroft are also located here. The subtle legibility of the pre-reclamation shoreline defines a zonal boundary which, once read, can stir a dormant imaginary of place in which the river and wetlands reassert their hold over the land. After periods of heavy rain the sight of waterlogged fields and drainage ditches ready to burst heightens this sense of a resurgent historical landscape, as if the past and its ghosts are seeping up through the soil.

As a cultural landscape, the aesthetic virtues of the canalised Dee, unlike some of its more picturesque locations upriver (in Cheshire or the Vale of Llangollen, for example), are perhaps not so readily apparent. In his Dee travelogue, *River Map*, for example, Jim Perrin writes,

the canalised cut … meanders across the dreariest of industrial landscapes to this loss of identity. … Let's skip a few miles and a period in time, because I do not want to impose any more than is necessary of that desperate landscape upon you.

(Perrin 2001: 4)

Yet insofar as the story of the estuary is, as Young suggests, one of tragedy, it is precisely this ellipsis in the river's spatial story that casts the longest shadow. Like the river, the mythopoesis of the Dee – the wellspring that Michael Powell had sought to draw from – has silted over; narratives and their geographies have been canalised, their spoil used to build embankments within which they are safely contained. The spirit of Nathaniel Kinderley looms large over this sealand-scape. The barriers need breaching; the river reclaiming.

Reclaiming the Dee

Flow back to your sources, sacred rivers,
And let the world's great order be reserved.
(Euripedes, *Medea*)

In a historical analogue to *The Elusive Pimpernel*, sometime around 1800 an émigré or asylum seeker from revolutionary France came to Chester from Normandy (perhaps passing through Mont St Michel). A relative of Quatremère De Quincey, we do not know much about this individual other than that he was the cause of mistaken identity, precipitating *Thomas* De Quincey's journey to Chester to return a letter which contained a banker's draft for 40 guineas mistakenly sent to the writer. In his account of his time in Chester in *Confessions of an English Opium Eater*, De Quincey describes a walk to an area of the city known as the Cop which is an open space overlooking the River Dee. Already in a state of some anxiety as a result of having to attend to the matter of his mistaken inheritance, the writer is paralysed by 'a sudden uproar of tumultuous sounds rising clamorously ahead' (1994: 80). He later realises it was the tidal bore which in De Quincey's day would have come in close to the city centre. Clearly affected by the phenomena – 'until that moment, I had never heard of such a nervous affection in rivers' (ibid.: 82) – De Quincey is moved to describe the river as 'hysterical', invoking the above-cited lines from Euripedes's play *Medea* (ibid.: 80).

In this moment of hysteria, the psychic connection De Quincey makes with the river strongly alludes to a state of inversion, transition and the suspension of established rules and societal conventions: qualities that we can quite readily characterise in terms of the liminal. Re-framed within the broader context of this chapter, the *Medea*'s injunction calls upon the Dee to reassert its dormant spirit of transition and flux. Retracing the footsteps of those who have trod before us – be it De Quincey, Charles Kingsley, Celia Fiennes, or the marshland wayfarers of the Book of the Dead – establishes a relationship of co-presence (Ingold and Vergunst 2008: 7) by which a psycho-topographic remapping of the Dee becomes possible. As a liminal practice it is instructive to think of this not so much in terms of the tripartite formulation of Arnold van Gennep and Victor Turner (the three stages of the ritual process), but in the more truncated terms which the artist Phil Smith (aka CrabMan) outlines in his book *Mythogeography*. Reworking the Situationist concept of the *dérive* or 'drift', CrabMan suggests:

If romantic walking … can be compared to the rites of passage defined by anthropologist Victor Turner … then the dérive … lops off the last of the three [stages] (re-integration) and short-circuits flux [the liminal phase] straight back into separation. And keeps doing that until the practice can stand no more repetition and throws off some new, mutant activity.

(Smith 2010: 118)

Reclaiming the Dee, the estuarine excursions I have set out in this chapter have sought to map the confluence of past and present geographies of liminality. These liminal landscapes are transitional in the sense of occupying a space 'betwixt and between', but also, as performative spaces, their affective carto-graphies map the latent energies that reside at these confluence points, offering the potential for transformation, but also for danger. The trope of drowning, while connoting death, can also serve as a metaphor for the saturation of an indurated land. To drown may be to go under, but it can also mean renewal.

Notes

1 www.airfieldinformationexchange.org/community/showthread.php?2989-Dee-Estuary-Burton-Marsh-decoy-for-Garston-Docks; www.airfieldinformationexchange.org/community/showthread.php?2988-Dee-Estuary-Heswall-Decoy-for-Liverpool-northern-dock-area; www.wikiwirral.co.uk/forums/ubbthreads.php/topics/330639/Hilbre_Island_WW2_Bombing_Deco.html (all accessed 27 April 2011).
2 news.bbc.co.uk/1/hi/wales/north_east/3847799.stm (accessed 28 April 2011).
3 Michael Shamburg, 'The Sands of Dee', www.kinoteca.net/Text/sands_dee.htm (accessed 21 June 2010).
4 In *Million Dollar Movie*, the second volume of his autobiography, Powell recalls how at chapel in school he often spent his time meditating 'on my favourite miracle, the parting of the Red Sea' (quoted in Conrad 1992).
5 This legislation was introduced in response to the Morecambe Bay tragedy. The purpose of the Act is 'to make provision for the licensing of activities involving the supply or use of workers in connection with agricultural work, the gathering of wild creatures and wild plants, the harvesting of fish from fish farms, and certain processing and packaging; and for connected purposes.' www.legislation.gov.uk/ukpga/2004/11/introduction (accessed 11 May 2011).
6 The Chester City Coroner Records can be viewed online at www.nationalarchives.gov.uk/a2a/records.aspx?cat=017-chec_2&cid=5–10#5–10 (accessed 30 March 2010).
7 This is also the Welsh name for the River Dee.

References

Anon. (1989) 'Saltney Marsh', in B.D. Clark (ed.), *Saltney and Saltney Ferry: A Second Illustrated History*. Saltney: Saltney Local History Group.

Armour, G. (1956) *The Trade of Chester and the State of the Dee Navigation 1600–1800*. Unpublished PhD thesis, University College London.

Augé, M. (2004) *Oblivion*. Minneapolis: University of Minnesota Press.

Bachelard, G. (1994) *The Poetics of Space*. Boston: Beacon Press.

Butler, C. (2008) 'Cockle pickers can return to Dee Esturay [*sic*]', *Daily Post*, 1 September, www.dailypost.co.uk/news/north-wales-news/2008/09/01/cockle-pickers-can-return-to-dee-esturay-55578–21645247/ (accessed 20 May 2011).

Christie, I. (2001) 'I Know Where I'm Going', *The Criterion Collection*, www.criterion.com/current/posts/95-i-know-where-im-going (accessed 20 May 2011).

Conrad, P. (1992) 'Prospero at Play', *Observer*, 11 October, www.powell-pressburger.org/Reviews/Micky/Prospero.html (accessed 20 May 2011).

De Quincey, T. (1994) *Confessions of an English Opium Eater*. London: Wordsworth Classics.

Dobinson, C. (2000) *Fields of Deception: Britain's Bombing Decoys of World War II.* London: Methuen.

Douglas, M. (1966) *Purity and Danger: An Analysis of Concepts of Pollution and Taboo.* Harmondsworth: Penguin.

Herson, J. (1996) 'Canals, Railways and the Demise of the Port of Chester', in P. Carrington (ed.), *'Where Deva Spreads Her Wizard Stream' – Trade and the Port of Chester*. Chester: Chester City Council.

hooks, B. (1990) *Yearning: Race, Gender and Cultural Politics.* Boston, MA: South End Press.

Ingold, T. (2007) *Lines: A Brief History.* London: Routledge.

Ingold, T. and J.L. Vergunst (2008) 'Introduction', in T. Ingold and J.L. Vergunst (eds), *Ways of Walking: Ethnography and Practice on Foot.* Farnham: Ashgate.

Jarman, D. (1992) *Modern Nature: the Journals of Derek Jarman.* London: Vintage.

Mason, D.J.P. (1987) 'Chester: the Canabae Legionis', in *Britannia*, 18: 143–68.

Owen, H.W. (1994) *The Place Names of East Flintshire.* Cardiff: University of Wales Press.

Perrin, J. (2001) *The River Map.* Ceredigion: Gomer.

Pritchard, T.W. (2002) *A History of the Old Parish of Hawarden.* Wrexham: Bridge Books.

Thacker, A.T. and C.P. Lewis (eds), J.S. Barrow, J.D. Herson, A.H. Lawes, P.J. Riden and M.V.J. Seaborne. (2005) 'Economic infrastructure and institutions: Roads and road transport', *A History of the County of Chester: Volume 5 Part 2: The City of Chester: Culture, Buildings, Institutions*: 73–83. British History Online. www.british-history.ac.uk/report.aspx?compid=57309 (accessed 28 February 2010).

Smith, P. (2010) *Mythogeography: a Guide to Walking Sideways.* Axminster: Triarchy Press.

Wainwright, M. (2010) 'Cockling on the Dee', *Guardian*, 15 July, www.guardian.co.uk/environment/2010/jul/15/cockling-dee (accessed 09 October 2010).

Williams, G. (2008) 'Morfa', in *Blood, etc.* Cardigan: Parthian.

Young, J.A. (1926) *The Physical and Historical Geography of the Dee Estuary.* Unpublished MA thesis, University of Liverpool.

Part III

Urban liminalities

Ritual, poesis, experience

8 Spinning Lhasa

Ritual circumambulation routes as liminal urbanscapes in China's 'Western treasure-house'[1]

Ivan Costantino

There is no spatiality that is not organized by the determination of frontiers.

(de Certeau 1984: 123)

It seems best, then, to conceive of the frontier as a zone rather than a line, one in which all possible boundaries of geography, race, and culture cross and overlap to form a ... transitional area of great complexity.

(Aris 1992: 13, cited in Epstein and Wenbin 1998: 123)

Introduction: Central Tibet's capital as a new frontier

In the lines above, Aris puts his finger on the transient, culturally multilayered nature of the frontier: the ultimate in-between space. Aris is referring to those areas of Eastern Tibet that border with Han-populated regions of China, but I argue that over the 60-odd years since Chinese takeover, Han migration, urban development, and tourism have also transformed central Tibet's Lhasa—the capital of the Tibet Autonomous Region (TAR)—into a frontier zone: a heterotopia[2] where different notions of urbanism and identity meet and are constantly renegotiated. In this essay, I look at how this process of encounter and renegotiation plays out in everyday place-making tactics (cf. de Certeau 1984) in contemporary Lhasa. I do so by focusing on one of Lhasa's ultimate liminal groups—young Tibetan migrants—and their use of the city's main ritual circumambulation (Tibetan: *skor ba*[3]) routes. The latter not only attract both Tibetan devotees and Chinese tourists (Buddhist believers and non), but also mark the frontier between the old city and the newer developments that have been sprouting up around Lhasa's historic centre over the past six decades, thus pointing to the *skor ba* routes as liminal zones in Tibet's capital.

The aim of this chapter is therefore to engage my ethnography of young Tibetans' practice of urban space—the result of 14 months of fieldwork in the Tibetan capital—in a dialogue with theories of spatial marginality and the liminal. Much has been written on sacred landscape, pilgrimage, and religious place-making in the Tibetan cultural world (cf. Huber 1999; Gutschow *et al.* 2003; Karmay 1994), but little has been produced in the social sciences on

Tibetan *urban* space.[4] Similarly, while a growing body of literature in anthropology, human geography, and urban planning points to the role of embodied practices in defining notions of place and identity (cf. Ingold 2004; Ingold and Lee Vergunst 2008; Massey 2005), so far only Ronald Schwartz (1994) has made an attempt to link Tibetan ritual circumambulation to notions of liminality in his study of non-violent forms of protest in the late 1980s. My ethnographic work follows on the path laid by Schwartz but, rather than on major historical events, I focus on the production of liminal space through everyday ritual practice: I present young Tibetans' prostrations and circumambulations as instances of the resilience of ritual in Lhasa's complex urban space, where ethnic and religious boundaries are constantly re-inscribed onto an increasingly divided and multi-layered cityscape.

In what follows, I shall first briefly discuss the Chinese construction of Tibet as a 'frontier' zone examining in particular how Lhasa and her circumambulation routes mark the new frontier of Chinese tourism. I will then turn to an in-depth ethnographic analysis of the practice of *skor ba* among young Tibetan rural migrants to the city and, in a dialogue with Victor Turner's theory of liminality and communitas as well as Csikszentmihalyi's work on flow and de Certeau's on walking in the city, I shall present the circumambulation routes as veritable liminal zones marking the boundaries of identity and preferred behaviour in Lhasa's urbanscape.

From 'lonely land' to 'holy land': Tibet fever and Tibetan religious space as a treasure-house of touristic attractions

In his introduction to a recent collection of essays on contemporary Tibet (2009), Robert Barnett claims that often Tibet is not only portrayed, but treated as one of those places that Theodore Roosevelt described as the 'lonely lands': a term referring to vast and deserted planes and used primarily to exalt the exploits of frontiersmen in America (ibid.: 1). Tibet has certainly always represented the ultimate political and economic frontier for Communist China.[5] The Mandarin Chinese word for Tibet, *Xizang*, literally translates as 'Western treasure-house'. Academics, travel writers, and members of Tibet support groups have often claimed that the term describes most aptly Tibet's natural resources, and in particular its mineral deposits, which Beijing is said to have been appropriating since 'peaceful liberation' in 1950.[6] Significantly, the second character of the term Xizang, *zang* (or *cang* in its verb form[7])—meaning storehouse, repository—is also the tail word of the Chinese term for mineral resources: *kuang-cang*.[8] In short, this expression seems to suggest that Tibet, as the Western frontier of China's modernization, is there as a repository of resources for China to explore and utilize.

Together with the exploitation of its natural resources came the sinicization of Tibet through both Han Chinese migration and a process of modernization and urbanization. Lhasa in particular has undergone dramatic changes since Chinese troops first entered the city in 1951: in 1948, the old town consisted of just 600 buildings and its population was around 30,000 people (Larsen and Sinding-Larsen 2001: 15). Chinese government statistics indicate that in 2008 the population of Lhasa's urban area (excluding the remaining seven rural districts that also make up Lhasa prefecture) was six times that, around 186,000 people. The townscape has also seen dramatic development, with Chinese-style high-rises sprouting up west, north, and east of the old town, but also on the islands on the Kyichu River, just south of Lhasa's historic centre. In contrast to official census data, which indicates that Han residents make up less than 1 per cent of the population of the TAR, Tibetans in Lhasa (as well as the Tibetan Government in Exile) claim that Han residents represent at least half of the population of Lhasa.[9] Tibet support groups have thus pointed to the risk of 'cultural genocide' as a result of the massive influx of Han Chinese migrants to the region, thus making population statistics a hotly contested issue.

Increasingly, however, Tibet, the last frontier of China's modernization project, is also becoming the ultimate destination for China's tourism industry; its natural and cultural 'treasures' attract an ever-increasing number of visitors, the vast majority domestic. Be they wealthy businessmen from China's Eastern seaboard who take their entire families on a tour of a mysterious land, or younger backpackers on a budget, it is undeniable that tourist presence in Lhasa is at an all-time high. The number of tourists visiting the TAR each year over the nearly 30-year period from 1980 to 2009, with a couple of notable exceptions, has been steadily increasing. The only two steep falls—in the years 1989/1990, and 2008—coincided with waves of protests and rioting in Lhasa and other Tibetan regions between 1987 and 1989 and in March–April 2008 respectively.[10] On those occasions, the Chinese media played a huge role in discouraging Han tourists from travelling to Tibet: they repeatedly showed footage of ethnic Tibetans vandalizing Han businesses, but downplayed the number of casualties amongst the protesters. Despite a certain degree of apprehension that I witnessed amongst a number of Han tourists travelling to Tibetan areas, however, visits to the TAR increased by a staggering 250 per cent in 2009: going from 2.25 million in 2008, the year of the riots, to 5.6 million and thus exceeding the previous four-million high reached in 2007 (XTJNJ 2009; ZGXL 2010).

Chinese-language newspapers and specialized publications like *Tibet Tour* (Chinese: *Xizang lüyou*), often use the expression 'Tibet fever' (Chinese: *Xizang re*) to describe and simultaneously promote this fascination for the 'land of snows'. The perception of Tibet as a sacred land of religion plays a major role in the construction of Tibet as a tourist destination, while Han Chinese visitors to the Tibetan plateau are increasingly showing an interest in religious experiences. Barnett (2009) writes that, starting in the 1990s, many Han Chinese, mostly from wealthier backgrounds, have developed a special interest in Tibet, its landscape, and religion and have come to regard Tibetan lamas as precious spiritual teachers (ibid.: 14). A 2006 *Tibet Tour* article entitled 'Lhasa, the Holy City' reifies similar notions by praising Lhasa's 'unique geographical location, surrounded by snow-capped mountains and shrouded in mystery', its 'religious atmosphere' and fame as a 'holy city' (Yuan 2006: 32). The author also claims that Lhasa has become a dream destination for many people. Similarly, a 2005 article entitled 'Impressions of Lhasa' (Chinese: *Lasa yinxiang*) in the magazine *West* (Chinese: *Xibu*) also points to Lhasa's distinctive geography: 'located at an altitude of 3,800 metres and also known as the "sunlight city" ... with a bright sun and blue sky as background, Lhasa is a beautiful city' (Xu 2005: 1). The author also reminds his readers of Lhasa's role as a 'political, economic, cultural, and religious centre' and refers to the meaning of the city's Tibetan toponym: literally translating as 'holy land' or 'place of the Buddhas'. Chinese touristic discourse on Lhasa and Tibet, therefore, seems to revolve mainly around two often-related tropes: that of Tibet as a distant land with unique and spectacular territorial features and the trope of Tibet as a holy land.

Particularly when writing of Lhasa, however, Chinese tourism magazines focus on religion and the practice of ritual circumambulation. Lhasa's old city is defined by its circumambulatory circuits: the inner circuit (Tibetan: *nang skor*) which leads around the Jokhang temple's main chapel, the middle circuit (Tibetan: *bar skor*), which leads around the whole temple, the circuit around the Potala Palace (Tibetan: *rtse skor ba*[11]) and finally the outer path (Tibetan: *gling skor*), which envelops the entire old city and most of its holy sites. Urban space in Lhasa saw, until 1951, organic development within the confines of these circuits, while pilgrimage, trade, and socialization thrived along the routes they defined. It is hardly surprising, then, that in Lhasa the attention of the tourist is drawn to the circumambulation routes, which thus become multilayered spaces, where touristic practices encounter those of Tibetan devotees.

In 2008, *Tibet Tour* devoted nearly an entire issue to Lhasa's circumambulation circuits, which they entitled 'Lhasa's Holy Routes' (Chinese: *Lasa shenglu*), with pictures from all four of Lhasa's main *skor ba* routes and a map. The year before, in 2007, the same magazine had already published another article— mostly a photographic essay—entitled 'Turning' (Chinese: *zhuanjing*), in which the author wrote of how 'charming' early mornings in Lhasa can be, when 'old Tibetan men and women, in an orderly manner, spin big and small prayer wheels inscribed with sacred mantras' (She 2007: 60). If Chinese-style modernization, Han migration, and tourism have transformed Tibet and Lhasa into a frontier zone of encounter and cultural complexity, then, the Chinese media freeze the circumambulation routes as the ultimate bastions of Tibetanness and religiosity. In an attempt to go beyond the exoticizing rhetoric of Chinese tourism discourse, the remainder of this chapter aims to look at the role of circumambulation in young Tibetans' practice of urban space in Lhasa: I present the *skor ba* routes not as the locus of a timeless tradition, but as the liminal spaces of ritual resilience where young rural migrants come to terms with the transitional state of frontier urbanism and attempt to establish communitas.

Ritual elation: Lhasa's youths, *skor ba* and communitas

Whilst performing *skor ba* on a busy summer evening, I asked one of my Tibetan young informants what he thought of all the tourists wearing mountaineering clothing and carrying expensive cameras—some with massive telephoto zoom lenses—who were also walking with us around Lhasa's most central and important temple, the Jokhang. He said that in a way he did not mind it as he wanted to become a tour guide, and the presence of more tourists would have done him good. He therefore tolerated the folkorization of Tibetan religion that occurs as a result of the heavy presence of Han Chinese tourists on Lhasa's *skor ba* route and which would appear to be in sharp contrast to Tibetans' own practice of *skor ba*. But what does this practice consist of exactly?

My first experience of circumambulation took place on a cold January evening, some three months into my fieldwork. Lobzang had just given me a call asking if I wanted to join him and some friends of his who were going to prostrate the entire length of the circumambulation route around the Potala Palace (Tibetan: *rtse skor ba*). As I arrived in front of the Potala, I spotted Lobzang and his friends immediately: all males in their early twenties, they were wearing elbow and kneepads, old gloves, and some of them even plastic sackcloth and facemasks. Friendly and enthusiastic, my young informants were all Tibetan rural migrants from nearby villages and had each spent at least a year in Lhasa. Some of them students, others skilled workers, they often spent their spare time in Internet cafes, pool parlours, Tibetan nightclubs, karaoke bars. They also regularly made religious visits (Tibetan: *mchod mjal*[12]) to temples, monasteries, and other sacred places and frequently got together to perform ritual circumambulations on Lhasa's *skor ba* routes.

On this particular evening, a few weeks before the Tibetan New Year, they decided to do something a bit more unusual: full-length prostrations (Tibetan: *phyag 'tshal*) along the nearly two-kilometre *skor ba* route that encircles the Potala Palace. Prostrations are among the crucial preparatory (Tibetan: *sngon 'gro*) practices tantric practitioners are to engage in. Full prostrations (Tibetan: *brkyangs phyag*) normally consist of throwing oneself flat on the floor in front of a sacred symbol with the arms outstretched (Powers 2007: 299), but they can also be performed while circumambulating a religious site, such as the Potala Palace or western Tibet's Mount Kailash.

All lined up and keeping a distance of some five metres between each other, by the time I arrived at the palace, my informants had already started their prostrations on the southern side of the circumambulation path. 'It was *rgan* Tashi-*lags*'s idea,' said Dhondrup, 'and we went along with. He knows so much about Tibetan religion!' A 27-year-old who works as an electrical technician for the state energy company, Tashi is a very charismatic figure. His friends call him *rgan lags*, a Tibetan polite term of address for teacher, as he often teaches Tibetan history and religion in a cramped classroom in the newly built courtyard in the old city where Lobzang runs a small private school. Tashi looked at me and asked: 'Are you also going to do prostrations?' 'Of course!' I replied. Nodding his head in approval, he told me to follow Dhondrup, who was already stretched out face down on the pavement in front of the palace, and to ask him any questions I might have about performing prostrations.

And so Dhondrup showed me: with his hands folded, he would reach over the top of his head, then touch his forehead, his mouth, his chest, slowly bend his knees, lower his body, and slide his hands over the pavement so as to throw his entire body onto the ground. He then stretched his arms in front of his head and brought the palms of his hands together, with the tips of his fingers facing the sky. I finally made an attempt myself and started to reflect on the significance of these gestures. Prostrations require a strong drive, a certain degree of conviction and resolve. When performing them, one has to lie face down on the ground and breathe through one's nose the dirt produced by the continual wave of residents, pilgrims, and visitors that have been finding their way to Lhasa for years. The perceived detachment from our surroundings that we are afforded by our bipedal position briefly vanishes into the dust that covers the pavement. It is an act of reverence, in which, notions of hierarchy are embodied and weaved into the practitioner's experience of physical space.

Martin Mills points to how, during prostrations, the body's movement through space determines a hierarchical orientation toward a sacred centre along a vertical axis, which involves the lowering of the highest point of the prostrator's body, the head (2003: 50). When prostrating, my young informants thus establish themselves in a deferential position with respect to the sacred ground of the Potala and the sacred geography of the city in general, reifying indigenous notions of religiosity and urbanism that predate Communist rule and mark the confines of the urban area of pre-1959 Lhasa. As I shall explore further in later sections, their ritual movements point to the resilience of traditional approaches

Figure 8.1 A young worshipper prostrates in front of the Potala palace.

to the practice of urban space at a time of great change; the circumambulation routes signifying the ultimate *limes* between contrasting notions of what a city Lhasa should be.

Continuing our prostrations in what was at once a communal and individual effort, we passed the three stupas (Tibetan: *mchod rten*) at the south-western end of the Potala and turned right, heading north on the circumambulation route that encircles the palace. We had covered about 550 metres and had reached the western side of the *skor ba* circuit, when Tashi decided it was time for a break. He took a few cans of 'Red Bull' and 'Coca Cola' out of his backpack and we all gathered around near a flowerbed on the edge of the pavement. The atmosphere was relaxed; we sipped our drinks and Dhondrup even lit a cigarette. 'Are you tired?' Tashi asked the group. 'Of course I am not tired,' our friend Choegyal replied defiantly and all of a sudden he stood up and started break dancing and doing push-ups on the pavement, right next to the prayer wheels that line the walls of the palace. Tashi, Dhondrup, and the others immediately joined in. They would push and thrust each other, laugh and shout: 'Wait! Look at me!' one of them said. 'Can you do that?' said Lobzang as he attempted a handstand. A quiet break from religious salutations thus quickly turned into an impromptu friendly contest, a manifestation of physical strength, skill, and bravado as well as a sense of camaraderie.

The patent, almost overstated, display of excitement and devotion marks the group's prostrations as both a very conscious, serious attempt at religious observance and as a moment of communal joy, elation almost. And the two things are in young Tibetans' experience of outdoor religious space correlated. As opposed to the quiet reverence with which I have seen members of this same group of prostrators enter chapels and shrines, outdoor circumambulation is often a chance for catching up with friends in an apparently nonchalant manner. While on their *skor ba*, if not so much when they are prostrating, young Lhasa Tibetans often speak loudly on their mobile phones, play music on them, chase each other, and even flirt at times.

This link between ritual and sociality is clearly not unique to the Tibetan cultural world. Victor Turner devoted much of his work to an analysis of how ritual sets the cultural terms for social living within a group. He looked, in particular, at the role of ritual in the formation of what he famously termed 'communitas', or the 'bond ... uniting people over and above any formal social bonds' (1974: 45).

In one of his many essays on ritual, liminality and communitas (1977), Turner describes ritual as work-like and obligatory: sooner or later everyone has to fulfil one's 'ritual duty' (ibid.: 39) in society and take part in so-called 'sacred work'. In the same way that my young informants' sense of comradeship was strengthened on the *rtse skor ba*, it is joint participation in ritual work that leads to the construction of communitas. Turner also claims that, if on the one hand ritual practices can be described as work-like, on the other these 'tasks' are also often supplemented by a strong ludic component: 'In many tribal rites, there is built into the liturgical structure, a good deal of what we and they would think of as amusement, recreation, fun, and joking.' (ibid.: 40)

What Turner is talking about here are more structured, ritualized forms of jocularity and recreation. His argument, however, resonates with what I observed on Lhasa's circumambulation routes, where serious religious observance, routinized and work-like, can quickly turn into jesting and fooling around. If prostrating the entire length of the *rtse skor* ba is a remarkable and exceptional feat, it is also simultaneously relaxed and commonplace.

One could go as far as saying that in their relaxed and yet regulated engagement with Lhasa's sacred space, my informants experience something akin to what Csikszentmihalyi calls flow. This term refers to activities characterized by 'peaks of involvement that produce intense feelings of enjoyment and creativity' (1988: 15). In a manner very similar to the experiences of my young prostrators, flow experiences would consist of a mixture of highly rewarding, regulated activities and momentary, playful interruptions, or interludes.

Flow is also crucially linked to an 'ability to perform', which in the case of my young informants is very much a *cultural* ability. Shared rules and ritualized actions, therefore, allow for flow experiences and a feeling of communitas to come about: 'one experiences flow most often in activities which have clearly established rules for action, such as rituals, games, or participatory art forms like the dance' (Csikszentmihalyi 1975: 45).

Sociality would thus appear to be inherent in communal ritual bodily practices like circumambulation and prostrations. In the context of their ethnography of walkers, Ingold and Lee Vergunst (2008) point to the importance of communal bodily movements in cementing relationships and creating a sense of unity:

> Sharing or creating a walking rhythm with other people can lead to a very particular closeness and bond between the people involved. ... This physical co-presence, emphasized by common movements, is also important...
>
> (Ingold and Lee Vergunst 2008: 69)

More important even is the connection between rewarding flow experiences and the actors' relation to their surroundings, in our case the circumambulation route around the Potala Palace. Csikszentmihalyi maintains that one 'is actively engaged in some form of clearly specified interaction with the environment' (1975: 43) thanks to specific skills and norms. Similarly these young Tibetans develop a respectful, deferential engagement with Lhasa's holy sites through their prostrations. This attitude is also accompanied by feelings of euphoria and enjoyment.

Circumambulation and distinction

After my first experience on the *skor ba* routes, I decided to explore the issue of ritual as recreation further and conducted a series of semi-structured interviews. I first asked Tenzin, a 23-year-old from a farming village in Malgro Gungdkar,[13] if it was not strange for young people to get together to perform *skor ba*, if they did not have something more 'fun' to do in their spare time. He responded that many young people in Lhasa do not care about religion; they do not work and spend all their time in teahouses and pool parlours. Tenzin said that he also likes going out to drink tea or to sing karaoke, but that it is very important to devote time to religion. A lot of his friends are monks and he likes spending time with them or going for *mchod mjal*, particularly in a place like Lhasa that is good for that.

Tenzin's words seem to suggest that these young migrants not only want to make the most of the spiritual opportunities Lhasa has to offer, but they also want to set themselves apart from other people their age, often from urbanite families, who generally avoid the circumambulation routes and spend most of their time in different parts of the city. These two groups, in fact, can be said to have very different practices of urban space, reflecting some of the tensions that animate Lhasa's recent development.

In this respect, Lobzang also made an interesting observation about how he prefers to devote time to religion—and thus make more use of Lhasa's religious spaces—when he is in a good mood. He said that if he is happy, he likes to go to temples, or to perform *skor ba* and *phyag 'tshal*. It is when he is not happy, if he has had a bad day at work, that he wishes to spend time in bars, pool parlours, or Internet cafés.

Just like Tenzin, Lobzang is a fun, outgoing young man and we cannot interpret his claim that, when in a good mood, he prefers to frequent religious spaces as a moralistic one. He also clarified that he would not just go to lay recreational places only when he feels unhappy and that *nang ma* (Tibetan traditional nightclubs) and karaoke are among his favourite pastimes. He does, however, make a distinction, in which he identifies ritual behaviour as *preferred* behaviour: something that, if in the right mood, he would often prefer over other activities. What is more, unlike some of my Tibetan informants from urbanite and particularly cadre families, Lobzang does not own a car. The few friends of his who do are largely drivers running a private service between Lhasa and the local township close to his home village. Differences in income levels, reflected amongst other things in car ownership, correlate with distinct leisure and residential geographies for different groups of young Tibetans in Lhasa. The motivations for the trajectories they trace in the urban-scape of the Tibetan capital are neither entirely pious for young migrants nor fully secular for wealthier urbanites. Rather, as we shall see in the next section, beliefs come up against prohibition for wealthier Tibetans and their families, whilst young migrants' ideal preference for ritual activities—as in Lobzang's case—may not always be realized. Both at the levels of discourse and practice, however, distinctions are reified and impact Lhasa's development.

These perceived and material distinctions as well as a preference for ritual practices or lack thereof translate into a spatial distinction between Lhasa outside and inside of the *gling skor*, especially the zone west of the Potala known in Chinese as *xijiao*. According to government statistics, between 2000 and 2008, the total floor space of residential buildings under construction each year in the TAR has increased by nearly 200 percent.[14] In Lhasa this has led to the sprouting of housing developments and the formation of new quarters outside of the *gling skor*. With their four-lane roads, high rises, restaurants, karaoke bars, and night-clubs, these areas resemble in style the cheap glass-and-concrete constructions of most other Chinese cities. While many Tibetans also reside in some of these new developments, the latter are mostly home to large communities of predominantly Han Chinese migrants. The *skor ba* circuits and the *gling skor* in particular, then, lie at the frontier of two different notions of urbanism: that of a sacred city of temples, market stalls and alleyways, mostly populated by migrants from countryside villages in both central and Eastern Tibet, and that of Lhasa as a modern Chinese urban centre, inhabited to a large extent by Han migrants and wealthier Tibetans.

This is not to say that Lhasa within the *gling skor* has remained unchanged, but that—especially for Tibetans of more devout inclinations—the Barkor and the rest of the old city remain veritable 'power-places'. The history of these places points to Tibetan people's vision of the relation that ties space, land-scape, religion, and architecture. The continual reproduction of this relation is probably best represented by the practice, for some daily, of *skor ba*, some-times combined with *phyag 'tshal*. Their circular movement and pedestrian nature are opposed in the minds of informants like Tenzin to the more linear taxi routes that take them on their lay pilgrimages to the Chengdu-like *xijiao*. Michel de Certeau claims that if on the one hand totalitarianism attacks indi-genous beliefs by labeling them superstitious, for walkers/practitioners 'local legends ... permit exits, ways going out and coming back in, and thus habita-ble spaces' (1984: 106). For my informants, the centripetal force of indigenous

Figure 8.2 View of west Lhasa (*xijiao*) from the Potala palace.

belief that ignites the *skor ba* reveals Lhasa's historic centre as the axis in a circular movement that, I believe, epitomizes the reproduction of habitable, familiar spaces.

Insofar as the routes open up both devotional and social opportunities, then, one could speak of a cultural delimitation of space. Paths are opened up that allow for both the expressions of devotion and the realization of more sociable and familiar activities. That my participants will often combine these, referring to a discourse of happiness is indicative of the enduring centrality of ritual space and practices for this group of urban residents. These youths define and distinguish themselves, among other things, by frequenting the *skor ba* routes and identifying them as places for the strengthening of communal bonds through joint participation in devotional practices as well as recreation.

Lhasa's *skor ba* routes: identity, mobility, and the limits of Tibetanness

So far, I have looked at mostly one side of the story, describing how and why a group of young migrants in Lhasa might decide to devote a considerable amount of time to outdoor ritual practices like prostrations and circumambulation. I have also hinted at how these activities make this group of migrant youths distinct from other Lhasans their age, whose practice of urban space and residential patterns lead them to make considerably less use of locales within the *gling skor* or of the *skor ba* routes.

One of these young Lhasans, a woman called Lhamo, proved to be very dismissive of my migrant informants' interest in ritual practices like *skor ba*. Lhamo, is a 25-year-old from Lhasa, who studied at university in inland China. She lives with her parents in an apartment in a recently built housing development and has landed a well-paid job with a government agency. During an informal conversation, I showed her on my camera some pictures I had taken the night before while circumambulating the Potala with Lobzang. I asked her what she thought of these young villagers and of their interest in religion. She replied that she does not normally spend a lot of time doing 'religious work', but that she does not think these people like Lobzang do it out of devotion. She points out that a lot of them are unemployed and just do *skor ba* to kill time: they stroll (Tibetan: *'cham 'cham*) on the Barkor because they do not have anything better to do, not because they really care about religion.

I said I agreed that *skor ba* can be a pastime, but I also added that some of these young migrants are busy, hard-working young people, who still often prefer to spend their evenings doing prostrations or circumambulations, rather than stay at home or go to a bar. Lhamo responded that maybe they did not have difficult jobs and were not as tired in the evenings.

Lhamo's attitude confirms the presence of a certain discourse of Tibetan indolence in Lhasa that Emily Yeh has also discussed (2007). Yeh describes how both Han *and* Tibetans often talk of Tibetans as being generally lazy, always sitting around in teahouses and bars, or just hanging out and wandering around the city. Yeh observes that older peri-urban villagers often blame the city for being a source of distraction with its 'many places to hang out' (ibid.: 605). Lhamo's attitude towards young, allegedly lazy Lhasa Tibetans adds to this contrast between urban degeneration and the industriousness of rural residents a further distinction between modern, hard-working Tibetans trained in China and lazy, unskilled Tibetans who have never left the TAR.

Thupten, who is 27 years old, also spent considerable time in inland China as a middle school and university student. He is an ambitious young man and is also preparing to sit the examination to join the Communist party. I once asked him if he was going to take part in the circumambulation around the Lingkor that is customary in Lhasa on the 15th day of the month of Sagadawa. He replied that he is not very religious and that he would not come. He also added that even if he wanted to come, he could not really; he explained that since his parents are Communist party members, if he were seen to take part in religious practices, this may get reported to his parents' 'leaders' (Tibetan: *mgo khrid*) who could issue a warning.

Thupten's words help us interpret the preference my migrant informants showed for ritual activities less in terms of a supposedly 'natural' Tibetan indolence. Thupten points, instead, to the negative correlation between social mobility and religious freedom, whereby my young migrant informants—mostly skilled workers and students—can 'afford' religious practice because neither they nor their close relatives (who are mostly farmers) have important jobs or hold positions of responsibility. This is obviously only one way of explaining a discrepancy in interests between Tibetan youths in Lhasa. I do, however, find it persuasive, particularly in light of a decline in the interest Lobzang and some of his friends started showing towards ritual practices at the end of my fieldwork, after joining a Chinese-run company in Lhasa.

Conclusion: the path and the thoroughfare

In the preceding section I claimed that not all young Tibetans in Lhasa manifest the same interest in religion and the ritual practice of *skor ba*. This simple distinction between two groups, while in itself reductive, has come up again and again in my ethnographic work, *skor ba* marking the however blurred confines between two major ways of spatially negotiating identity and mobility among 20-something Tibetans in Lhasa. Of course, adherence to religion and traditional practices present a very specific notion of what it means to be Tibetan and this is not to say that circumambulators are, in fact, any more Tibetan than people their age who are not as devout. More simply, the *skor ba* circuits mark a behavioural boundary between what my migrant informants perceive Tibetans to be as opposed to either the sinicized modernity of the new developments or the folklorized photographic aesthetics of the tourist gaze that I discussed at the beginning of this chapter.

In their movements between different sections of the city, between the circular paths of *skor ba* and the linear thoroughfares of west Lhasa, young Lhasans find themselves having to negotiate different notions of urbanism and identity. The space of the city is essentially composite, or as they would say *ra ma lug*: a humorous and sometimes derogatory Tibetan term that literally means 'neither goat nor sheep' and which refers to anyone or anything that is a mixture of two things, a hybrid. In his seminal discussion of van Gennep's 'rites de passage', Victor Turner describes how, once the ritual is consummated, the subject 'is expected to behave in accordance with certain customary norms' (1967: 94). In Lhasa one can say that the transition is never quite completed, but that its residents are often in a continuous state of flux. Corsín Jiménez (2003) describes how humans have a 'capacity' for creating space even in alien environments; similarly, I believe that circumambulation gives to some the cultural and spatial capacity to follow and reinterpret certain customary norms. This helps them to define themselves less as transitional beings in the multilayered heterotopia of tradition, tourism, and modernity that is contemporary Lhasa by spinning into place.

Notes

1 Research for this chapter was made possible thanks to generous grants from the Frederick Williamson Memorial Fund (Museum of Archaeology and Anthropology, University of Cambridge) and the E.O. James Bequest (All Souls College, University of Oxford).
2 Peter Bishop (1999: 381) was probably the first to describe Lhasa and in particular the Potala Palace—former residence of the Dalai Lamas—as what Foucault calls a 'heterotopia', or the 'juxtaposing in a single real place several spaces, several sites that are in themselves incompatible' (Foucault and Miskowiec 1986: 25).
3 The term *skor ba*—literally meaning to encircle, surround, to walk around—also refers to the practice of circumambulation: the ritual act of moving around a sacred site or object. The term can also be used to signify a circumambulation route.
4 With the notable exceptions of Robbie Barnett's (2006) seminal work on Lhasa's streets and Emily Yeh's (2007) piece on indolence and urbanism in the Tibetan capital, which I discuss later.
5 After the establishment of the People's Republic of China in 1949, reuniting Tibet with the 'motherland' was one of the 'prime targets' of the Chinese Communist Party (Goldstein and Rimpoche 1989: 623).
6 Explorer and travel writer Ian Baker, for example, claims that 'The Chinese call Tibet Xizang, the Western Treasure-House, and since their 'liberation' of Tibet in 1950 they have systematically plundered its vast forest reserves and ravaged its earth for uranium, gold, and other precious metals' (2004: 266). Similarly, economist Peter Navarro also maintains that 'The treasure in question refers to the fact that Tibet is a repository for some of the world's largest deposits of boron, borax, chromite, iron, lithium, and uranium' (2008: 137).
7 Meaning to hide, to conceal, to save.
8 Literally meaning the minerals that are hidden.
9 Apart from having serious political implications, however, Ma Rong and Tenzan Lhundup (2008) report that this discrepancy is also due to the fact that most Han in Lhasa are temporary migrants (mostly from Sichuan and Gansu), who try to avoid government registration to dodge fees and management charges. While the public

security bureau, work units and residential committees should be responsible for keeping count of these temporary migrants, they are often disorganized and lack personnel. More recently, however, a survey carried out by the Family Planning Committee of Lhasa City estimates Han temporary migrants to the city to be in the region of 80,000, a lot closer to the estimates of Tibet support groups and the Tibetan government in exile (ibid.).

10 In March 1989, martial law was imposed in Lhasa, lasting a total of 13 months.

11 This term—literally meaning the circle around the peak/the top (*rtse*)—refers to the circumambulation route around the Potala Palace. The latter is also known in Tibetan as *rtse pho grang*, meaning 'palace on the top', given its location perched on top of the Marpori hill, at the northwestern end of the old city.

12 This Tibetan compound word made of *mchod* (to make offerings) and *mjal* (the honorific form of the verb to meet) refers to the act of visiting a place of worship.

13 A rural county roughly 70 km northeast of Lhasa's urban area.

14 Going from 869,800 m^2 in 2000 to 2,566,300 m^2 in 2008 (XTJNJ 2009).

References

Aris, M. (1992) 'Introduction', in M. Aris and P. Booz (eds) *Lamas, princes, and brigands: Joseph Rock's photographs of the Tibetan borderlands of China*, New York, China House Gallery: China Institute in America.

Aris, M. and Booz, P. (eds) (1992) *Lamas, princes, and brigands: Joseph Rock's photographs of the Tibetan borderlands of China*, New York, China House Gallery: China Institute in America.

Baker, I. (2004) *The heart of the world: a journey to the last secret place*, New York: Penguin Press.

Barnett, R. (2006) *Lhasa: streets with memories*, New York: Columbia University Press.

Barnett, R. (2009) 'Introduction', in L. Wang and T. Shakya *The struggle for Tibet*, London: Verso.

Bishop, P. (1999) 'Reading the Potala', in T. Huber (ed.) *Sacred spaces and powerful places in Tibetan culture: a collection of essays*, Dharamsala, H.P.: Library of Tibetan Works and Archives.

Certeau, M. de (1984) *The practice of everyday life*, Berkeley: University of California Press.

Corsín Jiménez, A. (2003) 'On space as a capacity', *The Journal of the Royal Anthropological Institute*, 9(1): 137–53.

Csikszentmihalyi, M. (1975) 'Play and intrinsic rewards', *Journal of Humanistic Psychology*, 15: 3, 41–63.

Csikszentmihalyi, M. (1988) 'The flow experience and its significance for human psychology', in M. Csikszentmihalyi and I.S. Csikszentmihalyi (eds) *Optimal experience: psychological studies of flow in consciousness*, Cambridge, New York: Cambridge University Press.

Csikszentmihalyi, M. and Csikszentmihalyi, I.S. (eds) (1988) *Optimal experience: psychological studies of flow in consciousness*, Cambridge; New York: Cambridge University Press.

Epstein, L. and Wenbin, P. (1998) 'Ritual, ethnicity, and generational identity', in M.C. Goldstein and M.T. Kapstein (eds) *Buddhism in contemporary Tibet: religious revival and cultural identity*, Berkeley: University of California Press.

Foucault, M. and Miskowiec, J. (1986) 'Of other spaces', *Diacritics*, 16(1): 22–7.

Goldstein, M.C. and Rimpoche, G. (1989) *A history of modern Tibet, 1913–1951: The demise of the Lamaist state*, Berkeley: University of California Press.

Gutschow, N., Michaels, A, Ramble, C. and Steinkellner, E. (eds) (2003) *Sacred land-scape of the Himalaya: proceedings of an international conference at Heidelberg, 25–27 May 1998*, Vienna: Austrian Academy of Sciences Press.

Huber, T. (ed.) (1999) *Sacred spaces and powerful places in Tibetan culture: a collection of essays*, Dharamsala, H.P.: Library of Tibetan Works and Archives.

Ingold, T. (2004) 'Culture on the ground', *Journal of Material Culture*, 9(3): 315–40.

Ingold, T. and Lee Vergunst, J. (eds) (2008) *Ways of walking: ethnography and practice on foot*, Aldershot: Ashgate.

Karmay, S. (1994) 'Mountain cults and national identity in Tibet', in R. Barnett and S. Akiner (eds) *Resistance and reform in Tibet*. London: Hurst.

Larsen, K. and Sinding-Larsen, A. (2001) *The Lhasa atlas: traditional Tibetan architecture and townspace*, London: Serindia Publications.

Massey, D.B. (2005) *For space*, London: SAGE.

Mills, M.A. (2003) *Identity, ritual and state in Tibetan Buddhism: the foundations of authority in Gelukpa monasticism*, London: Routledge Curzon.

Navarro, P. (2008) *The coming China wars: where they will be fought and how they can be won*, Upper Saddle River, NJ: FT Press.

Powers, J. (2007) *Introduction to Tibetan Buddhism*, Ithaca, NY: Snow Lion Publications.

Ma, R. and Lhundup, T. (2008) 'Temporary migrants in Lhasa in 2005', in *Journal of the International Association of Tibetan Studies*, 4, www.thlib.org/collections/texts/jiats/#jiats=/04/marong/ (accessed 11 April 2011).

Schwartz, R.D. (1994) *Circle of protest: political ritual in the Tibetan uprising*, New York: Columbia University Press.

Turner, V.W. (1967) *The forest of symbols; aspects of Ndembu ritual*, Ithaca, NY: Cornell University Press.

Turner, V.W. (1974) *Dramas, fields, and metaphors: symbolic action in human society*, Ithaca: Cornell University Press.

Turner, V.W. (1977) 'Variations on a theme of liminality', in S.F. Moore and B.G. Myerhoff (eds) *Secular ritual*, Assen: Van Gorcum.

Yeh, E.T. (2007) 'Tropes of indolence and the cultural politics of development in Lhasa, Tibet', *Annals of the Association of American Geographers*, 97(3): 593–612.

Chinese-language sources

She, M. (2007) 'Zhuan jing' ('Turning'), *Xizang lüyou (Tibet Tour)*. (accessed 11 April 2011 through China Academic Journals Full-text Database).

Xizang lüyou (Tibet Tour) (2008) 'Lasa shenglu' ('Lhasa's holy routes').

XTJNJ [*Xizang tong ji nian jian*] (Tibet statistical yearbook) (2009) Beijing: Zhongguo tong ji chu ban she. Online. (accessed 11 April 2011 through All China Data Center, China Data Online).

Xu, C. (2005) 'Lasa yinxiang' ('Impressions of Lhasa'), *Xibu (West)*. (Accessed 11 April 2011 through China Academic Journals Full-text Database).

Yuan, M. (2006) 'Shengcheng Lasa' ('The holy city of Lhasa'), *Xizang lüyou (Tibet Tour)*. (Accessed 11 April 2011 through China Academic Journals Full-text Database).

ZGXL [*Zhongguo guigu Xizang lüyouwang*] (China Tibet travel network) (2010) 'Xizang lüyou jing yu gaoduan pinzhi you' (Tibet tourism specializes in high-quality travel), 30 October, www.tibetcn.com/news/2010/05301582.html (accessed 11 April 2011).

9 Urban exploration as adventure tourism

Journeying beyond the everyday

Emma Fraser

> *I came to Chernobyl to visit the ruins.*
>
> *For someone intent on the situated experience of decay, this site, when detached from its past, is a model for the process of the decline of the built environment.*
>
> *But it would be a mistake to ignore the inevitability of Chernobyl—its ongoing, insistent presence in the landscape. The reality that it will be thousands of years before the threat of further nuclear disaster ceases to be real, and the fact that we collectively fail to do anything much to prevent such an outcome, have an impact so immediate and solid, when standing in the sun on a peaceful spring afternoon, that they are not easily forgotten, or, more exactly, recovered from.*[1]

Pripyat was a purpose-built 'atomograd', a Soviet-era city designed to house the workers of the nearby Chernobyl nuclear power plant. The city was occupied for just seven years before the entire population of 50,000 was evacuated in 1986, following the accident at Reactor 4.

To visit Chernobyl as a tourist is not a comfortable experience. Besides the potential exposure to radiation, the three-hour trip from Kiev on deteriorating roads, or the process of passing through military checkpoints and radiation scans, I was not comfortable with visiting Chernobyl as a disaster zone, and I am not comfortable with fascination in relation to human suffering.

The discourse on Chernobyl (and by association nearby Pripyat) is often one of catastrophe, told in measures of radioactivity, body counts, clinical language of cancers and birth defects. None of these things speak in my experiences of the site:

> *Faded, washed out colours, nothing vibrant except the leaves on the trees. Modern buildings in a Soviet style removing them once from familiarity, removed again by broken windows with ragged curtains, and the scattered personal remnants of fifty thousand lives.*
>
> *Overgrown paths, half-obliterated mosaics. Classrooms in disarray, an empty pool with an impotent diving board suspended above. Finally, we reach the iconic amusement park, its rusting dodgem cars still waiting patiently behind the fence, a rotting wooden-seated roundabout, photographed against the backdrop of equally rotten buildings, and the red and yellow Ferris wheel, appearing from a distance as if it could still function, if only there were people here to use it.*

Figure 9.1 A swing in the abandoned amusement park, Pripyat (Chernobyl). Despite featuring in iconic images of the city taken since the disaster, there are questions as to whether this park was fully operational prior to the evacuation.

Images go some way to expressing the complexity of the site. They reflect the experience itself, the tactility. They remind me of the slight breeze, the spring warmth, the very tangible presence of absences and the strange taste of radiation—like touching your tongue to a battery.

This wasn't somewhere static; this was a place where one thing happened once.

Pripyat, along with Gunkanjima in Japan, is one of the few relatively untouched landscapes of large-scale modern ruin in the world. Modern ruins are those architectural sites where long-term neglect has led to a state of visible decay, and in which the functionality of the place is compromised so that the dominant impression becomes one of uselessness and absence. Unlike historically significant sites (remnants of prior cultures and eras), these everyday ruins are the persistent detritus of the culture that generated them, existing both within and outside that culture. If space is socially and culturally produced, as Lefebvre suggests, then a contemporary ruinscape is a void of production—its status as a place is called into question by material decline that signifies the end of its life as an actively inhabited (and therefore continually produced) space. The modern ruin becomes dead space because death '...has a location, but that location lies below or above social space', which is 'a space of society, of social life' (Lefebvre 1991: 35). Another way of framing the space/place distinction is in de

Certeau's iteration of Merleau-Ponty's phenomenology, in which he frames space as a site of movement and action, ever ambiguous, while place 'implies an indication of stability' (de Certeau 1984: 117). De Certeau also notes that death 'falls outside the thinkable' (de Certeau 1984: 190), which, when applied to modern ruins as dead spaces, partially explains their sudden shift from dynamic to inert sites of social production: modern ruins are the unthinkable 'dead' sites of the contemporary era, existing, but unstable—not yet gone, but implicitly excluded from society because of their uninhabitable and unpredictable presence.

As a destination that is between place and space, between being and unbecoming, the contemporary ruinscape holds a shifting transience—hardly a tautology, this notion considers the inherent possibility of such a space, which at any moment might face demolition, reconstruction or renewal; a transience that must be acknowledged because it renders the space fundamentally precarious.

The problematic nature of such precariousness can be seen in some early encounters with 'modern ruins', such as the aftermath of the Franco-Prussian war and the subsequent battle of the Paris Commune in 1871. The burnt-out shells of sites including the Hotel de Ville and Tuileries Palace stood for years in a recognisably modern (post-Haussmann) Paris, and were subject to fascination on the part of visitors, who avidly consumed postcards of the city in ruins (see Luxenberg 1998). Since then, the decay or destruction of modern cities has been repeated in world wars, natural disasters and acts of terrorism, which serve to make us no less fascinated, but decidedly uncomfortable about the ruins of the present era. Similarly, large-scale decline and abandonment has lead to landscapes of ruin, which are equally uncomfortable spectres in an urban setting.

The dominant perception of abandoned buildings classifies them as pejorative wastelands, eyesores that have no place in a modern setting. Disused and decaying buildings disrupt efforts to maintain order and aesthetic unity, and manifest as problems to be dealt with through demolition or renovation. There is little discourse within which to attribute value to such sites, with the exception of local sentiment and heritage, which tend to elevate select locations to the status of 'historical site', while other structures are denigrated. The mainstream view of modern ruins does not see any value in these discarded remnants of the recent past—at least, not as they stand. For most, such sites remain unnoticed in the everyday landscape (for example, Hollander (2009) and Gallagher (2010) resolve to fix the problems presented by modern ruins through demolition and erasure from the landscape, or incorporation into projects of renewal).

However, a growing body of literature on contemporary ruins attempts to deal less reactively with decay and abandonment. Some emphasise the individual or personal value of the sites themselves, and many assess modern ruins as both a product of recent history and a bellwether for a post-capitalist or even apocalyptic future. In their relation to the present they can be seen as post-industrial ruins (Edensor 2005), detritus of recent history (Hell and Schönle 2008, on the ruins of modernity), postmodern or post-Fordist ruins (High and Lewis 2007; Cowie and Heathcott 2003, on deindustrialisation), or as memorial and palimpsest (Huyssen's present pasts (2003)). As sites they can be scapes (Berger's drosscape, 2007; Hell and Schönle's ruinscape, 2008); spaces (Edensor's interstitial spaces (2005: 60), Turner's liminal landscapes (1986: 33–44), and de Certeau's espaces (1984: 117)); and states (terrain vague and shrinking cities (Oswalt 2005)). As place they can be defined by what they were (as in Boym's nostalgia (2001)), or what they might become (Vergara's 'American Acropolis' (1999: 15)).

Recently, there has been a growing fascination with urban and industrial decay, and ruins are increasingly acknowledged as a contemporary phenomenon. Images from Marchand and Meffre's *Ruins of Detroit* featured in a 2009 Time article on the decay of the city (see Marchand and Meffre 2009 and 2010). Paiva and Manaugh's *The Art of Urban Exploration* (2008); O'Boyle's *Modern Ruins* (2010) and Drooker, Woodward and Brinkley's *American Ruins* (2007) join earlier publications such as Vergara's own *American Ruins* (1999); Skrdla's *Ghostly Ruins* (2006); Seidel, Sack and Klemp's *Underworld* (1997) and Hamm, Steinberg and Jungk's *Dead Tech* (2000), each concerned with relatively contemporary sites of recent ruin, as well as obsolescence. Polidori depicts the decay of Pripyat and Chernobyl in his *Zones of Exclusion* (2003).

Most of these publications are little more than coffee table books depicting confronting, yet increasingly typical, images of decay. This emphasis on the aesthetics of decay reflects the preoccupations of the emerging practice of urban exploration. Whether mainstream (as in the case of Marchand and Meffre, and Vergara) or independently published in print and online, these texts represent the core products of a growing sub-culture.

'Urban Exploration' (hereafter UE) is an umbrella term for a practice in which participants seek to enter locations that offer experiences beyond the everyday. Most commonly, urban explorers visit sites of abandonment and decay, or forbidden locations (such as drains, sewers and subway tunnels). The term can also refer to related practices in which participants gain access to active sites (rooftops, building sites, bridges and otherwise restricted areas). The practice can involve trespassing, forced entry, and exposure to dangers including structural instability, asbestos and other contaminants. There is an element of personal risk with regard to the methods of access (which can include climbing, rappelling, tunnelling and so on), as well as encounters with security or police, or others who make use of such locations (the homeless, those engaging in illicit activities and 'salvagers', for example). Practices encompassed by UE include the Japanese practice of *Haikyo* (from the Japanese term for 'ruin', and a practice which is specific to ruinscapes) and Infiltration, which focuses on trespass and subversive aspects of UE.

Exploration in spaces of decay continues to be the most common form of UE. As one veteran explorer notes: 'Among the most delightful targets you'll find are abandoned sites, probably the most popular locales among urban explorers' (Ninjalicious 2005: 88). Thus, this chapter is concerned with the kinds of touristic experiences one can find in contemporary ruins, as opposed to popular ruins of antiquity; disaster zones in a state of disruption; the risks of adventure tourism, or the standard urban tourism of cities like New York.

UE consciously operates by subverting conventional attitudes towards abandoned or forbidden spaces, challenging notions that such sites are useless or unimportant. The explorer attributes personal, collective and aesthetic value to these sites as worthy destinations, sites of a particular kind of experience.

The UE community operates most evidently online. The web provides an ideal platform to share both images and privileged information between explorers, while maintaining anonymity. Through online networks, a sense of a worldwide community has been fostered and it is this community, more than anything else, that allows for the possibility of contemporary ruin tourism.

Formally, there are no UE tours—though such things could be said to exist via websites including CouchSurfing, GlobalFreeloaders and individual UE sites. Exceptions might include guided tours of Pripyat in the Ukraine (soon to be expanded), Haikyo tours of Gunkanjima in Japan, New Orleans 'Katrina tours', and tours of Catacombs and other similarly 'dark' sites. Considering any sanctioned tourism as UE is problematic, however, because the core element of UE—trespass—cannot apply. Conversely, as there is no way to access Pripyat in particular without prior consent, explorers must make use of sanctioned tourism to pursue their practice there. Further, few of the contemporary ruin photographs in print are taken without prior permission, although many of them are the work of confessed urban explorers.

Therefore, the notion of UE as a touristic practice must be considered—seeking the foreign or unfamiliar, destination specific travel for the purposes of UE, and the global nature of UE communities all suggest that there is an element of tourism—particularly in Pripyat and America's rust-belt cities, which have achieved high status in the community as must-see destinations for the dedicated explorer. Further, as with many tourist sites, iconographic images emerge: the Ferris wheel in Pripyat, or Michigan Central Station in Detroit. Even the increasing proliferation of literature focusing on contemporary ruinscapes cannot do without images. The work of Trigg (2006), Edensor (2005) and Hell and Schönle (2008) exemplifies this: these highly academic publications are filled with black and white shots of miscellaneous decay, as if their words are not enough to describe the state of things.

> *Something about the search for this place, signalling to us from a distance, long before we get close to it, makes it seem epic and static ... it is holding its breath—as are we.*
>
> *We approach the front fence of Michigan Central Station, awed. Take pictures. The smashed windows are gaping, angular, dark and opaque, a random pattern within the criss-crossed window frames.*

The relationship between tourism and consumption is well established, with Urry in particular providing a relation between western leisure practices, consumer culture and the escapism or exoticism of the tourist/travel experience. However, Urry suggests that tourist sites 'are fundamentally places of service and material consumption' (Urry 2004: 209), a quality which cannot easily be associated with the kinds of destinations sought by urban explorers. In fact, in the case of UE, the opposite is the case—modern ruins are sites which have fallen out of the world, they do not figure on any tourist map and are by definition absent of the kind of material consumption that generates a commodification of place.

However, Urry also suggests that 'the minimal characteristic of tourist activity is the fact that we look at, or gaze upon, particular objects, such as piers, towers, old buildings, artistic objects, food, countryside and so on' (Urry 1995: 131). Thus the visual component of UE, souveniring images of decay from abandoned locations, becomes consumption of place in a touristic sense—the images generated by the explorer are the productions of a visitor's gaze, and thus a 'tourist activity'. In this context, modern ruins are tourist destinations.

Contemporary ruins as tourist destinations stand somewhere between the romantic sublime and the uncomfortable notion of disaster tourism, which 'values extreme cultural experiences' as transgressive acts (Garoian and Gaudelius 2008: 124). As with adventure and disaster tourism, UE seeks to indulge in risk-taking activities, and perhaps also to imagine 'apocalyptic scenarios of the world turned upside-down' (Huggan 2010: 101) and 'to see and experience it in situ, to claim that one was physically present in the midst of it all' (Garoian and Gaudelius 2008: 124).

'Unfortunately, such transgressions are imperialistic', observe Garoian and Gaudelius (2008: 123), and Huggan argues that adventure tourism is potentially linked to 'a crisis in masculinity' and a 'quest for progress' (2010: 102). A similar reading of UE culture reveals an overt masculinity, particularly in the emphasis on exploring and conquering, physical strength, imperviousness to danger, and survival. The pursuit of real or authentic experiences, as opposed to the contrived spectacle of traditional tourism, is also a common element between the UE traveller and the adventure/disaster tourist (see Huggan 2010: 100–103, in particular).

In relation to adventure and disaster tourism, Bell and Lyalls's accelerated sublime incorporates vastness, stillness, extreme feats, 'dark' sites (here Bell includes Chernobyl) and risk for pleasure (2002: 188–200), which are also common to UE. The accelerated sublime is inverted, however (as is traditional tourism) by the covert and subversive nature of UE. Where the accelerated sublime accounts en masse for those who want to experience sublime qualities in authentic and impressive ways, UE continues to be a preoccupation of independent groups who make their own itineraries and maps, and are their own guides.

In considering 'toxic tours' (including Chernobyl), Pezzullo wonders if the benefits of tourism in disaster affected areas, run-down neighbourhoods and polluted sites raises a 'tension between engagement and objectification' (Pezzullo 2007: 31), an exploitation of people and places in the interests of a political or educational drive to occupy, physically, a space of risk in which something must be confronted. However, Pezzullo believes in the substantive power of this form of disaster tourism to counter 'mass commercial tourism' (Pezzullo 2007: 37), and in doing so, move away from the usual binaries of self and other or home and away, and avoid the sense of alienation and privilege of traditional tourism. A thinking engagement with the unacknowledged or spoilt spaces of everyday life, as a tourist, is less problematic than a tourism spectacle that emphasises foreignness and turns the potential for education into consumption.

Because UE operates as an unsanctioned and unguided engagement with spaces that are not the commodified sites of either traditional, disaster or adventure tourism, if it is a tourist practice at all, it must be said to be a participant generated consumption of the aesthetic and experience of modern ruins, which exists in opposition to commodified, mass-tourist practices.

When arguing for the potential of alternative practice in modern ruin spaces in this chapter, I take on two theoretical approaches. The first is Walter Benjamin's 'redemptive critical practice'; the second is de Certeau's notion of spatial practice.

Benjamin and de Certeau identify dominant perceptions and conditions within modern and spatial paradigms of the material world. They propose an active rejection of the experiences engendered by particular ways of seeing and existing. The practice of UE similarly rejects the control of the built environment by actively seeking sites in which such control is suspended, diminished, and challenged.

One could think of Benjamin as an early urban explorer—taking to the streets of foreign cities, and in his travels seeking locations and experiences that do not usually figure in a typical tourist account. Benjamin's experiments with hashish in Marseilles, for example, and his short pieces on Moscow and Naples, were aimed at altering the usual perceptions of the city, both as experience and as representation. A pertinent reading of Benjamin's city portraits suggests that

> [t]he fragmentary style pursued by Benjamin in his writing on the city is in keeping with his understanding of the modern urban complex as the locus of the disintegration of experience and with his recognition of the need to salvage the disregarded debris of contemporary society. The city is a vast ruin demanding careful excavation and rescue.
>
> (Gilloch 1996: 23)

Benjamin's writings, concerned often with the rejected, lost, and ephemeral are described by Caygill as 'littered with the remains and traces of abandoned works', with a great deal of his legacy made up of 'ruins', 'fragments' and 'Uncompleted/uncompletable projects' (Caygill 1998: 3). One such work is the voluminous Arcades Project, which is significant because it focuses on the semi-derelict shopping arcades of 1940s Paris. In wandering the ruins of the recent past, I share with Benjamin a fascination for the outmoded and obsolete detritus of capitalism, which he discovered in the then-decaying arcades.

In using a Benjaminian approach to contemporary ruin landscapes, I admittedly avoid engaging closely with notions of space and place, urban renewal, embodiment, affect and other equally significant understandings of the built environment and its decline (as outlined above). The reason for privileging

Benjamin's methodology is the extent to which it provides the necessary perspective to return potential and value to a site that is normatively beyond redemption in itself. Where other approaches place one at the centre of the ruin, or account for experience in terms of broader social and cultural contexts, Benjamin finds a use for the neglected and liminal refuse of modernity, for, as he states: 'Overcoming the concept of "progress", and overcoming the concept of "period of decline" are two sides of one and the same thing' (Benjamin 1999: 460). For Benjamin, as for myself, and for the practice of UE more generally, the forgotten and neglected aspects, the rejected elements of contemporary modernity provide an experience and understanding through which the notion of progress can be overcome; and by association the dominance of renewal, consumption, commodification, linear histories and the attribution of value within this framework might be (at least temporarily) suspended.

As a reaction to dominant perceptions, the experience of exploring ruins takes on the quality of a collective and subversive set of acts against a perceived spatial dominance in which our actions are prescribed by a constructed order. One reading of Urry suggests that 'tourism as a form of consumption starts to become hegemonic and organize much of contemporary social and cultural experiences' (Shaw and Williams 2004: 114). The second approach in this chapter, using de Certeau's Spatial Practice, presents an argument in favour of UE as more than an alternative and thrill-seeking hobby, instead considering it to be a tactical intervention in the built environment, and rightfully termed a 'practice'.

Urban explorers make use of the process of decline and renewal that prevails in cities in particular. Of New York, de Certeau says '[i]ts present invents itself, from hour to hour, in the act of throwing away its previous accomplishments and challenging the future' (1984: 91). Here, de Certeau shares a vision in common with Benjamin: he sees in progress and accelerated modernity a tendency toward catastrophic ruin. Gazing at the city, 'The spectator can read in it a universe that is constantly exploding ... a gigantic rhetoric of excess in both expenditure and production' (de Certeau 1984: 91).

This is the readable text of the city, against which de Certeau pits an everyday spatial practice that is migrational and mobile. Within this notion of the everyday, Certeau posits a challenge to the administrative power of the concept city. Vitally, the 'networks of order' dominate this concept city, in which 'there is a rejection of everything that is not capable of being dealt with in this way and so constitutes the "waste products" of a functionalist administration (abnormality, deviance, illness, death, etc.)' (de Certeau 1984: 94–95). Modern ruins are such 'waste products', excluded from order and network, and in de Certeau's argument, these products (if not reintroduced and transformed via the force of progress) can manifest 'effects contrary to those at which it aims' (de Certeau 1984: 94). Thus, ruins, like unpredictable articulations of walking in the city, provide a tactical alter which cannot be accounted for in the organisational principles of an idealised built environment, allowing for myriad possibilities which are often unseen within the constructed order.

Regarding travel and the possibility of exiting the ordered city, de Certeau states that '[t]ravel (like walking) is a substitute for the legends that used to open up space to something different.' Here, he suggests that the practice of travelling provides an exoticism of the everyday, 'walking exile produces ... the effect of displacements and condensations'. Such practices in turn 'invent spaces', that is; they provide the same potential as walking to subvert the everyday, to bring about new perspectives, new stories and new narratives about place (de Certeau 1984: 106–107).

Where unpredictable movement of citizens through city space might undo the hegemonic regulation of urban life (for example, the spatial practices of walking, travelling and narrating), UE adds several dimensions of resistance within the construct of the everyday. Each step over a threshold takes the explorer away from crowds, away from newness and sameness, away from the codes that regulate public behaviours; away from the watchful eye of police and fellow citizens, away from the safety of the ordered city. To crawl through a hole in the fence is to disarm the powers that assumed a fence could keep you out. To lower yourself into a dark basement, and light it with a torch is to rediscover a forgotten world that you would otherwise never see. To capture a moment of death with pictures of smashed windows, flooded lift-shafts and crumbling plaster is to challenge any idea of stability and constancy of the built environment.

In framing UE as practice, the act of urban exploration is legitimised as an interventionist strategy. Like the play and psychogeography of the Situationists, designed to 'take action over the city' (Sadler 1998: 15), the practice of UE reveals the potential of modern ruins to interrupt and subvert dominant conceptions of ideal, modern space, as well as the expectations and aims of traditional or 'everyday' tourism. 'In the ruin we confront an alternative aesthetic, one which rebukes the seamlessness of much urban design and opens out heterodox possibilities for appreciating beauty and form' (Edensor 2008: 134).

The consciousness of this activity is revealed in shared codes and rules of the UE community. I refer here to two seminal texts on the subject, collated by early participants in both the online and real-life culture of UE that began to emerge in the mid-1990s.

The co-creators of *Jinx* 'World Wide Urban Adventure' magazine, record the adventures of their 'agents' in *Invisible Frontier* (Deyo and Leibowitz 2003). In addition to abandoned sites, the frontier of which they speak is to be found in any restricted, uninhabited or difficult to access location in New York. This includes underground (sewers, subways, aquifers), government buildings (UN headquarters), bridges, rooftops, and the usual urban ruins.

While the *Jinx* crew is a community of secret agents adventuring in a hostile urban wasteland, Jeff Chapman (aka Ninjalicious) considers a more serious practice (or 'art') of UE. He emphasises preparedness, and advises the aspiring explorer to get fit, stop smoking and cultivate an ethical attitude to what he sometimes terms 'infiltration'. Like the writers of *Jinx*, Ninjalicious self-published independently (in photocopied 'zine' format, and online) during the early development of the international UE community.

Both of these texts significantly influenced core tenets of UE culture, largely accounting for the unity of practice that is reflected in the following core principals of UE:

> Show respect for sites by not breaking anything, taking anything, defacing anything or even littering while exploring.
>
> (Ninjalicious 2005: 20)

> Explorers use the motto 'take nothing but pictures, leave nothing but footprints'.
>
> (Ninjalicious 2005: 26)

> While no equipment is actually essential, there are three pieces of basic equipment that I regard as the explorer's best friends: the flashlight, the camera and the moist towelette.
>
> (Ninjalicious 2005: 51)

Though there are variations on this last theme (the recent adage of GPS enabled electronics, for example), the fundamentals remain the same: despite the occasionally exaggerated anarchism of UE, there are rules and codes which are followed by most, if only in the interests of personal safety and preserving the site itself.

Such rules are a curious development, and occasional criticism, for a culture that otherwise takes the stance of pioneers against pretentious aestheticism and state or hegemonic control of space. However, such rules exist in part to distinguish explorers from vandals, graffiti artists and partying teens, and in part because these locations are, realistically, often unsafe.

The stories of the Jinx crew, Ninjalicious and other explorers reflect my own experiences in modern ruins—surreptitious entry, a sensation of smells and sounds which differ totally from everyday encounters with space and place; sites littered with remnants, personal effects, animal (and human) faeces. Locations defined by what is missing – floors and roofs, doors and walls, windows, furnishings and, crucially, people. They are marginal sites, on the fringe and the outer, quietly fading from life.

> *We visited Staten Island three times while in New York. The advanced deindustrialisation and population decline of the island provided easy access to a vast playground of modern ruins. Each day we took the ferry past the Statue of Liberty, and landed with residents and a few other tourists at the terminal, seemingly worlds away from Manhattan, despite the fact that we could see the city clearly across the water.*

Urban explorers are those who visit and pay attention to such sites, not out of historical or personal interest (or not that alone), but for the sake of a particular kind of experience. Anyone who visits a site of modern ruin leaves behind an everyday world of assumed stability to step into a highly unusual universe where decay and disorder dominate. In contrast to the regulated spaces with which we are most familiar, modern ruins stand out as a challenge in two senses: they offer an alternative to the regulated and mediated spaces of daily life, and thus the possibility for opposition; and they are not easy to find or access.

> *This building, once a standard brick structure with reinforced concrete flooring, is now devoid of most doors and all windows. Possibly, the person who made the hole we climbed in through also stripped the place of anything of value. Probably, the windows fell out after a few years of a freeze-thaw cycle and no maintenance.*
>
> *We gain the roof (the urban explorer's Everest), and are rewarded by a sunset view of the Brooklyn Bridge—a reward made sweeter because there is no one else there to interrupt the moment, no other tourists taking happy snaps, no screaming children or ticket sellers.*

There is a great deal of repetition amongst the UE community regarding these sites as forgotten, forsaken, silent and so on. To a more thorough analysis, this vision fails to comprehend the complexity of urban decline and renewal—alternative uses by squatters, homeless, graffiti artists; havens for criminal or illicit activity, as well as sites of sentimental histories for local citizens. The signs of 'life' in modern ruins are often summarily ignored by the urban explorer who insists on the static, empty and isolated qualities of abandoned locations. What is

Figure 9.2 Interior of an abandoned factory on Staten Island (view towards the Verrazano-Narrows Bridge).

significant about this wilful ignorance is the special privilege it places on the explorer as the only presence in the ruinscape. It makes sense in the context of a culture of subversion that, though potentially risky and dangerous, only takes the practitioner away from the safety of their home for the brief incursion into the forbidden. To acknowledge that others might have more right to these sites, or that they might not in fact be as marginal and excluded as the explorer perceives them to be, would diminish the assumed authority that presents their experiences and legitimises their practice.

Fundamental to the experience of the abandoned, disordered, and rejected sites of recent history is the nature of their appeal to those who seek them. Writing about this appeal without grand statements and clichéd generalisations can be challenging because these are sites in which human culture is absent, locations where there is little discourse within which value might be attributed. Part of the appeal is also in the confronting impact of decay, which is also challenging to communicate without emotive generalisations. New language must be found—that is to say, existing terms must be applied to the experience itself. To say an abandonment is wild, beautiful, colossal, epic and confronting in its decay is to say it is sublime, in the classical sense of an ancient ruin, and speak also of a romantic ruin aesthetic. To say a ruin is lost and forgotten, full of history or holds memories is to speak of an urban palimpsest in the sense of Huyssen's politics of memory (2003), of Gordon's ghosts and haunting (2008), and also echoes Benjamin's critique of progress as a force which obliterates the past. The idea of an unacknowledged or lost past, of untold stories, also relates to Stewart's poetics and affect (1996 and 2007), and Crinson's urban amnesia (2005). The observable fascinations with peeling paint, broken and smashed windows and objects, discarded rubbish and unidentifiable substances are the stuff of Kristeva's uncanny and abject (1982) or Trigg (2006) and Edensor's (2005) aesthetics of decline.

> *On our final day, we bring a native New Yorker and a GPS and trek through the rain to a complex of active and disused hospital buildings. In what is one of our more successful expeditions, we find an array of unwanted objects and rotting, yet accessible interiors. The decay is pervasive, and the building seems tired out and used up, as if it is resigned to its fate of demolition by neglect. The rain outside enhances the sense of isolation and intimacy, and as we creep out into the darkening day, I'm sorry to leave.*
>
> *This is how we come to know New York—through dark, smelly, slimy, rusty, holey, disappearing places. Places that few others see. Places which are never guaranteed to be there the next time you visit; which are sometimes already gone before you arrive.*

In his rumination on the value of urban ruins, Leary questions the potential of abandoned buildings, and refers to urban explorers as 'ruin fetishists' (Leary 2011). It is perhaps an apt term in the sense that many ruins achieve iconic status amongst explorers, as indicated by the repetition of certain images in the online archives as well as in print, and particular reverence for sites of significance (usually based on their size, and thus the scale of decay, as well as level of accessibility). But Leary also refers to 'ruin porn', suggesting that these images gratify some desire, perhaps voyeuristic, to uncover the ruin, to lay it bare and to indulge in the pleasure of a ruin aesthetic.

In interrogating my own reactions to ruins, I must admit a certain amount of pleasure in decay. As much as I want to deny that I am a voyeur of other people's broken lives and failures, it is an unavoidable aspect of an obsession with the rejected, obsolescent wreckage of modernity. However, in considering ruin gazing as practice, it becomes a method that might legitimise an otherwise uncomfortable inversion of tourism. The practice of UE is not necessarily one of conquering uncharted territories so much as collecting the fragments of a vanishing past, to explore the ruin is to acknowledge that '[t]he true method of making things present is to represent them in our space. ... We don't displace our being into theirs; they step into our life' (Benjamin 1999: 206).

Bringing the lost and forgotten back into the world is a redemptive act. As Benjamin proclaims in his *Theses on the Philosophy of History*, 'nothing that has ever happened should be regarded as lost to history' (2003: 390). He also asserts that 'The past carries with it a secret index by which it is referred to redemption' (ibid.). The diversity of these ruins, their accessibility in being neglected and outcast, allows them to be reclaimed. Not in a possessive, material sense or even in the sense of rescue and rebirth which might redeem discarded objects, but in the more abstract sense of encountering and knowing the secret index of history which Benjamin considers to be vital to salvaging lost and threatened pasts.

Salvaging such sites need not be a colonising act, glorifying their heritage, or beautifying their decay. It may be enough to be aware of their existence, to experience them in their final stages of life, to meet them and know them at that place and time. In a Benjaminian sense, modern ruins should be met at the stage of their fate (or, to use another of Benjamin's phrases, their 'future fate'). In this case, their fate is abandonment, decline, and ultimately, insignificance. As important as any detailed history is their liminal status as the ruin.

Turner's last words on liminality, though still in reference to van Gennep's rites of passage, open up the term for a broad engagement with ruins as ambiguous sites 'detached from mundane life' (Turner 1986: 41), a space in which ordinary experience is suspended, where a 'fructile chaos, a storehouse of possibilities ... a gestation process' (ibid.: 42) bears the potential for both a post-liminal state (in which the ruin can become something else, razed or rejuvenated) and a unique or unusual experience which stands against tradition. This is particularly apparent in connection to what Turner terms the 'aesthetic form' and the role of disparity and resistance in the struggle for equilibrium (ibid.: 37–38).

Ruins as liminal landscapes, therefore, are sites that provide the necessary 'stage ... for unique structures of experience' (Turner 1986: 41). Like Benjamin's Erlebnis (shock experience) or de Certeau's Spatial Practice, what is significant about contemporary ruins is the way in which they can interrupt, fracture and disturb ritualistic responses, in this case, the reactions to the dead, undesirable or dangerous. By penetrating a contemporary ruinscape, a dead space, one is confronted with many things that are not of the dominant modes or perceptions, and thus, 'erupt from, or disrupt, routinized, repetitive behaviour' (ibid.: 35), particularly when 'we try to put past and present together' (ibid.) as we do when encountering modern ruins.

In their contemporaneousness, as modern ruins, the sites of which I speak are undoubtedly 'betwixt and between the structural past and structural future' (Turner 1986: 41), though not so much in terms of humanity's biological development, but rather in relation to presumed progress and teleological histories, both of which naturalise ends and means, and envision the future positively in terms of material progress (rather than Benjamin's rubble and wreckage). The normative view of history posits constant renewal—contemporary ruins are the absolute antithesis. In their ambiguity as not-what-they-were, but not-yet-gone, ruins not only symbolise and signify, they offer an experience to the visitor which is seldom found elsewhere.

Note

1 The italicised sections in this chapter are excerpts from my travel notes from 2009. While most of the details about Chernobyl were gathered from tour guides when visiting Pripyat, see also Mould (2000: 143–147) and Beresford and Smith (2005: 290–293).

References

Bell, C. and Lyall, J. (2002) *The Accelerated Sublime: Landscape, Tourism, and Identity*, Westport, Connecticut and London: Praeger.

Benjamin, W. (1999) *The Arcades Project*, Cambridge, Mass. and London: Harvard University Press.

Benjamin, W. (2003) *Walter Benjamin, Selected Writings Volume 4, 1938–1940*, Cambridge, Mass. and London: Belknap Press of Harvard University Press.

Beresford, N.A and Smith, J.T. (eds) (2005) *Chernobyl – Catastrophe and Consequences*, Berlin: Springer-Praxis.

Berger, A. (2007) *Drosscape: Wasting Land in Urban America*, New York: Princeton Architectural Press.

Boym, S. (2001) *The Future of Nostalgia*, New York: Basic Books.

Caygill, H. (1998) *Walter Benjamin: The Colour of Experience*, Abingdon, Oxon and New York: Routledge.

Cowie, J. and Heathcott, J. (eds) (2003) *Beyond the Ruins: The Meanings of Deindustrialisation*, Ithaca, New York: Cornell University Press.

Crinson, M. (ed.) (2005) *Urban Memory: History and Amnesia in the Modern City*, New York: Routledge.

de Certeau, M. (1984) *The Practice of Everyday Life*, Berkeley and Los Angeles, Calif.: University of California Press.

Deyo, L.B. and Leibowitz, D. (2003) *Invisible Frontier: Exploring the Tunnels, Ruins and Rooftops of Hidden New York*, New York: Three Rivers Press.

Drooker, A., Woodward, C. and Brinkley, D. (2007) *American Ruins*, London and New York: Merrell.

Edensor, T. (2005) *Industrial Ruins: Space, Aesthetics and Materiality*, Oxford and New York: Berg.

Edensor, T. (2008) Walking Through Ruins, In: Ingold, T. and Vergunst, J.L. (eds) *Ways of Walking*, Aldershot, Hampshire: Ashgate Publishing, 123–143.

Gallagher, J. (2010) *Reimagining Detroit: Opportunities for Redefining an American City*, Detroit, Mich.: Wayne State University Press.

Garoian, C.R. and Gaudelius, Y.M. (2008) *Spectacle Pedagogy: Art, Politics, and Visual Culture*, Albany, New York: State University of New York Press.

Gilloch, G. (1996) *Myth and Metropolis: Walter Benjamin and the City*, Cambridge, Mass.: Polity Press.

Gordon, A.F. (2008) *Ghostly Matters: Haunting and the Sociological Imagination*, Minneapolis and London: University of Minnesota Press.

Hamm, M., Steinberg, R. and Jungk, R. (2000) *Dead Tech: A guide to the archaeology of tomorrow*, Santa Monica, Calif.: Hennessey + Ingalls.

Hell, J. and Schönle, A. (eds) (2008) *Ruins of Modernity*, Durham: Duke University Press.

High, S. and Lewis, D.W. (2007) *Corporate Wasteland: The Landscape and Memory of Deindustrialisation*, Ithaca and London: Cornell University Press.

Hollander, J.B. (2009) *Polluted and Dangerous: America's Worst Abandoned Properties and What Can Be Done About Them*, Burlington, Vt.: University of Vermont Press.

Huggan, G. (2010) *Extreme Pursuits: Travel/Writing in an Age of Globalization*, Ann Arbor: University of Michigan Press.

Huyssen, A. (2003) *Present Pasts: Urban Palimpsests and the Politics of Memory*, Stanford, Calif.: Stanford University Press.

Kristeva, J. (1982) *Powers of Horror: An essay on Abjection*, New York: Columbia University Press.

Leary, J. P. (2011) Detroitism, *Guernica,* January. Available at: www.guernicamag.com/spotlight/2281/leary_1_15_11/ (accessed 10 March 2011).

Lefebvre, H. (1991) *The Production of Space*, Malden, Mass. and Oxford, UK: Blackwell Publishing.

Luxenberg, A. (1998) Creating Désastres: Andrieu's Photographs of Urban Ruins in the Paris of 1871, *The Art Bulletin*, 80 (March 1998), 113–137.

Marchand, Y. and Meffre, R. (2009) Detroit's Beautiful, Horrible Decline, *Time*. Available at: http:/www.time.com/time/photogallery/0,29307,1882089,00.html (accessed 10 March 2011).

Marchand, Y. and Meffre, R. (2010) *The Ruins of Detroit*, Göttingen: Steidl.

Mould, R.F (2000) *Chernobyl Record The Definitive History of the Chernobyl Catastrophe*, Bristol: IOP Publishing.

Ninjalicious (2005) *Access All Areas: A Users Guide to the Art of Urban Exploration*, Canada: Infiltration.

O'Boyle, S. (2010) *Modern Ruins*, Pennsylvania: Pennsylvania State University Press.

Oswalt, P. (2005) *Shrinking Cities*, New York: Hatje Cantz.

Paiva, T. and Manaugh, G. (2008) *The Art of Urban Exploration*, San Francisco: Chronicle Books.

Pezzullo, P.C. (2007) *Toxic Tourism: Rhetorics of Pollution, Travel, and Environmental Justice*, Tuscaloosa, Ala.: The University of Alabama Press.

Polidori, R. (2003) *Zones of Exclusion Pripyat and Chernobyl*, Göttingen: Steidl.

Sadler, S. (1998) *The Situationist City*, Cambridge, Mass.: MIT Press.

Seidel, P., Sack, M. and Klemp, K. (1997) *Underworld: Sites of Concealment*, Santa Monica, Calif.: Hennessey + Ingalls.

Shaw, G. and Williams, A.M. (2004) *Tourism and Tourism Spaces*. London: Sage Publications.

Skrdla, H. (2006) *Ghostly Ruins: America's forgotten architecture*, New York: Princeton University Press.

Stewart, K. (1996) *A Space on the Side of the Road: Cultural Poetics in an 'Other' America*, Princeton, NJ: Princeton University Press.

Stewart, K. (2007) *Ordinary Affects*, Durham and London: Duke University Press.

Trigg, D. (2006) *The Aesthetics of Decay: Nothingness, nostalgia and the absence of reason*, New York: Peter Lang Publishing.

Turner, V.W. (1986) Dewey, Dilthey, and Drama: An Essay in the Anthropology of Experience, In: Turner, V.W. and Bruner, E.M. (eds) *The Anthropology of Experience*. Urbana and Chicago: University of Illinois Press, 33–44.

Urry, J. (1995) *Consuming Places*, London and New York: Routledge.

Urry, J. (2004) Death in Venice, In: Urry, J. and Sheller, M. (eds) *Tourism Mobilities: Places to Play, Places in Play*, London and New York: Routledge.

Vergara, C.J. (1999) *American Ruins*, New York: Monacelli Press.

10 Another place or just another space?

Liminality and Crosby Beach

Hazel Andrews

The purpose of this chapter is to explore the ways in which Crosby Beach in the north west of England can be understood as a liminal landscape, to probe if by mere geographical location – being on the edge – does actually make it liminal. Crosby Beach makes an interesting study because it is different from most other beaches in that it is home to an art installation called *Another Place* by the British artist and sculptor Antony Gormley. As such this chapter discusses the way in which the presence of the art installation intertwines with understandings and practices of the beach and the impact or not on the liminality of the space. The discussion is based on several short periods of participant observation and a number of semi-structured interviews conducted during the autumn of 2009. The chapter proceeds as follows: first I will make a short comment about the study of beaches. Second, I will very briefly outline the role of public art in regeneration projects. Third, I will detail the background to the study providing the context of the local regeneration initiatives, geographic setting, details of the art installation, and follow this with the ethnographic detail. The penultimate section will discuss the issue of liminality both in relation to the space of the beach and the role the installation plays in that setting before I draw the chapter to a conclusion.

Beaches

Beaches carry with them a number of what Shields (1991) describes as 'spatial assumptions'. He argues that to think of a beach conjures up not just images and understandings of its material nature 'but also of a particular *kind* of place, peopled by individuals acting in a specific manner' (1991: 60, emphasis in original). Shields uses the seaside (and its obvious association with beaches) as one example to explore the development of liminal spatial areas based on the transgressive behaviour associated with places seen to be marginal. So, for example the southern UK coastal town of Brighton emerged as a zone in which dominant discourses could be subverted. The change in the use of the beach from the days of Brighton as a fishing village, through sea-bathing for medicinal purposes, to a site for the conduct of extra-marital affairs allowed the beach to be associated with the carnivalesque and associated upturning of societal norms. Beaches then are fertile grounds for exploring social and cultural practices and inversions. Indeed, beaches can be perceived as different spaces and linked to a qualitatively different experience compared to that encountered off-beach. For example, feeling hotter and lying down are touristic practices that make the beach different and special for many (Andrews 2011). In addition, Baldacchiono contends that beaches are the main public environment in which adults can regress to childhood. Indeed 'adults are at liberty, and are even expected, to fool around, build sand castles, dig canals, and perform other "childlike acts"' (2010: 773). Further, Obrador-Pons notes in connection to beaches as sites for naturism that 'there are few other public places in western societies in which nakedness is so accepted' (2007: 124), and that beaches are not just sites for hedonistic, playful behaviour but are also sites for providing 'evidence of how the contemporary world still inspires deep and powerful attachment' (ibid.: 138).

It is not a particularly profound point to note that beaches vary in form and popularity (Löfgren 1999) but there is a need to acknowledge that they have a strong allure and that this is in part built up by the tourism industry, which in the creation of its many images draws on the western imagination to such an extent that 'sandy beaches have become amongst the most heavily consumed sites of this predatory industry' (Baldacchino 2010: 768). However, despite their importance to the economies of tourism and the foreshore more generally (Boissevain and Selwyn 2004) beaches have been somewhat ignored as sites of inquiry. As Urbain contends, beaches are 'still relatively unexplored' (2003: 5). This chapter seeks to help to redress this imbalance whilst at the same time bringing into focus the connection between beaches and the concept of liminality. The discussion will proceed by providing background to the beach in question along with some detail regarding the art installation situated there. Although it is not the purpose of this chapter to address issues relating to the use of public art in urban regeneration projects or indeed the complexity of the term 'public art' (Hubbard *et al.* 2003 and Sharp *et al.* 2005) in terms of providing context for Crosby Beach, it is worth outlining some of the main points relating to its use.

Regenerating a sense of place

According to Miles (1997: 5), since the 1960s contemporary works of art have found their way increasingly into public spaces from government buildings, hospitals and schools to outside spaces including parks, city squares and the external walls of houses. Public art has been used in urban regeneration projects since the 1980s, with champions of its use claiming its positive role in a range of social issues including: developing a sense of place and identity, encouraging civic pride, addressing community needs and issues of social exclusion, etc. (Hall and Robertson 2001). The use of culture as a product and means for local economic development is now well established (McCarthy 2006). Hall and Robertson argue that public art does not just provide an economic function but also has a role in the 'material relations and reproductions of society' (2001: 5). As such it can have a role in creating a sense of place.

That a sense of place emerges through people's interaction with a space as an ongoing creative process – rooted in and connected to memory and history throwing up multiple interpretations of places – is now well rehearsed in cultural geography and social anthropology (for examples see Relph 1976; Tilley 1994; Bender 1993 and 2002; Bender and Winer 2001; Rodman, 1992). The *Another Place* installation fits well this understanding of place because as an artwork its meaning and the engagement with it is also open to being made and re-made. As Gormley comments:

> Each person is making it again ... for some it might be about human evolution, for others it will be about death and where we go, where our bodies finally belong, do they belong to the earth and the elements? And I think that's what's amazing about in a way the work now – contemporary art, it's no longer representing the ideology of a dominant class it's actually an open space that people can make their own.[1]

The statues have also had a role in creating a sense of place[2] in that prior to their arrival Crosby Beach was not a widely known visitor attraction. Indeed, the Chief Executive of Sefton Council claimed in 2007 that 'The "Iron Men" have placed Crosby and Sefton firmly in the spotlight'.[3]

As such the installation is a marker of place in line with that discussed by MacCannell (1976) as the statues and the information attached to them both on-site and off-site appear more important than the beach or surrounding area but nevertheless inform the narratives associated with Crosby Beach and Sefton Council. The next section picks up on some of these issues in relation to regeneration initiatives in Sefton whilst at the same time providing some contextual information for the site of enquiry before proceeding to the ethnographic detail.

On Crosby Beach

Crosby Beach is part of the Merseyside coastline and is in the local authority of Sefton located near the mouth of the River Mersey, north west of Liverpool England. The beach forms part of a coastal park which runs along the coastline in linear form for 6.76 km and covers an area of approximately 920 hectares. The beach itself is 4.8 km long, running from the north west of Liverpool's Royal Seaforth Dock through to Waterloo. The coastal park is a nature reserve and site of local biological interest. The medium through which Gormley mainly works is that of sculpture. He is one of the UK's most successful and celebrated artists, winning the Turner prize in 1994 and being awarded an OBE[4] in 1997 amongst other honours and prizes. Gormley's work is widely exhibited both in the UK and overseas. One of his most renowned exhibitions in the UK is that of the *Angel of the North*, erected in 1998 on the A1 road near Gateshead, north east England. Like much of Gormley's work it is modeled on the human body and expresses the artist's interest in the relations between the human body and space. *Another Place* is another example of the exploration of this relationship.[5]

The statues that make up *Another Place* are cast iron models of Gormley's own body. They number 100 in total and are spread over 3 km of the coastline.

Figure 10.1–2 Crosby Beach and another place. Stills from *Another Space* (Les Roberts and Hazel Andrews, 2010, 5 mins).

The statues are situated on the beach near to land as well as further out on the foreshore which means that some of the statues are submerged either fully or partially as the tide comes in. All of the statues face seaward as if staring at the horizon. They first appeared on the German beach of Cuxhaven in 1997 from where they moved to Stavanger, Norway (1998) and De Panne, Belgium (2003), arriving in Crosby in June 2005. The installation was due to move on again to New York in 2006 but was retained in the area following a public campaign. The statues were first brought to Crosby Beach by the South Sefton Development Trust as part of a regeneration programme for the area as a whole with the view to boosting jobs and training opportunities for local people, encouraging visitor numbers to the area and generally raising the area's profile. The project was supported by a number of different programmes and agencies in the region including the North West Development Agency, Mersey Docks and Harbour Company, The Arts Council, and Mersey Water Front program. The last of these programmes is under the auspices of The Mersey Partnership. The remit of the programme is as follows:

> Mersey Waterfront is a far reaching programme set up to regenerate the Liverpool City Region's 135 km (84 mile) coastline. It connects the waterfront's communities and assets across the districts of Sefton, Wirral, Liverpool and Halton, with the objective of creating an internationally acclaimed waterfront alongside the likes of Toronto and Sydney.[6]

Another of the installation's supporting mechanisms is the government initiative. The Northern Way,[7] a regionally led regeneration programme covering both the north east and north west of England with an aim to change both the economic and aesthetic appeal of the landscape. With regard to the latter, part of the methods used to achieve this include the use of public art installations. *Another Place* then is among a number of other installations whose purpose is to highlight the culture and art of the region.

With regard to Crosby Beach the success of the installation was recognised in The Mersey Partnership commissioned visitor attraction survey in 2006.[8] The purpose of the survey was 'to evaluate the profile, satisfaction and spend of visitors to the Another Place installation'. As part of this work, visitors' perceptions, reactions and satisfaction with the attraction were also assessed. A total of 131 people were questioned for the research. The survey found that the installation attracts more females than males, an older aged group (55+) of visitors, and that visitors tended to be from the more wealthy end of the social spectrum (A/B/C1). Further, 66 per cent of informants visited the beach as part of a family group. The majority of these visitors were also shown to hail from the Merseyside region itself. The results of the survey demonstrate that only 23 per cent of respondents cited coming to see the statues as their main reason for visiting the area. The overall methodological approach adopted in the survey is firmly based within the positivist paradigm utilising quantitative techniques and data analysis. Whilst perceptions that lend themselves more to a post-positivistic paradigm were invited from informants the data were not, it seems, analysed within an interpretative framework. Responses were merely counted, thus missing the opportunity to analyse their meanings. The survey was clearly designed to assess the success of the attraction in terms of visitor numbers and as such serves as a measurement of its regeneration potential. I will now proceed with data drawn from the current project.

Crosby Beach is a long sandy beach. At one end it is reached by taking one of several paths through sand dunes. At the more northerly end it is possible to drive to the concrete promenade which runs alongside but above the beach and can be followed to the Marina at the beach's southerly end. Sited behind the promenade are two council run car parks. The beach is also within walking distance of three train stations that serve the Crosby area. Buses, again as part of the local network, also serve the area. The proximity of two car parks next to the beach in its northern end makes this section of the beach attractive to view the statues. At this point the beach is backed by a concrete wall with access via steps or a boat ramp. The promenade sits atop this construction. On the landward side of the promenade is a large green area the other side of which is housing. When visits to the beach coincided with the summer months, bank holidays and weekends both car parks are busy with parking space a premium. Access to the statues is not necessarily easy as signage at the southern end of the beach is misleading and, as will become apparent in the proceeding discussion, knowledge of the tides is necessary. As one informant comments in response to a question about the presence of the statues bringing benefit to the local area,

> well I don't think so no, I don't think so, because people find, you often get stopped in the early days, 'where are the men?', so you'd direct them here, so if they had that much trouble getting here following all the signs, I don't think they're gonna go off back to the shops, cos they've gone past them shops on the way in really.

There are no facilities to speak of at the site apart from ice-cream vans and toilets. Again this is the focus of some of the responses to the installation by local people as another respondent suggests,

> They spent so much money putting the statues here, that it would have been a good idea to er, put something like a cafe, for the people that come to see them, and it can give them, well they can spend some money here, because nobody is spending money here.

The promenade allows views across the Crosby Channel to the north east of the Wirral peninsula, the docks of Liverpool, the shipping lane that leads along the Crosby Channel into the River Mersey, and numerous wind farm turbines. Apart from these the view to the horizon is clear. At this end of the beach the sand becomes quite mud-like and even at low tide quite large pools of water can remain on the beach. Like any coastal area the tide comes in and out which naturally affects how much of the beach is visible and in this case how many of the statues and how much of each statue is visible. At particularly high tides none of the statues can be seen.

At the beach's northern end at the point where the promenade ends there is information about *Another Place*. The information is a commentary on the art and quotes Gormley himself. The text has not been updated since the art's permanent installation and the message conveys the advice that the statues are due to move in 2006. The board becomes a focal point for visitors to the attraction, especially if an in-tide means the statues are not visible. It is not unknown for visitors to come to the beach looking for the statues only to find that they cannot be viewed. Indeed one respondent who took part in the interviews was visiting the beach for the first time with a friend who has visited the beach before. When asked what they liked about the statues the first time visitor comments: 'if it was me I would probably like them but unfortunately I can't see them. I would've liked to have seen them, I am disappointed'. There are occasions when the tide is in when the statues are not completely submerged but the presence of the sea means that people cannot get up close to them.

Reactions to the statues vary and not all responses can be classified as positive, particularly from people who visit the beach and are local to the area. It is an

Figure 10.3 Information board Another Place. Still from *Another Space* (Les Roberts and Hazel Andrews, 2010, 5 mins).

obvious point that the beach had its uses before the statues were sited there. Such uses have continued even with the presence of the art work, for example dog walking, fishing, sunbathing, picnicking and so on. As one female informant in her 70s (she no longer lives in the area but is discussing how she uses the beach during her visit and how she used it when she did live nearby) advises that she comes 'to walk the dog, but if I haven't got the dog I would still come because I like to see the shells that are washed up and the seaweed ... I've always walked down to the beach' and a younger male interviewee who uses the beach primarily for fishing states: 'I'm local, I live in Maghull [I've been coming to the beach] erm about 40 years, yeah ... no thoughts on it [*Another Place*] whatsoever. It does encourage more people which limits our fishing.'

Even visitors to the beach do not always come for the express purpose of seeing the statues. As one day tripper claims the purpose of his visit is 'for a walk so it wasn't necessarily to come and see the installation just for a walk and some fresh air'. His trip to Crosby is to visit friends and so the walk on the beach is incidental to his visit. A member of the friendship groups explains 'we're going for a walk and I have a kite on my back so we're going to fly that'. The use of the beach for recreational reasons other than to see the statues is echoed by other interviewees, 'my partner has a three year old son so we bring his football down and have a kick around'.

The views discussed thus far do not mark Crosby Beach out, or indeed the statues, as being special in anyway and although comments from informants do show appreciation of the art, as one elderly female local suggests: 'I think it's very good art work actually ... it is what people do, they come and stand and look out to sea and think about things ... it is representative of what people are doing.' So, the use of the beach is part of the everyday and for some, as in the case of the fisherman, the presence of the statues does not provoke or invoke any particular thoughts or feelings. As one respondent explains about the statues:

> Never really had any feeling about them you know they are just there. It's not like the Yellow Submarine in the town centre or the Lamb Banana like that. You know they are a laugh. They [*Another Place*] are just iron work if you know what I mean. ... Yeah but I have gone up and looked. I can't really see the point of them, maybe it's just me.

However, other beach users and visitors find the statues meaningful and thought provoking and acknowledge their potential for inspiration as one middle-aged local man comments, 'it does bring art to the people and if they are interested they might progress in other ways, and they may want to do it themselves, or try to. Bring their kids up to do it.' For example a female tourist from Birmingham when asked about her thoughts and feelings regarding the beach and the presence of the statues explains:

> I quite like the way they're all staring out to sea ... there's more than I thought ... I think they're really nice. Erm, feelings I don't know, it's kind

of thoughtful though, the way they're all staring out to sea isn't it? It's kind of waiting for the tide, I like that.

For a local male in his 50s the statues reflect aspects of life and are representative of 'trial and tribulation, when you're going through shit [he laughs] sort of reminds you of that when your neck's just above water. Or at this time, just peaceful, looking out to sea.' His wife comments

> it takes your mind away from the hustle and bustle of life doesn't it, when you're seeing all the likes of this, it's the same as having buskers in town … some people don't like it, most people do, because you're seeing something different, it takes you away from your shopping.

Other informants find the statues particularly stimulating:

> I think it's just thought provoking to think that somebody can just do that and leave them there and it makes I don't know – mortality and everything – a person, it makes you think of all sorts of things. It made me think of those poor fishermen on Morecambe Bay cockle picking.

This quote is from a female tourist visiting from Bristol with her friend who also acknowledges that the presence of the statues is what brought them to the beach: 'it makes the beach more interesting, we would never have come here if it weren't for those' and in response to the likelihood of a repeat visit 'not high on my priority it's one of those things for me because I am not a beach person really. I've seen it now I might see it again but it's not something I would rush back to.'

However, another visitor who had returned to Crosby for a second time specifically to see the statues observes: 'I think maybe it makes you more contemplative, contemplative about being here rather than just coming here for the beach and it adds a dimension to being here.' Another visitor comments 'I guess they are kind of still and contemplative a sort of pensive feeling really I get with them … quite peaceful.' Some of the thoughts that arise in reaction to the statues by both visitors and locals are with regard to other public art by other artists and Gormley, most notably the *Angel of the North*.

With regard to specific thoughts about what the statues might represent a dominant theme to emerge from the data relates to mobility, the idea of movement through and across the water and in relation to that the role of the statues as protectors: 'sitting here and looking at the statues, they're looking at the ships coming in, which to me again they're like guardians, I suppose in a way.' Another informant advises 'the men looking out to sea, as a seagoing nation and a port, er brings it all back, but er a sign for the future.' The notion of movement and particularly of moving on is also recognised in the words of one participant who says of the statues 'Gormley should have painted them green for leaving Liverpool and going to Ireland'. Movement is also associated with the way in which the statues change in situ as one female interviewee suggests: 'I like going up close to them seeing the way they have been weathered the rusting and actually how the different ones have been weathered in different ways that's what I like the most.'

Concomitant with this idea of watching and moving are thoughts relating to waiting. One interviewee comments that the statues invoke thoughts and feelings on 'looking out to sea, life ... as if they are waiting for someone ... they just seem to be waiting'. For others they enjoy interaction with the statues either by themselves or by others:

> I like the humour of people putting things on the statues like bikinis. There was one particular day we came here and I'm just a bit nosey, so I noticed that all the beach was clear, there was hardly anybody there and there were just loads and loads of footprints just going up there and somebody had painted a bathing cap on one and erm a bikini and it was so beautifully done.

And for one female tourist the statues were an invitation to engage in a particular sort of way:

> Last time I came, obviously no children were present and we did perform a few sexual activities with the men probably because of the parts on them [laughs] I don't know I suppose it just makes your mind think a little ... I think your mindset is a little bit different isn't it, like I was saying ... you wouldn't really think about doing the same things.

For other respondents the presence of the statues changes their attitudes towards the beach in terms of feelings of safety and comfort:

> If you look at them for long enough ... we've got one over there I call him George, you can convince yourself that George was walking around, you know you can actually imagine that sometimes.
>
> (Female local aged 50)

> I feel that if I were walking along the beach on my own with nobody else here I would feel that with these statues I had company that there was someone here. I feel quite safe with them here.
>
> (Female visitor in her 20s)

> I think it probably makes you more relaxed and wanting to explore around the beach more rather than staying in one place.
>
> (Male visitor in his 40s)

However, there is also a feeling of threat and fear attached to the statues as a possible cause of danger that they are related to drowning and in reactions to the statues as one informant reports 'I have to say that the three-year old does not like them he is scared of them'.[9]

As one would expect the use of the beach and reactions to the statues vary between people. For some the statues are an added attraction, the purpose for visiting the beach; for others, and particularly local people, the statues have had little impact on their behaviour. Similarly the thoughts and feelings that the statues invoke among both locals and visitors are also varied. What any of this says about Crosby Beach as a liminal landscape is the subject of the next section.

Discussion

What liminality is and its development as a concept has been explored elsewhere in this volume and in detail by Thomassen (2009). It is not the intention to re-rehearse these discussions in this chapter but to explore the ways in which Crosby Beach (with the *Another Place* installation) can be understood as a liminal landscape or not. In terms of what Crosby Beach represents, or what any beach represents, one interpretation could be that it symbolises a state of liminality in relation to the element of transition. I mean this in terms of the physical aspects of beaches in relation to their role as markers between sea and land, they are 'betwixt and between' land which is habitable and the sea. The movement of the sea across the surface of the beach and the alterations that it will make to the beach in so doing (new debris deposited, existing debris washed away, erosion of the beach material by the action of the water and the changes in the position of the material composing the beach). Wind and rain might also cause similar changes by weathering. So the idea of transition is very pertinent to beaches and in the case of Crosby Beach and the *Another Place* installation it is possible to make this connection. First, the beach is like any other beach in being subject to the vagaries of natural processes and the statues are subject to similar processes. As one informant notices she is interested in the way that the statues are changed by the elements and for other informants they invoke ideas of movement.

There are many ways in which the statues themselves can represent aspects of liminality as set out by Turner (1969, 1982): their homogeneity, anonymity, absence of property/status, nakedness and for some an association with danger.[10] That is, the statues could be mistaken for someone drowning, the fear that they interfere with shipping lanes and so on. As Allen observes 'the beach is perhaps nature's greatest expression of the liminal, as the physical space has a shifting status between high and low tides, neither land nor sea' (2008: 56). However, like all symbolic tools the meanings attached to the beach and statues are poly-vocal. As such they represent the opposite of danger making the beach a more inviting space to explore and they counter issues of loneliness. In addition, the nakedness of the bodies (and that it is based on that of an identifiable person) draws attention to their gender, maximises it and their sexuality. At the same time the way that some of the statues have been dressed, or had clothes painted on them, distinguishes them from those which have not be altered. In addition, the fact that individual statues are singled out as friends, as in the local woman who identified one statue as George, is not invocative of the absence of status and equality that is said to be experienced by neophytes during the liminal stages of rites and rituals.

A key aspect of liminality is the element of potential. The ambiguous and unstable state that liminality provokes invites transformation and potential for becoming. Again the beach and the statues might be interpreted as representations of such ideas, in terms of the notion of moving on, of waiting for something to happen and the 'as if' or subjunctive nature of that. In addition the creativity associated with the dressing up and painting of some of the statues could be understood as the marginal nature of being on the edge of the land resulting in the conditions that invite the production of symbols and works of art. Indeed, as Gormley himself notes about the installation 'each person is making it again … for some it might be about human evolution, for others it will be about death and where our bodies finally lie.'[11] The association with death was highlighted by one informant in relation to the Morecambe Bay cockle pickers disaster in 2004. Death is a liminal state between the world of the living and the world after either in terms of religious belief or the incorporation into the world of the living in memory or the relics of the deceased. As the statues invite contemplation on such issues they are associated with liminality as they allow reflection on the individual's relationship with society, nature and culture.

Representation is but one strand of the dynamics of the beach and in this case the statues. An assessment of the degree to which this can be argued as a liminal landscape emerges in the practices and performances of beach users. What is notable from the responses gained from the interviews is that local informants report no change to their usual beach practices of walking, walking the dog and fishing. The changes that have resulted are found in qualitative aspects of the beach in terms of numbers of people, feelings of company and something to look at. In this respect the beach is no different from many other public spaces and the statues do not impact on behaviour. However, there is evidence that the statues encourage or invite transgressive performances in terms of the sexual activity enacted with a statue reported by one informant. But is sex on the beach in reality that transgressive? Certainly in terms of a moral framework of where sexual activity should take place it is possible to say that sex on the beach would appear to work against the norms established by such a framework[12] but at the same time the associations between beaches and sex (to the extent that there is a cocktail called 'sex on the beach' (Andrews, 2011)) would seem to suggest that this in itself is not that out of place. In addition to reiterate Shields's observation 'we learn that bare, carefree and relaxed are not only appropriate but also *natural* attitudes towards specific spaces such as a beach' (1991: 60, emphasis in original).[13] The playful aspect of sex on the beach as a cocktail, or with statues conforms to what Turner describes as a move from understandings of sex as the work necessary for procreation to sex as play. It is play which he argues is a feature of post-industrial worlds.

For Turner the idea of play is linked to the liminoid which is different in character from the liminal. According to Turner the liminoid is the product of societies based on organic solidarity in which social relations are contractual and the emphasis is on the individual rather than the collective. Another feature of the liminoid is that the cyclical nature of rites and the expression attached to those are given less importance in favour of a continuous generation of the possibilities of becoming. As such *Another Place* fits a liminoid 'model' as in Gormley's own words 'each person is making it again.' In addition another characteristic of the liminoid is the connection to the emphasis placed on the individual creator and it is clear from the discourses surrounding *Another Place* that it is strongly linked to its artistic creator. These aspects of the installation and their location on a beach which, in this case, is separate from work and a zone of leisure activity in which choices are exercised (that is there is no obligation to visit the beach or its statues, although the statues might encourage a form of obligation to see a much discussed piece of art work), further marks this as space with liminoid characteristics rather than liminal in which there is no collective reaction or meaning associated with either the beach or the art.

Another element of the liminoid relates to commoditisation. Turner notes: 'the liminoid is more like a commodity – indeed often *is* a commodity ... one *plays* with the liminoid' (1982: 55, emphasis in original). Although there is no monetary price attached to viewing the statues or using the beach – and Turner recognises that some liminoid entertainments are 'free' – they are used as commodities in terms of 'selling' Crosby and the surrounding area. In addition there is a desire in some cases for financial transactions to be attached to a visit to the beach: the need for a coffee shop, economic rationales behind regeneration projects and not-with-standing the required expenditure to actually visit the beach. Further, as some of the interactions with the statues indicate, there is an element of play associated with their presence. The liminoid is also characterised by permanence and in the case of *Another Place* the statues have become a permanent fixture at Crosby Beach.

Conclusion: another place or just another space?

This chapter has examined a space that is often associated with the liminal based largely on its geographical location of being on the edge of the land or as being 'betwixt and between' land and sea. I have observed that beaches by their peripheral nature have been discussed in relation to transgressive behaviour but the question I pose relates to whether this is enough to claim Crosby Beach, or any beach for that matter, as a liminal landscape. My conclusion drawn from the data collected for this research would suggest not. Crosby Beach is part of the everyday, it could be argued that it is different or special in terms of its hosting of public art, but rather than adding to ideas of the liminal the presence of the liminoidal-like statues serves to detract from notions of liminality. *Another Place* appears like many other public art installations underwritten by the desire to regenerate an area (and it is not the intention here to criticise such endeavours). However, in providing a permanent home for the statues, along with their actual fix in place and their representation of waiting and arrested movement suggests that Crosby Beach rather than being a liminal landscape is, to borrow from Allen, a 'confirmation of entrapment and stasis as opposed to a symbol of transformation' (2008: 57). Beaches then are not as marginal as they might at first appear and the siting of *Another Place* on Crosby Beach may help to construct a sense of place, but in all other respects it is just another space.

Acknowledgements

I would like to express my thanks to Donna Mckeown and Claire Clark, two undergraduate students at Liverpool John Moores University who were responsible for the collection of the interview data used in this chapter as part of a Research Informed Teaching project.

Notes

1 www.bbc.co.uk/liverpool/content/articles/2005/07/05/art_antony_gormley_feature. shtml (accessed June 2011).
2 Cf. Hubbard *et al.* (2003), who comment on the role of public art in the creation of a sense of place in Coventry.
3 www.sefton.gov.uk/Default.aspx?page=7218 (accessed June 2011).
4 Order of the British Empire.
5 www.antonygormley.com/#/biography/antony-gormley. (accessed June 2011).
6 www.merseyside.org.uk (accessed June 2011).
7 www.thenorthernway.co.uk (accessed June 2011). This project closed in March 2011 as part of the closure of regional development agencies in 2012.
8 The Mersey Partnership (TMP) is a local organisation which brings together both public and private interests and is charged with 'developing the economy of the Liverpool City Region' (www.merseyside.org.uk, accessed June 2011).
9 When I first visited the beach one of my children was only about three-years old and was scared of the statues, refusing to go near them. On subsequent visits, when he was older, he lost his fear and engaged with the installation.
10 It is also worth noting that beaches can be dangerous places.
11 www.bbc.co.uk/print/liverpool/content/articles/2005 (accessed June 2011).
12 See, for example, discussions about beaches in Andrews 2011.
13 However, we might counter that by noting Obrador-Pons' observation that the practice of nudism on a beach in Menorca 'there is a strict code of behaviour that … represses sexual urge' (2007: 129).

References

Allen, S. (2008) 'British Cinema at the Seaside – the Limits of Liminality.' *British Cinema and Television*, 5(1): 53–71.
Andrews, H. (2011) *The British on Holiday. Charter Tourism Identity and Consumption.* Bristol: Channel View.
Baldacchino, G. (2010) 'Re-placing Materialitiy. A Western Anthropology of Sand.' *Annals of Tourism Research*, 37 (3): 763–778.
Bender, B. (1993) 'Introduction: Landscape – Meaning and Action', in B. Bender (ed.), *Landscape: Politics and Perspectives*, Oxford: Berg: pp. 1–17.
Bender, B. (2002) 'Time and Landscape.' *Current Anthropology*, 43: 103–112.

Bender, B. and Winer, M. (eds) (2001) *Contested Landscapes Movement, Exile and Place*. Oxford: Berg.

Boissevain, J. and Selwyn, T. (eds) (2004) *Contesting the Foreshore. Tourism Society and the Politics of the Coast*. Amsterdam: Amsterdam University Press.

Hall, T. and Robertson, I. (2001) 'Public Art and Urban Regeneration: advocacy, claims and critical debates'. *Landscape Research*, 26 (1): 5–26.

Hubbard, P., Faire, L. and Lilley, K. (2003) 'Memorials to Modernity? Public art in the 'city of the future'.' *Landscape Research*, 28 (2): 147–169.

Löfgren, O. (1999) *On Holiday. A History of Vacationing*. Berkeley: University of California Press.

MacCannell, D. (1976) *The Tourist: A New Theory of the Leisure of the Class*. London: Macmillan Press.

McCarthy, J. (2006) 'Regeneration of Cultural Quarters: Public Art for Place Image or Place Identity.' *Journal of Urban Design*, 11 (2): 243–262.

Miles, M. (1997) *Art Space and the City. Public Art and Urban Futures*. London: Routledge.

Obrador-Pons, P (2007) 'A haptic geography of the beach: naked bodies, vision and touch.' *Social and Cultural Geography*, 8 (1): 123–141.

Relph, E (1976) *Place and Placelessness*. London, Pion.

Rodman, M.C. (1992) 'Empowering Place: Multilocality and Multivocality.' *American Anthropologist*, 94: 640–565.

Sharp, J., Pollock, V. and Paddison, R. (2005) 'Just Art for a Just City: Public Art and Social Inclusion in Urban Regeneration.' *Urban Studies*, 42 (5/6): 1001–1023.

Shields, R. (1991) *Places on the Margin. Alternative Geographies of Modernity*. London, Routledge.

Thomassen, B. (2009) 'Uses and Meanings of Liminality.' *International Political Anthropology*, 2 (1): 5–28.

Tilley, C. (1994) *A Phenomenology of Landscape, Places, Paths & Monuments*. Oxford, Berg.

Turner, V. (1969) *The Ritual Process*. Harmondswort: Penguin.

Turner, V. (1982) *From Ritual to Theatre. The Human Seriousness of Play*. New York: Paj.

Urbain, J.-D. (2003) *At the Beach*. Translated by Catherine Porter. Minnesota: Minnesota University Press.

Part IV
Liminality and nation
Marginality, negotiation, contestation

11 Shifting borders and dangerous liminalities

The case of Rye Bay

Tom Selwyn

Introduction

Coastal landscapes, their metaphors and symbolic structures

Jean Didier Urbain (2003) writes 'the beach is a place where society puts itself on show'. Andrews (2011), Weber (2010), and Rogelja (2004) have re-worked this sharp observation for the broader fields of the anthropology of tourism and coastal studies. Whilst Andrews has described how British charter tourism reveals features of British society itself, Weber and Rogelja have shown how readings of the seascapes of Montenegro and Slovenia point towards contours of the societies, cultures, histories, and politics of the countries and regions that they border. The present chapter builds on, and develops, these lines of thought by offering a reading of some of the material sites and associated symbolic markers of a stretch of 'liminal landscape' in South Eastern England, namely the coast of Rye Bay between the town of Hastings in East Sussex and Dungeness in Kent.

The chapter also builds on work in the fields of the political archaeology, geography, and anthropology of landscape by such authors as Bender (1993), Crouch (1990, 2010) and Selwyn (1995, 1996, 2001).

Discourses we use to understand the landscapes around us and to mobilise opinion about their management (whether or not to erect wind turbines in certain sites and not others, for example) derive as much from the realm of symbolic features of landscapes as they do from material ones. For example, the 'u-turn' in 2011 by the British coalition government on whether or not to privatise forests (the government wished to do this, the public did not) owed a considerable amount to the symbolic significance of trees in the public imagination. Forests and woods appeared to many so essential to British identity and association with the land that the idea of them being privatised was, and remains, anathema.

Exploration of liminal landscapes thus requires us to focus, first, on their natural and built sites (hills, rivers, buildings, spaces, significant objects, and so on), second on the metaphorical and symbolic connotations these generate, and third on the social relations within which both the material and symbolic are embedded.

A walker in Rye Bay

The chapter proceeds by imagining a walker following a route along the coast from Hastings to Dungeness. Like most walkers, he or she spends much of the journey observing and responding to the material, symbolic, and social surroundings as these appear on the way. Once again like most travellers, our walker will be keenly aware, both consciously and unconsciously, of the relationship between landscapes and the senses of self that they generate (Selwyn, 2010). After all, members of the Ramblers Association go on mountain walks partly or mainly because by doing so they affirm or re-affirm senses of themselves as these relate to, and are shaped by, open spaces and the values, such as the rights to roam freely in the countryside, that go along with them. In this sense ramblers have something in common with the kite surfers of Camber Sands, who we will meet below, as they too link their own style of movement along the seashore to senses of freedom that help define who they are.

In short, the present chapter is concerned with how a walker in Rye Bay might relate its coastline actually and metaphorically to his or her sense of self as a citizen of Britain in the world today. Indeed, in this regard, we are also concerned to use the insights generated here to reflect on the nature of contemporary Britain.

Our walker is, in a sense, everyman (or everywoman): a traveller who might, perhaps, keep a diary, a local citizen, tourist, or both, blessed with an average amount of wit and thoughtfulness and with a wide field of material and symbolic markers to select from during the journey. To give it some preliminary shape we may suggest that this field may be divided into three interpenetrating layers. To start with there is a layer containing a benign collection of holiday beaches, amusement parks, the cobbled streets of Rye itself, and other tourist related 'heritage' narratives. Then there is layer of landscape of fishing boats, lifeboats and their memorabilia, churches (the two appearing here are at Rye and Rye Harbour), war memorials, tales of the links between the Cinque Ports, Ancient Towns and royalty, and so on, that all seem to evoke narratives about an English identity of pragmatic individualism, heroism in the face of stormy seas, Anglicanism, royalty, antagonistic relationships between England and France, and so on. A third layer contains sites and symbols that connote more unsettling structures and forces. There is the power station at Dungeness whose cooling system some believe to be compromised by shifting shingle deposits. Then there are the firing ranges at Lydd, owned by the Ministry of Defence. These are reported to have had, at various times, realistic mock-ups of the streets of Belfast and Baghdad as aids to the training of army personnel in responding to snipers. Additionally, there are other manifestations and reminders elsewhere about deaths caused by some of the past millennium's wars, including the most recent ones in the Middle East. Underlying all of these our walker cannot but be aware at every turn of the ubiquitous sea defences that speak materially, metaphorically and accurately enough of anxieties about rising sea levels and the propensity for parts of the land behind the coast to be flooded.

We may make the point simply. In travelling along the coast our walker will be faced with the task of working out how Camber Sands in summer, Rye Harbour lifeboat, Dungeness nuclear power station, and the fallen of the Iraq war, are related to each other, and to him or herself.

Shifting borders

Visitors to Lime Kiln Cottage, the Rye Harbour Nature Reserve Information Centre, will be aware of a rumbling sound towards the sea some half a mile to the south. This is the sound of lorries and their mechanical shovelling equipment collecting shingle from the shore at Terminal Groyne, the area adjoining the river Rother's western bank as the river runs into the sea, and setting off with their loads along the sea road to the west in order to empty the pebbles out at Cliff End, Winchelsea Beach near Pett, some miles along the coast. This sound is to be heard almost every day of every year for the Sisyphean task of transporting shingle from one end of the beach to the other is one of the consequences of the permanent eastward drift of sand and shingle along the coast. If left to drift without the daily intervention of fleets of lorries, the mouth of the river would silt up rapidly. Further east along the coast, shingle also piles up on the western side of the point at Dungeness where it tends to curve round, extending the point in the process. Some believe that accumulating shingle interferes with the cooling water outlets of the nuclear power station. The shingle, duly removed from around the power station, is used in the refurbishment of shingle beaches elsewhere on the coast including Cliff End.[1]

The drifting and accumulation of shingle that, if left unchecked, could lead to the silting of the mouth of the Rother which, in turn, would result in a shift of the river's course, brings to mind the history of the shifting borders and courses of sea and rivers in and around the Rye Bay area. Rye itself, for example, together with Winchelsea, used to be on the sea until the storm of 1287 diverted the waters, leaving both towns high and dry and Rye itself looking over the marsh with only the course of the Rother winding towards the harbour some two miles away to link it to the sea.

It is these shifting borders of river and sea that are expressed in the title of the chapter, the remainder of which will consist of a more considered description of some of the features encountered on our walker's course along the bay's coastline. This, in turn, will be followed by a suggestion about how we might make preliminary sense of the coast's 'dangerous liminality' of which the title also speaks and what this might have to do with aspects of the state of contemporary Britain in the world.

Walking the coast from Hastings to Dungeness

We will imagine our walker starting out from the shopping mall in Hastings town centre. Surrounded by such names as Mothercare, BHS, Next, and Waterstones there is a sculpture here of a cricketer and a plaque that records that the shops stand on ground that was formerly one of the best cricket grounds in England. The municipality explains in its web site that the Queen unveiled the sculpture the Spirit Of Cricket in 1997 'to celebrate the opening of Priory Meadow Shopping Centre' and to mark the fact that 'the mall is on the site of the former Central Cricket & Recreation Ground on which the game was enjoyed for over 130 years'.

The sculpture and the longevity of the cricket ground it commemorates inevitably provoke thoughts about the history of Hastings itself and its character as a site for summer visitors. Photographs of the time when the cricket ground was at its most serenely popular (late nineteenth/early twentieth century) show the beach itself as crowded with masses of straw boatered holidaymakers, bathing machines, deck chairs, sailing and rowing boats drawn up on the shingle, Punch and Judy shows, lines of people shown on the promenade above the beach. Such photographs are powerful reminders to us today of a time when rhythms of holidays were closely linked to the rhythms of manufacturing: times when whole factories closed for limited summer periods during which workers came, *en famille* and *en masse*, to the beach.

Walking eastwards along Hastings promenade and beach, our walker passes a fun fair, with notices proclaiming 'family amusements': big (or medium) dipper, roundabouts, and an installation called 'Showtime' which promises an encounter with stars and legends of the cinema as it was in the starry days of the 1950s.

Beyond the fair there are several fishing boats drawn up on the shingle beach, often surrounded by nets and lobster pots. The Rye Bay fishing fleet is composed of squat, distinctive, and tough looking clinker built boats that seem to announce in no uncertain terms capacities to withstand the routinely rough seas of the English Channel. The fleet is one of the very few – perhaps the only one – in England that routinely makes use of boats that are dragged up on, and launched from, the beach. We will return to them later but it is worth recording at this stage the symbolic potency, as well as the Masefieldian connotations, throughout a long period of English historical imagination and memory, of fleets of small boats in this part of the English coast.

Though possible to scramble along the sea shore from Hastings to Winchelsea, probably best or only at low tides, most walkers will take a slightly interior route and miss parts of the dramatic overhanging eroding cliffs – and the nudist beach – to the west of Fairlight.

Back on the seashore at Pett Level, on the edge of Winchelsea Beach, our walker will be struck, at low tides, by half buried evidence of the wreck of the English warship *Anne*. She suffered substantial damage in June 1690 when she came under fire from French ships during the engagement between the French and an Anglo-Dutch fleet. She was run ashore and grounded between Fairlight and Winchelsea Castle. Having experienced the attentions of treasure hunters in 1974 she is now protected under the ownership of the Nautical Museum's Trust.

The footpath from Winchelsea Beach to Rye Harbour, mostly within the boundaries of the Rye Harbour Nature Reserve, passes the Old Lifeboat House where an interpretation board recounts the loss, whilst attending to a ship in trouble during a fierce storm, of the lifeboat, the *Mary Stanford*, in 1928, as well as gravel pits, bird watching spotsf, and the groyne on the bank of the Rother referred to earlier.[2] As to the *Mary Stanford* herself, she and members of her crew are remembered at a grave in Rye Harbour churchyard by individual head-stones inscribed with the names of the crew. The grave also has a collective memorial stone carved with a dramatic portrayal of a lifeboat captain in oilskins and souwester. The grave and this striking carving seem clearly to speak of the heroism of the lifeboat crew in the face of stormy seas.

Another feature of Rye Harbour village is the caravan camp. This camp is one of several on the coast of Rye Bay that (together) house around 5000 caravans. Caravan owners and their families constitute one of the most significant groups of consumers on the coast. However, most of the camps are partially hidden from view and not all are in good condition. For example, looked at from Limekiln Cottage, Rye Harbour camp appears positioned behind a bank of sea defences. Elsewhere (at Camber, for example) one caravan park is positioned in fields behind, and at a lower level than, the coastal road running along the top of the sea defence mound, whilst another is (astonishingly) found underneath electricity pylons further along this road towards Lydd. The caravan camp at Pett Level appears in a collection of photographs on the net entitled 'Shit Britain'.[3] The point, to which we will return, is that the half hidden caravans are one feature of a coastal landscape that is clearly spatially structured by class relations and divisions.

And so our walker enters Rye itself. Tourism South-East,[4] in collaboration with the Countryside Agency and the Environment Agency, sets the mood when writing about Rye and Winchelsea:

> These captivating little towns have always been special. The picture-postcard beauty of Rye's Georgian buildings, Tudor houses, and cobbled streets provided an inspiring home for authors such as E.F. Benson and Henry James, whilst Winchelsea's placid streets of tile-hung houses and distant glimpses of French shores attracted artists such as Millais, who fea-tured it in his painting *The Blind Girl*. Old Winchelsea was actually reclaimed by the sea after a savage storm in 1287, but it was rebuilt and – together with Rye – it prospered as an Ancient Town attached to the Cinque Ports of Sandwich, Dover, Hythe, Romney and Hastings, receiving privi-leges in return for providing the king with fighting ships and men.

As another Ancient Town attached to the Cinque Ports,[5] Rye is one of the archi-tectural jewels of the south coast, and England more generally, and is, unsurpris-ingly, visited by many people. Thus most days in the spring and summer coach-loads of pensioners are to be seen dismounting near the market square on the railway station forecourt, many pausing for a cup of tea at a small café, the 'Fat Controller',[6] which is attached to the station, before they mount towards the High Street and the Anglican church to be found at the top of the town.

Rye Church itself is the central and highest point of reference of the town, both as our walker approaches Rye from outside and/or as he or she ascends to the top of the town from inside. For several miles away (from all directions) the church appears to stand at the pinnacle of a more or less symmetrical pyramid of buildings underneath the dark red roofs of houses. The church is *the* dominant symbol of the city. In the small streets outside the West door are teashops ('Simon the Pieman' is one) where afternoon cream teas are served. On the east side there is a graveyard and war memorial in which the fallen of the two world wars are commemorated. More recently, names have been added to the memorial of Rye men killed in action during the wars in the Gulf and Iraq. At the centre of the memorial is a large cross within which is inscribed a sword (an arrangement routinely found in the memorials of Commonwealth war graves throughout the world). This seems a powerful enough announcement and/or reminder of a conceptual unity of sacred and secular power, with connotations of justice deriving from force of arms authorized by the Anglican Church.

As our walker moves down from the church through the streets of Rye he or she will encounter shops and cafés rigged out in various types of mostly inter-, or just post-, world war paraphernalia that serve to decorate a 'heritage' face of the town that is otherwise framed by references to a rich architectural townscape in which Tudor-beamed Sussex houses play a determining role. Although, of course, 'Heritage' is a chameleon word it is found, confidently displayed in bold white letters against a brown background, on one of the larger road signs at the entrance to the town. This sign directs the visitor to the Information and Heritage Centre which is, in itself, a treasure trove of items of 'heritage' in which eras of Rye's history are skilfully blended into collections of brochures, information sheets, fridge stickers, and postcards, as well as a model of the town that serves as foreground to an audio introduction to its history.

'Heritage' comes in many forms. For example, there are a number of shops in Rye containing photographs and images of the town proclaiming its *visual* 'heritage' in displays of paintings and photographs. One of the most pervasive and persuasive aspects of the *literary* 'heritage' of the 1920s and 1930s is associated with the novels by one of Rye's former mayors and best known authors, E.F. Benson. Benson's most popular novels feature lives of upper class (or nearly upper class) Rye citizens, the misses Mapp, living in Lamb House (former home of Henry James and now a National Trust property) and Lucia. Mapp and Lucia are extremely mannered ladies, who spend much of their time exercising a commanding linguistic and cultural etiquette that invites us to assume that Rye is at, or nearly at, the apogee of English upper or nearly upper class refinement. Trollope did not write of Rye but (as it were) he might have done.[7] Benson's own work became a television series, *Mapp and Lucia*, graced by immaculate performances by Prunella Scales, Geraldine McEwan, and Nigel Hawthorne.

Our walker may choose to leave Rye by crossing the bridge over the river near the town staithe, refurbished with funds from the European Commission, where the Rye fishing boats are moored. This has an adjoining marina of pleasure craft. There is also a fish shop that (prominently) advertises scallops recently dredged by Rye Bay fishing boats. He or she would then set out towards Camber past fields of sheep and wind turbines.

Approaching Camber on the road from Rye towards Lydd, Rye Golf Club appears on the right. Notices near the entrance helpfully inform passers by to 'Keep Out' adding that there is no way through the golf course to the sand dunes or sea beyond. Here we are deep into the pleasure landscape of the English upper class. The golf club itself is said to have a 15-year waiting list. Members include those from the upper reaches of the English legal and/or financial establishments. Opposite the club is a green field with pond and, frequently, elegant looking horses, making the area feel every inch out of Stubbs or even Gainsborough.

It is possible to link, in a Veblen-like way, the golf club with the Yacht Club at Rye Harbour and the Tennis Club on the road out of Rye towards Appledore. All are leisure sites for the wealthy and moderately wealthy – but in this particular landscape, statuses are organised slightly more precisely on a golf/tennis/yachting axis (for example, a man, recently rich, might have less difficulty becoming a member of the yacht or tennis clubs than the golf club). To one degree or another, however, all are sites patronised by members of the 'leisure classes', in Veblen's sense of this term.[8]

Just before reaching Camber itself, Pontin's Holiday Camp looms to the left, painted blue, with gates and security guards. Here we are in the territory of industrial tourism for working class families who have purchased inclusive packages of accommodation, food, and entertainment. In Camber itself, to pursue for a moment the class *motif* into a distinctively middle-class space, there is a relatively new development of town houses with solar panels, near which is a café serving organic and healthy food: Camber as Islington so to speak. Back in 'old Camber', the village shops sell visitors beach gear such as lilos, buckets and spades, and brightly coloured plastic windmills, decorated with Union flags, attached to wooden sticks. There is also a car park and amusement centre and fried food restaurant that leads on to the working class section of Camber Sands and the sea.

Climbing to the top of the sea defence mound, the walker will find the road to Lydd running above Camber's shingle beach which, on the seaward side, runs down at low tide into one of the broadest and longest sandy beaches in Europe, but which, at the highest tides of the year, witnesses the sea virtually lapping the edge of the road. On the landward side of the road is the caravan park referred to above. As noted, the park is found in fields beneath the defences – precisely in the front line of any future breach of the sea defences in the area.

Lively exchanges of contrasting views are to be found by correspondents on the SEKA[9] and BPS[10] websites (both devoted to wind kiting on Camber Sands) about the plans by local authorities in the Camber region to plant large concrete boulders on the upper beach as a new effort at sea defence. One respondent writes:

> It's the fear of sea level rise and another storm that's making the council shit a brick that the marsh will soon look like that map again that's prompted all this. Any breach along that black line and the marsh is fucked!!

Another replies in a different vein:

> I say that the sea take back what was once its own, the land started off as salt marsh and from what I remember of bible lessons at school the wise man built his house on a hill made from bricks.

Progressing eastwards the walker arrives at a part of the beach entitled 'Jury's Gap'. We are at the eastern end of the publicly accessible part of Camber Sands. It is an area patronised more by middle and upper-middle class families than working class ones (although, of course, kite surfers at low tide navigate their crafts across all class borders as they sail from one end of the sands to the other).

The name 'Jury's Gap' is derived from an earlier name of 'Jew's Gap'. Spector (1987) writes:

> The earliest reference to Jewry in post-resettlement Sussex appears in the records of fees, duties and Rents of Assizes of the harbour of Rye dated 1670: 'The Bailiff received one shilling head money on every Jew leaving or entering the harbour'. Until about 1840 there was an inlet east of Rye known as 'Jews Gap', but the name has since been corrupted to 'Jury's Gap'. It is possible that it obtained its original name by being a place of landing or exit for those who chose not to pay this impost.

This intriguing mixture of fact and conjecture serves to suggest how boundaries and relations between social categories (here defined by ethnicity and/or religion, elsewhere by class), on the one hand, and regional and/or national authorities, on the other, were historically formed.

The coastal area that includes Jury's Gap is arguably best known in the area for the long tradition in and around Romney Marsh and Rye Bay of smuggling. This aspect of the bay's history has been incorporated into 'heritage' narratives of the region in a way that makes smuggling into an activity that appears slightly exotic and which, in this respect, is comparable to Guy Fawkes' attempt to blow up the British Houses of Parliament. Guy Fawkes Night is celebrated in a more dramatic way in parts of Sussex, particularly Rye and Lewis, than other parts of England. The large bonfires, fireworks, burning barrel throwing, 'bloater boats' and other rituals and public entertainments effectively merge the gunpowder plot itself with other Christian and pre-Christian references. Additionally, also in this respect like the folding of the Guy Fawkes story into Bonfire Night, the history of smuggling seems safely located in the distant past.

This will be another topic to which we will return in the concluding reflections of the chapter. We may note at this stage, though, that smuggling played a major role in the history in this area of law and order, as well as the legitimacy of local and national authorities.

The Ministry of Defence firing ranges, whose jurisdiction extends to the seashore, interrupt the coastal walk to the east of Jury's Gap. Within the area of the firing ranges there is a built stage-set used to train marksmen in urban warfare. It is reported that there have been times when the buildings of this set have been built to resemble Baghdad. There are, clearly, multiple connotations here, over and under written by those flowing from the position of the range in the path of German planes during the Second World War. The reference to the Baghdad mock up, however, especially when linked to the war memorial to the fallen in Iraq in Rye Church, does obviously raise all the familiar issues about the status, legality, and political wisdom of the ongoing wars in the Middle East. We will come back to the debates about these later.

Skirting round the firing range, past the caravan site, with its plastic classical Roman columns either side of the entrance and under the pylons and electricity lines that emit a permanent humming noise over the caravans, and past the town of Lydd – known, *inter alia*, for army barracks routinely hired out by the army for use as film sets – our walker will arrive in the dramatic landscape in which is found the littoral between Lydd and Dungeness: salt marshes, artificial reservoirs, sea grass, a building housing the regional centre of the Royal Society for the Protection of Birds (RSPB),[11] a race track for a certain class of slightly beaten up cars, Lydd Airport, the Dungeness power stations and lighthouses,[12] shacks used by fishers and lugworm collectors, and the former house and garden of the late and distinguished film director Derek Jarman.

Dungeness itself is one of the largest expanses of shingle in the world and falls under several official conservation designations for its international geomorphologic importance. It is a National Nature Reserve (NNR), a Special Protection Area (SPA), a Special Area of Conservation (SAC) as well as being part of the larger area of Rye Bay Site of Special Scientific Interest (SSSI).

But this part of the bay is also a highly contested landscape fought over by a number of competing interests. There are, for example, the arguments surrounding the development of Lydd Airport,[13] presently more or less run down and only operating flights to Le Touquet and Jersey for approximately 3000 passengers annually. Its relatively new Saudi Arabian owner has put forward plans to open up and extend the airport to cater for 500,000 passengers in the short term and two million passengers in the longer term. These plans have found favour amongst some in the town of Lydd on the grounds that a refurbished airport will bring employment to the area. The RSPB, however, is running a campaign to prevent any redevelopment of the airport, saying that this would damage the bird population of the area. The RSPB campaign is supported by Greenpeace, British Energy, Council for the Protection of Rural England, Kent Wildlife Trust and the British Hedgehog Preservation Society. Then there are the bitter debates about the future of energy production stimulated by the looming presence of the nuclear power stations at Dungeness. Fresh from the wind turbines in the fields of Romney Marsh, and with the recent tragedies in mind of the combined forces in Japan of a boiling sea and nuclear power that wreaked such terrible havoc, there our walker cannot help but be faced by the issues raised by these discussions as he/she approaches the power stations. The competing forces supporting and opposing the commissioning of the third power plant are clearly not restricted to the area of East Kent but range throughout both private and public sectors in Britain as a whole.

Some of the features encountered by our walker at Dungeness Point, the end of the journey, are likely to include the following.

There is, to start with, the southern terminal station of the Romney, Hythe, and Dymchurch railway (RHDR). This is the narrow gauge railway running between Hythe and Dungeness that boasts some wartime involvement in its carriage of anti-aircraft guns during the Second World War. The railway also has a starry association being re-opened after the war in 1947 by Laurel and Hardy.

Being the easternmost point of the bay there are several Rye Bay fishing boats drawn up on the shingle, some resting on launching strips laid out between the sea and the highest point of the shingle. Our walker may see these silhouetted against the sky effortlessly symbolising a character and disposition of sturdy individualism and independence in the face of what is often a treacherous sea.

Near the beached fishing boats, and scattered over a large part of the surfaces of Dungeness Point, are black wooden shacks. These are used by fishers, some associated with the fishing boats, to store nets and other fishing tackle. Others are used by those who dig out lugworms from the sand and mud around the point at low tide. Lugworms are used as bait for pleasure line fishing off the shore and the diggers tend to wrap them in newspaper in bundles that they then sell to the fishing stores of Lydd and New Romney. This is extraction at its most raw from one of the most barren looking (and feeling) landscapes in England. Furthermore, digging worms at Dungeness is about as far away as is possible to get (though only a few kilometers away) from playing golf at Rye Golf Club: two poles defining the same country.

And finally to the house and garden that belonged to Derek Jarman.[14] His small shingle garden, which is the most famous part of his home, consists of circles of large pebbles, containing and interspersed with marsh plants and flowers, with oblong stones standing up in the centre of the circles, clearly resembling, and representative of, erect penises.

Reading the landscape

How may we read this landscape?

Several observations made during the above account serve as clues. Following these we may suggest that the natural and built landscapes of Rye Bay, together with their symbolic associations, reveal issues that we may group under five interrelated thematic headings: energy and its production, consumption and conservation, order and governance, Britain's relation with the world, and finally, in some senses encompassing the others on both material and symbolic levels, the sea itself.

Energy

Nuclear power clearly dominates the bay in the shape of the power station at Dungeness. However this plant is not the only source of energy as the wind turbines in the marsh and the solar power panels throughout the area demonstrate.

The 'nuclear lobby' (starting from elements of the private sector backed by parts of the regional and national public sector) and some citizens of surrounding towns and villages, are vocally supportive of the nuclear industry while other local people, other sections of local and regional authorities, together with voluntary and third sector societies and associations,[15] are equally vocally opposed to the proliferation of nuclear power in the area. The recent tragedies in Japan have added urgency to the debates. This is not the place to rehearse the various arguments for and against nuclear power, many of which are well known as such intertwined issues as climate change, energy efficiency, and the governance of energy. Our walker might reflect that each of these issues raised the overriding question about the respective roles of the private and public sectors in the financing, building, operation, and decommissioning of any past, present, or future nuclear power plant not to mention the task – until the end of time after all – of physically shifting the shingle from around the plant. Our walker might ask whether there could be a Japanese style tragedy at Dungeness and, if so, whether the causes come from the land, sea,[16] or air? One voice picks out a possible scenario. The chartered consulting engineer advising the organisation opposing the Lydd Airport development has suggested that although the reinforced concrete vessel of each reactor at Dungeness B would be likely to withstand an aircraft crash, subsidiary equipment failures caused by the crash could lead to a very significant radiological release, mirroring the situation at Fukushima.

The issue of nuclear power thus raises questions that cross the boundaries of scientific, economic, and political judgment. After Japan, and given the attributes of the physical location of the Dungeness plant, anxieties about the danger of the enterprise are understandable. But the widespread opposition to nuclear power in the area suggests an additional sense of unease about decision-making processes determined by private and public operators struggling to relate and/or conflate evidence, profit, and public responsibility.

Consumption and conservation

Barry Yates, the Head of Rye Harbour Nature Reserve, observes that there are many different and conflicting interests on the coast of Rye Bay. Amongst a host of others, these include families on holiday, kite surfers, water sports enthusiasts, car and motor cycle racers, caravans, dogs, houses and housing developers, wildlife, fishers, leisure sailors, farmers, walkers, schools and educational institutions. Furthermore, there are divisions between actually and potentially conflicting parties: landowners and conservationists, those favouring turbines and those opposing them, the nuclear and renewable lobbies, EC fishing quota regulators and fishers themselves.

In a nutshell, Yates points towards the fact that there are many different possible ways of using, or consuming, the bay, and that these are underpinned by fundamentally divergent social, cultural, economic and environmental interests. He goes on to suggest that there is an obvious need for a well-designed and implemented overall coastal zone management. In his view there is little evidence of this.

Our walker who, after all, set off from Priory Meadow Shopping Centre in Hastings, might also wish to point to the consumerist symbolism (in both town and countryside) that connotes the fundamental shift from an economy based on production to one based on consumption. In such a context, leisure is no longer defined in opposition to work for in a sense it *is* work. *En passant* we may notice that a society and economy based on consumption has less time and space for leisure pursuits that are not themselves part of the consumption process. It is no wonder that the Sussex cricket pitch (in an area of prime property values) had to go elsewhere. But if consumption is production (hardly an original idea) what happens to conservation? Or, to put it in a slightly different way, does not the type of conservation manifestly needed in Rye Bay depend precisely on the types of complex systems of regulations and institutional controls that the coalition government of 2011 seemed dedicated to stripping away in the name of giving consumers and developers greater 'freedoms'?

Order and governance

With all this in mind, and understandably wishing to pause for a coffee and reflective chat in Rye Harbour Nature Reserve or the café attached to the RHDR station at Dungeness, our walker's attention is inevitably drawn to questions of order and governance. How, for example, are such potential dangers as the overuse of the coastal zone by elements of the leisure/tourist industries and other building developments effectively to be addressed if, at the same time, a political programme of privatization and reduction of systems of civil governance is pursued? Anxieties about such questions are heard everywhere in the bay and beyond – from Lime Kiln Cottage to the heart of the National Trust itself. As Simon Jenkins[17] has argued, the government is

> attempting to resolve these nuances with peculiar brutalism with the localism bill which on the basis of nothing but assertions of the development lobby that local planning is a bar to growth wishes to steer the planning regime towards building and against countryside conservation in the name (at clause 124) of 'local financial considerations' that promote development.

There is, of course, nothing new (except in the form they take) about these anxieties. In the sense that overweening private entrepreneurs (smugglers old and new, irresponsible developers, and so on) have routinely threatened stability in the bay, law and order have always been issues of significance.

Britain in the world

People smuggling from war zones into Rye Bay and the responses of the police and local authorities is staple fare in local newspapers.[18] In this context, the Lydd ranges, with their erstwhile mock up of Baghdad, will remind our walker that many of the war zones have been a consequence of the actions of the British government and that the illegality of refugee smuggling is arguably trumped by the questionable legality of the wars and invasions themselves.

But our walker might justifiably argue that the logic underlying the wars is all too clearly revealed by the spatial proximity of the ranges to the Dungeness nuclear power station. Are not the wars, he or she might ask, concerned with gaining (and/or losing) power over sources of, and means of producing, energy? And if that is acknowledged, are not the fallen of the Iraq war who are commemorated in Rye also victims of the struggle for energy? Furthermore, Lydd Airport is, in its way, also linked both to the firing ranges and the power station. Whatever political or ideological side our walker may be on, he or she cannot but be struck by the irony of an owner, enriched by his ownership and control over sources of energy, also being a source of local contention and disputation about the airport's development and consequent employment prospects.

In a specific sense, therefore, the three sites – the ranges, airport, and power station – weave a narrative about a former colonial power and its changing relationship with the Middle East and beyond. The icing on the cake, the cream on the irony, comes with the fourth site in the area, the Lydd army barracks. As these appear on the web for hire to potential film makers, our walker would be bound to ask, precisely as Derek Jarman did, whether such manifest juxtapositions between war, oil, nuclear power, and the loss of British political power, make for a type of scenery that he had in mind in making his best known film, *The Last of England*.

The sea

The presence throughout the walk of sea defences has been emphasized. Sea walls, groynes, breakwaters, concrete boulders, the incessant movement by lorry of shingle, and so on, have all been described. They speak of the sea as an actual and potential threat to the area in the bay behind the coastline itself. In short, the sea carries with it a very considerable sense of danger. One of the underlying aims of the present chapter is to feel a way towards thinking through how the danger of the sea is also a metaphor for other types of danger. The question is danger to what? Let us explore in the following way.

If our walker had consulted the website viewsfrombesidethesea.com[19] before setting off he or she will have read that

> Camber Sands keeps its stunning beauty a secret, hidden behind huge dunes, that the beach beckons you to climb, in order to be faced with seven miles of sandy beach – half a mile wide at low tide. The sea sparkles in the sunshine of a beautiful summer's day, inviting you to paddle in its blue flag awarded waters. This beach is beautiful in all weathers and seasons.

Comparable sentiments are to be found throughout the official and semi-official promotional media about the sea in Rye Bay.

Such sentiments link directly to a mainstream of discursive and artistic traditions in and beyond Europe that have used the sea to express ideas and feelings about beauty and well being. Botticelli's Venus and Picasso's Mermaid are cases in point. Unwrapping a picnic on Camber Sands in high summer at low tide our walker may recall the words of the mid-nineteenth century English poet, Thomas Campbell, who wrote:

> *Yet potent sea*
> *How placidly thy moist lips speak even now*
> *Along yon sparkling shingle. Who can be*
> *So fanciless as to feel no gratitude*
> *That power and grandeur can be so serene*
> *Soothing the home – bound navy's peaceful way*
> *And rocking even the fishers little barque*
> *As gently as a mother rocks her child.*
>   (Quoted in McClatchy, 2001)

Later in the year, though, if our walker were to return to Camber, at Jury's Gap perhaps, at a time of high tide in winter, with the red flag denoting stormy weather flying over the beach and with the firing ranges alongside, the words of the prophet Isaiah might seem more appropriate:

> Ah, the thunder of many peoples, they thunder like the thundering of the sea! Ah, the roar of nations: they roar like the roaring of the mighty waters! The nations roar like the roars of many waters, but God will rebuke them.
>   (Isaiah, 17.12)

Isaiah speaks, of course, to another part of the tradition that has used the sea to denote fearfulness, danger, and death. Paintings of storms at sea by such artists as John Singer Sargent and Turner, and tales from the Odyssey and elsewhere of Sirens and other sea monsters, are obvious examples.

For centuries, therefore, the sea has clearly been used as a powerful metaphorical force in the framing of ideas. Where does it leave our walker in Rye Bay? What insights might have come from the walk about his or her identity and sense of self as a British citizen? And where are we as we reflect on what the experience may have informed us about the state of Britain itself? The answer to both questions is the same: on the edge, that is in the liminal and dangerous landscapes with which this book and chapter are concerned.

Thus our walker will have been impressed both by the sheer beauty of the bay's towns and countryside and the complexity of the social and legal frameworks devoted to their protection and conservation. The view from Lime Kiln Cottage is of a landscape researched, known, nurtured: one that is organised and managed and into which the next generation of school students and visitors are welcomed. Furthermore, the turbines and solar panels dotted about in the bay speak of energy efficiency and moderated consumption.

On the other hand, much of the landscape described above speaks of wars of questionable legality fought to control energy supplies, of part privatised and possibly unsafe nuclear expansion, of consumerism and hyper individualism (demanding a limitless need for energy), historical and contemporary examples of civil destabilisation, and of a localism bill that promises potentially uncontrolled development in the area.

All of which points towards the appropriateness of us taking the last words from a film critic of the magazine *Village Voice* who wrote of how Derek Jarman's *The Last of England* described the death of a country following the economic and political restructuring started by the Thatcher government and continued by a succession of governments after hers. According to this review Jarman's film speaks of 'a world violated by greed and the irrevocable damage that has been wrought on city, countryside and soul'[20] which (we might add) an increasingly fragmented 'heritage' industry might find increasingly difficult to conceal.[22] Here, perhaps, lies the real danger of the sea.

Notes

1 I am indebted to Christopher Strangeways for much of the information presented here on coastal erosion, shingle accumulation, power generation, and local democracy. I would also like to thank him for asking his colleagues in the Rother Environment Group (REG) to allow me to sit in on the group's meetings.

2 Rye Harbour Nature Reserve Booklet, www.naturereservc.ryeharbour.org.

3 www.flickr.com/photos/worthingwanderer.

4 'Escape into the Countryside' booklet published by visitsoutheastengland.com (2004).

5 These were established by the Crown in 1155.

6 The Fat Controller is the fictional head of the railways in the popular children's book series on Thomas the Tank Engine.

7 *Conde Nast Traveller* (July 2007) writes of the George Inn in Rye's High Street 'A classic coaching inn on Rye's high street, straight out of the pages of Trollope'.

8 Veblen (1899) did not define 'leisure classes' being composed of people who did not work but whose work or occupation involved time and space for pursuit of particular types of leisure activities.

9 South East Kiting Associations (SEKA), www.seka.org.uk, last accessed 20 July 2011.

10 Boarderline PowerKite School (BPS), www.learntopowerkite.com, last accessed 20 July 2011.

11 The RSPB boasts the largest body of voluntary support of any charity in Britain.

12 There are two power stations, Dungeness A (which is in the process of being decommissioned) and Dungeness B, an active plant. Plans for a third in the future are on hold in the anxious atmosphere following the Japanese disasters and the continuing arguments about the safety of nuclear power plants on Dungeness Point in the first place. There are also two lighthouses in recent history. The older one, with its remarkable internal system of reflecting glass that gave out a particularly searching beam of light, was replaced as the active lighthouse by a more modern version in 1961.

13 Cf. RSPB, Autumn 2010, 'Stop Lydd Expansion'.

14 Amongst the best known of Derek Jarman's films were *Caravaggio* (1986) and *The Last of England* (1988) to which reference is made in the main text of the chapter. His garden at Prospect Cottage, his house at Dungeness, has attracted something of a cult

following. Jarman was a well-known campaigner for the rights of homosexuals until his death from HIV/AIDS in 1996.

15 The topic is frequently raised at the REG, for example. In one meeting I attended in 2009 the balance of opinion within the group was against nuclear power although countervailing views were also expressed.

16 According to an online 2010 BBC News report 'the coastline at Dungeness is volatile. With global warming, more frequent and powerful storms and their associated waves and surges are possible and might increase the instability of the Dungeness headland' (29 January 2010).

17 Simon Jenkins is Chair of the National Trust. The words quoted here are from the fourth Boydell lecture given on 20 July 2011.

18 The *Rye and Battle Observer* (17 January 2002) reported that a refugee had been discovered clinging to the underside of a trailer as it drove through Rye. According to the report, police stopped the vehicle and the man fell out onto the road. The man, believed to be an Afghanistan national, was taken into custody. Immigration officials at Dover have warned that the focus for smuggling illegal immigrants could switch to smaller places, such as Rye, as controls in larger ports are tightened.

19 Last accessed 14 August 2011.

20 en.wikipedia.org/wiki/Derek_Jarman#Films (last accessed 31 December 2011).

21 In writing of the British on holiday, Andrews (2011) refers to an underlying presence of war in some of the metaphorical connotations of some of the activities in Magaluf.

References

Andrews, H. (2011) *The British on Holiday*, Bristol: Channel View Publications.

Bender, B. (1993) *Landscape: Politics and Perspectives*, Oxford: Berg.

Crouch, D. (1990) 'Culture in the Experience of Landscape', *Landscape Research*, 15 (1): 11–19.

Crouch, D. (2010) *Flirting with Space: Journeys and Creativity*, Aldershot: Ashgate.

McClatchy, J.D. (ed.) (2001) *Poems of the Sea*, New York/London: AA Kopf.

Rogelja, N. (2004) 'Izola's Fishermen between Yacht Clubs, Beaches, and State Borders: Connections Between Fishing and Tourism', in J. Boissevain and T. Selwyn (eds) *Contesting the Foreshore*, Amsterdam: University Press.

Selwyn, T. (1995) 'Landscapes of Liberation and Imprisonment: Towards an Anthropology of the Israeli Landscape', in E. Hirsch and M. O-Hanlon (eds), *Anthropology of the Landscape*, Oxford: Oxford University Press.

Selwyn, T. (1996) 'Atmospheric Notes from the Fields: Reflections on Myth-collecting Tours', in T. Selwyn (ed.), *The Tourist Image: Myths and Myth Making in Tourism*, Chichester: John Wiley.

Selwyn, T. (2001) 'Landscapes of Separation: Towards an Anthropology of By-pass Roads in Israel/Palestine', in B. Bender and M. Weiner (eds), *Contested Landscapes*, Oxford: Berg.

Selwyn, T. (2010) 'The Tourist as Juggler in a Hall of Mirrors: Tourist Brochures, Social Relations, and Philosophical Positions', in S. Watson and E. Waterton (eds), *Visual Representations of Cultural Heritage*, London: Routledge.

Spector, D. (1987) 'Brighton Jewry Reconsidered', *Jewish Historical Society of England*, Vol. 30.

Urbain, JD. (2003) *At The Beach*, London: University of Minnesota Press.

Veblen, T. (1899) *The Theory of the Leisure Class*, New York: Macmillan.

Weber, I. (2010) 'Flower, Food, and Holywood: Maritime Identities and Tourism in Montenegro', unpublished conference paper presented at the Tourism and Quality of Life Conference, University of Promorska, Portoroz-Turistica, Slovenia.

12 'Danger zones'

The British 'road movie' and the liminal landscape

Simon Ward

Liminality and the 'road movie'

The 'liminal' is an attractive, if not seductive, concept when contemplating the 'road movie'. The journey narrative of such movies has a structure that bears a strong resemblance to Arnold van Gennep's description of the rite of passage, which involves a pattern of separation – liminal phase – reaggregation (van Gennep 1960). In films as diverse as *Badlands*, *Little Miss Sunshine*, *Sideways*, *The Straight Story* and *Thelma and Louise*, the protagonists move away from a secure domestic environment into an uncertain 'liminal' space of 'testing', before confronting, at the end of their journey, the question of reassimilation within a collective.

What constitutes, however, this liminal phase? In Victor Turner's appropriation of Arnold van Gennep's conception of 'liminal' in his work from the 1960s and 1970s, he places increasing emphasis on the ludic dimension of this phase (Crosby 2009: 10–12), the 'human seriousness of play', as one of Turner's book names it (Turner 1982). This focus on the ludic divorces the liminal rite from the fact that, for van Gennep, it has its origins in the *sacred*, the eruption of which is produced by the process of transition and threatens the cohesion of the social structure (van Gennep 1960: 13). For van Gennep, 'sacredness as an attribute is not absolute: it is brought into play by the nature of particular situations' (ibid.: 12). Van Gennep's example is that of physical displacement: 'A man at home, in his tribe, lives in the secular realm, he moves into the realm of the sacred when he goes on a journey and finds himself a foreigner near a camp of strangers' (ibid.).

The fundamental and ultimately reductive equivalence of each road movie's journey narrative needs to be considered against the way each particular road movie configures the ludic but also the sacred qualities of the encounter with the 'liminal landscape'. In road movies such as those listed above the sacred is brought into play through the nature of each particular situation which the film sets up. The contrast is established in each film between the ostensible order of a domestic situation and the 'liminal' space of 'testing', where the protagonists encounter 'sacred' landscapes and people that have been placed beyond the boundaries of their 'home' culture's ordering system, and which present challenges to the protagonist's prior sense of identity. To enter a liminal land-scape is to open up a space of free play, but also to open up oneself to experi-ences beyond the boundaries normally set by society, to confrontations with what that society has placed *beyond* its boundaries, with the abject that 'disturbs identity, system, order [and] does not respect borders, positions, rules' (Kristeva 1982: 4).

In her brief survey of the British 'road movie', Susan Picken equates the road with the seaside as both are 'liminal space[s], with [their] own laws and con-ditions; neither one place or the other but always somewhere in-between' (Picken 1999: 222–223). This equation needs to be re-examined. One of the key family resemblances shared by all these films, and those under discussion in this chapter, is the 'chance encounter', something which is enabled precisely by the space of the road, and its own laws and conditions of encounter. These encoun-ters form a key element in the 'testing' of the protagonist. In the American road movie, the space of the road is the *mise-en-scène* of a liminality that is already structured by modern industrialization. These encounters 'on the road' may be beyond the boundaries of what would generally be experienced in the 'secular realm' – for example, the rape scene in *Thelma and Louise* is in a roadside bar car park, Louise's later seduction takes place in a motel – but the landscape is still determined by the automobile infrastructure. Hence the transgressive power of heading beyond the boundary of the road (often figured as literally driving through a fence) and into the desert, in films such as *Easy Rider*, *Badlands*, *Van-ishing Point* and *Thelma and Louise*. In doing so, these films frame the sacred quality of their liminal landscapes within the American pioneer myth, its iconog-raphy of boundless opportunity, and the possibility of forging a new community.

The absence of such a mythologically-charged landscape is perhaps one of the reasons why there is no tradition of the British road movie, but the films col-lected for discussion here not only share the road movie's archetypal journey narrative, but also a concern with two forms of off-road space: the wood and the sea. There is, as we shall see, the wood, a mythologically-charged interior space that is beyond the boundaries of the secular realm, but in the British road movie, the end of the road means an encounter with the sea. If, as Picken suggests, the road does indeed symbolize a liminal space 'in-between' two secular states, then, in arriving at the sea*side*, the protagonist encounters a space between civilization and oceanic indifferentiation, a place where the boundaries of the land (the nation), and of the protagonist's subjectivity, are not simply being tested, but are one step away from ultimate dissolution. Here the threat of the 'sacred' at the core of the liminal phase has the potential to make itself manifest.

Thus, in thinking about the concept of the 'liminal' in relationship to the British road movie, it is not just enough to think about the fundamental liminal-ity of the films' narrative structures, but how the films configure both the world of domestic order and the particular sacred qualities of the landscapes within which the liminal phase is enacted: what kind of tests emerge from the land-scape, and what are the consequences for the subjectivity of the protagonist who encounters them?

Genevieve: liminality and the ludic preservation of the domestic order

Genevieve (1953) may seem like an odd place to start an investigation of the threat posed by the liminal landscape, but it allows us to see the way in which potential crisis is managed through a socially-sanctioned rite of passage. In *Genevieve*, the everyday domesticity of marriage is coded as a mild form of masculine imprisonment, from which the London to Brighton car rally (explicitly coded as a traditional ritual) promises to form an escape route. The road is a landscape in which the unexpected erupts (accidents, breakdowns, chance encounters), but such tests are always overcome as the protagonists ultimately arrive at their ostensible goal, Brighton, which is in fact only a staging-post on the way to the ultimate goal, the reassertion of domestic harmony in London.

Genevieve is cited by Picken as one of a range of British films where the seaside is 'the last resort of the *carnivalesque* where everyday reality is turned upside down' (Picken 1999: 222). It is indeed not the sea, which remains at a secure distance beyond the railings of the promenade, but in *Genevieve* the sea*side* which is a liminal landscape that provides for carnivalesque moments played out on the seafront and in a hotel, lacking all domestic comforts, which is presented as a site for erotic play – an 'emotional event', as the film euphemistically puts it. The seaside shares this mild evocation of disorder with the film's

Figure 12.1 A brief interlude in the woods in *Genevieve* (courtesy of Granada Ventures/ ITV DVD).

other 'off-road' space of a 'green glade' into which the participants are drawn for a brief interlude of transgressive pleasure (cigarettes, alcohol, erotic play).

Given the generic conventionality of the film as a romantic comedy, it is not surprising that the narrative arc here ultimately follows the conventional framework of a rite of passage, taking its spectator and protagonists on a journey from separation from the secular realm through a liminal phase of 'crisis' to a reassuring social reaggregation back into the domestic environment. It is a film set in the secure world of the 'Home Counties' in the south of England that, for all its fascination with 'playing away', never imagines leaving the secure bounds of those Home Counties, and indeed barely leaves its Pinewood set. In *Genevieve*, the 'liminal landscapes' of road and seaside are only ever sites of ludic play without any sense of any darker threat.

Radio On: encountering the sacred

It is of course possible, and perhaps all too easy, to read *Genevieve* against the grain, seeing in its celebration of the 'classic car' and its male driver a backwards-looking fantasy that represses the then recent experience of wartime destruction and post-war mass production in favour of a nostalgic vision of an older, better Home Counties. Perhaps it is best to treat it now as a museum piece, much like the classic car museum visited by the protagonist towards the end of Christopher Petit's 1979 film *Radio On*. *Radio On* otherwise shares only the coastline as a location with *Genevieve*; it is a film that belongs to an utterly different tradition and historical moment. Part-funded by Wim Wenders's production company, shot by one of Wenders's cameramen, Martin Schäfer, and employing one of his most frequent female leads, Lisa Kreuzer, the film is also deeply thematically and cinematographically indebted (not least in its use of black-and-white film) to Wenders's mid-1970s road movies, *Alice in the Cities* and *Kings of the Road*.

The film establishes the unnamed protagonist's (David Beames) mundane existence as a DJ, whose routinized life is played out within a media-saturated, bleak and monochrome (post-)industrial urban setting. While there is an ostensible quest narrative (the protagonist investigating the circumstances of his brother's death), any plot summary would do severe injustice to the film's elliptical editing and to its use of long takes, which invite us to examine the phenomenological integrity of the predominantly urban landscapes (motorway intersections, factories, pubs, snack bars) that it frames.

Once the protagonist's journey has begun, *Radio On* takes from Wenders in particular the road's enabling of the chance encounter as part of its deliberately loose framework, which gives the journey the quality of a psychogeographical *dérive*, 'an unhindered unstructured wander through the restrictive landscapes of everyday space' (Bonnett 1991: 32), something which is enhanced by the film's refusal of clear narrative signposts. The protagonist encounters societally-marginal figures in marginal locations that are nevertheless not quite 'beyond' the post-industrial landscape; he discusses music and drugs with a young boy at

an outdoor snack bar (another Wenders allusion), the absence of erotic possibility on a pier with a German woman (Kreuzer) who is in search of her daughter,
and the car crash death of Eddie Cochrane with a musician (Sting) at the door of
a caravan at an apparently derelict filling station.

While such encounters might be classified as 'playful', in that there is little
sense of threat or disorder (other than in Cochrane's road death), there is one
chance encounter in which the protagonist nearly loses control. At one point, he
returns to his car, only to find the passenger seat occupied by an uninvited hitch-
hiker. This encounter does not, however, lead to the conventional 'buddy'-
dynamic (as with George Hanson's emergence in *Easy Rider*) or an opportunity
for satirical humour (as with the lesbian couple in *Five Easy Pieces*), but rather
to the eruption of something altogether more disturbing. The hitch-hiker appears
to be a soldier who is planning to go AWOL. It becomes clear that his psychological state is unbalanced, and we are led to draw the connection between this
and his traumatic experiences as a soldier in Northern Ireland (the film's diegetic
soundtrack, often taken from radio reports, refers to this ongoing conflict, alongside other ways in which the borders of the society are being policed: the exclusion of pornography and prostitution).

This figure, then, who emerges uninvited out of the liminal landscape of the
road, and whose life follows the trajectory of the industrialized body, first
adapted to factory work, then war, is the abject product of a society which is currently engaged in defending its borders against the unclean (the Irish are
described as throwing faeces at the soldiers in Belfast). The road, then, in *Radio
On*, becomes a space not only of ludic encounter, but of encounter with the dangerous, opening the protagonist out to experiences of which he knows little (he
claims never to have understood what the dispute in Ireland was about). This

Figure 12.2 Repelling the Intruder in *Radio On* (courtesy of BFI).

encounter is a microcosm of the larger narrative framework of the film, the protagonist's investigation into his brother's death, which leads him unintentionally into the subterranean, threatening and duplicitous world of state surveillance and the circulation of pornography. If the borders of the brother's identity became ambiguous in this world (it is unclear whose 'side' he was on), then it seems to leave the protagonist emotionally untouched, just as he secures the borders of his own car by repelling the soldier's attempts to get back into the passenger seat.

The protagonist's journey ends 'off road', where he leaves his car like a redundant relic, suspended on the edge of a disused quarry's cliff. We then see him walking along a beach (not a seaside promenade), but there is no romantic dissolution of the subject into this landscape, rather a blank, resigned reassimilation within the modernity which he left behind. The protagonist ends up (in true Wenders fashion) alone on a train, travelling to the electronic rhythms of Kraftwerk's 'Ohm Sweet Ohm', a playfully reflexive allusion to the film's awareness of its dependence on the structure of separation – liminal phase – reaggregation.

Gallivant: recording the ritual

There seems to be no alternative space beyond the disenchanted modernity of an incipiently post-industrial Britain in *Radio On*, or at least, if there is, then the protagonist cannot perceive it; for him, the only reserve of a past romanticism seems to be in the music and lives of early rock 'n' roll.

Andrew Kötting's 1997 film *Gallivant* is much more attuned to marginal spaces beyond modernity. Kötting's film follows the rite of passage structure of separation and reaggregation – travelling away from and returning to Bexhill on Sea. Indeed it is an indication of the film's reflexive engagement with ritual and rites of passage that the place is signed not as Bexhill, but as 'home' by Kötting's daughter in the film's concluding sequence. Rather than taking a journey *to* the extremity of the island that is Britain, *Gallivant* undercuts the idea of starting from a secure home by beginning on the beach at Bexhill. The film remains on the littoral extremity, perpetually within sight of the sea as its protagonists, Kötting, his daughter Eden and her grandmother Gladys travel along the coastline in a campervan.

Remaining physically on the margins is an indication of the film's commitment to the marginal landscapes of the island, and the people and rituals that remain to be encountered there. Picken, in her analysis, argues that 'the only certainty in this turbulent landscape is in tradition, in history' (Picken 1999: 227), and Kötting does indeed record the presence and indeed performance of pre-modern rituals that he encounters on this journey through these marginal reasons throughout the film (it is not only pagan, as Picken suggests, for the film recalls the fate of St Catherine on her wheel).

If the seaside postcard that *Gallivant* mimics at one point is a ludic-erotic field of play, albeit industrially limited to an A5 piece of card, then the film is also true to a ludic spirit throughout; embracing an absence of structure within its highly-determined route – Eden and her grandmother frequently leave the journey for a brief time to gather fresh strength; Kötting uses time lapse cinematography, fake archive footage, Brechtian epic alienation strategies and frequent intrusions of camera consciousness to disrupt any sense of a coherent narrative journey or a transparent gaze upon the coastal landscapes.

The fact that the film is also committed to the ludic nature of its cinematic enterprise means that the past is not presented as a secure ground that film simply records. Rather, as one of the ironic commentaries of the pseudo-weathermen who 'narrate' the film notes: 'the past is hidden beyond the intellect, in some object of which we have no inkling'. There is a playful reflexivity to the process of documenting ritual sites and events: standing stones (such as Gop Cairn) are approached throughout the film with production microphones, as if their 'speech' could be technologically registered; the folk dances that recall the Viking raids on the north east coast are presented through faux archive footage. If there is a mythical (perhaps Celtic) Britain that has been marginalized, then it can only be conjured up in playful fashion, its survivals in dance and play (such as mud dancing on an unnamed beach in a film which is otherwise pedantically accurate in its topographical naming), or appropriated in the voiceover that relates the myth of the sleeping King Arthur and his knights over the image of a standing stone (and sound boom with operator) in Cornwall. For all this, Kötting clearly takes his job in registering and giving voice to the presence (and oral testimony) of these marginalized ritual practices and people seriously. Thanks to the film's loose narrative structure, these rituals seem to emerge unbidden from an unprejudiced encounter with the landscape. Kötting avoids overt verbal editorializing, a strategy which lends an odd weight not only to his own few interventions, which reflect on the way in which travelling undoes conventional forms of subjectivity: 'The travelling was working well as a mental distraction and a means of understanding, and by the time we passed Land's End I was struck by an incredible sense of loss and yearning'. Kötting's scepticism is more directed towards the limitations of what can be documented by his own technological medium. Indeed the film itself constantly plays with forms of communication (Eden, suffering from the genetic disorder Joubert's syndrome, speaks in sign language) and telecommunication.

Kötting is equally committed to the ritual dimensions of the journey, and its opening out of a liminal space, as the boundaries between the generations become fluid during the journey. The protagonists' identities are also marked as being 'in flux': in narratively-unmotivated sequences they adopt carnivalesque costumes that ironically allude to 'sacred' figures (if this is obvious in the case of Eden as the Virgin Mary and Kötting as a monk, then Gladys as a lollipop lady can be read as a figure who negotiates the in-between space of the road).

Yet, for all this sense of the ludic spirit of the liminal, the journey also opens on to spaces of encounter with the threatening. Many of the rituals evoke bloody experiences/legends from the past (the Viking invasions in the north east of England, a giant who bled to death in Cornwall). Predominantly, however, the threat comes in the form of the sea, alluded to in the commentaries of others (such as Gladys's observation, 'water is the worst thing you can ever have, fire you can fight, but water you cannot'). Danger is invoked by the recollection of a suicide at Beachy Head ('there is no road here', one tourist voice comments), by the discussion of the way the sea that has caused coastal villages to disappear, by the weathermen discussing the fog which envelopes the English coastline, and in one of Kötting's interlocutor's remarks on monks (Kötting's chosen alterego) that 'they live in them places, you never know what they do, dangerous'. This conversation, towards the end of the film, is followed by grainy footage of a shadowy figure, who appears to be Kötting, wading out into the ocean, accompanied by Gladys's remarks about a man who 'reckoned he had nothing to live for'. As the image turns to a black sea at night, we hear a phone message, seemingly from Kötting's partner, saying: 'I don't know what's going on, but, can you just phone me and let me know about that'. The sense of dangerous disorientation is immediately reinforced by chaotic, violent scenes from the 'Jack of the Green' rite in Hastings. If this is the closest the film comes to implying a kind of dissolution of the subject into a primal landscape (one that evokes both the sea and the earth), then it is swiftly averted by a return to the final sequence of the road journey and 'home', as Eden signs it.

Gallivant is a reflexive filmic essay on the status of ritual in contemporary Britain, but beyond documenting the survival of ritual on the margins of the island, it is also the enactment of a rite of passage that is profoundly attuned to the ambivalence of the liminal landscape, which on the one hand provides a condition of ludic possibility, but on the other also a dangerous state of instability, where the borders of the self become undone in role-play and in the encounter with the possibility of the loss of the differentiation on which the borders of the

Figure 12.3 The traveller disappears into the sea in *Gallivant* (courtesy of BFI).

self are founded. It does not resolve that ambivalence, but returns to where it began, on a beach.

Butterfly Kiss: the sacred in the midst of the profane

On the surface, Michael Winterbottom's *Butterfly Kiss* is a more conventional 'road movie' than either *Radio On* or *Gallivant*, in its playful dialogue with its generic predecessors (most obviously *Thelma and Louise* with its female serial killer configuration, but also *Badlands*, with its deadpan retrospective narration). The film also follows the structure of a journey narrative, framed within Eunice's (Amanda Plummer) quest for the quasi-mythical figure of Judith, as it traces its protagonists' flight from their imprisonments, be it Miriam's (Saskia Reeves) chains of domesticity or Eunice's self-imposed chains of self-punishment. It follows them to the point where Miriam's assumption of the role of Judith leads to Eunice's ritualistic death and Miriam's subsequent reassimilation within the confinement of a white-tiled secure unit, from which she narrates their journey.

If the conventional narrative structure of the road movie, as we have seen in the three films discussed so far, involves protagonists moving from a secular realm into a liminal landscape, then Winterbottom's *Butterfly Kiss* complicates that structure in an important way. In *Butterfly Kiss*, there are two protagonists: Miriam and Eunice. Miriam leaves behind her domestic security when she finds herself in thrall to the dynamic Eunice, who emerges in a series of disorientating cuts at the start of the film from the landscape of the motorway, first as a pair of feet, then legs, and then finally a recognizable figure. For Maszierska and Rascaroli, she appears 'so suddenly at the beginning of the film that she looks like an embodiment of that specific motorway [the M6]' (2006: 186). Eunice is however not the embodiment of the motorway network; she is a body at odds with that network, and emerges as a transgressor of the rules of the road, walking alongside the motorway, and remaining at odds with it, and what it represents, throughout the film.

For all the pseudo-sensationalism and post-*Thelma and Louise*-reflexivity of its horror plot, Winterbottom's film can be read as a critical interrogation of the spiritual emptiness of the motorway landscape, emblematic of a service-sector 'world in motion', to cite the song for which Eunice is searching. To reinforce this, the motorway landscapes of the north of England are rendered in muted washed-out colours, penned in by the film's televisual 4:3 format, with only the occasional isolated tower block framed in an ironic nod towards the mountainous iconography of the generic road movie. There is, to begin with, no escape from the 'bleakly banal' (Picken 1999: 227) world of service stations that 'sell tapes, not records as such', and certainly not the record for which Eunice is searching.

This interrogation of a spiritual emptiness is achieved not from a position of critical authority, above the landscape, but emerges, with an amoral energy, from within it, in the figure of Eunice. Winterbottom reframes the encounter with the sacred in the liminal landscape of the motorway. It is not a protagonist from the secular realm who is encountering the sacred on her journey. Rather, it is those, such as Miriam, who encounter Eunice during her journey around the motorways of northern England who come across that which does not belong within the conventional social order.

The question of what Eunice 'embodies' has been central to most of the critical discussion of Winterbottom's film. For Picken, she is 'like some latter-day self-flagellating saint' (Picken 1999: 228), whose religious devotion appears 'in the post-modern, post-Christian cynicism of the late twentieth century, like obsessive masochism'; for others, she is the 'priestess of the sacred, a sacrificial religion that has not yet tempered the fascination of murder' (Maszierksa and Rascaroli 2006: 179). Eunice's 'religious' practice is clearly important to an understanding of her function in the film. While it may be correct to assert that her sacrificial actions (including her concluding self-sacrifice) are 'not a meaningful part of a spiritual practice which connects her to a collective social project' (Chedgzoy 1999: 57), this misses the point that in this culture there is no collective social practice that would bind her rituals of sacrifice *within* a functional social cohesion. The absence of such a collective practice in the blankly secular motorway landscape means that Eunice embodies the eruption of the 'sacred' into a secular landscape which has no collective place for ritual, and the

Figure 12.4 The Motorway Bridge as Liminal Landscape in *Butterfly Kiss* (courtesy of BFI).

sacred is thus an untrammelled force for social disorder. Her transgressive performances (performing the motorway wrong, committing murder, blurring the lines between masculine and feminine, heterosexuality and homosexuality) reveal what the society's ordering system cannot tolerate, or has placed beyond its boundaries, highlighting a previously invisible boundary. To read, and exclude, Eunice in terms of an *individual* psychopathology is precisely to reinforce the boundaries about proper and improper that are inherent to the society from which she emerges and whose profanity her behaviour renders visible. It is not so much that 'she' has no place, but that the sacred has no place in a society that is, as the film suggests, founded on a motorway network.

One startling sequence, where she bemoans the fact that she is never punished for all the crimes she has committed, reveals the motorway and its infrastructure as the *mise-en-scène* of Eunice's imprisoned body. Eunice's sense of having been abandoned, and her plea for transcendental recognition, in essence the basis of her spiritual quest with all the bloody murder it entails, is set off against the enclosed white-tiled space of a service station motorway bridge, hermetically sealed in between two areas of service-sector consumption. It is not just that she has 'not performed the shift from sacrifice to taboo as imposed by the Bible' (Maszierska and Rascaroli 2006: 183), but rather that her actions have no 'meaning' in a world devoid of ritual practice.

It is not just that, as Winterbottom's film presents it, the motorway, as a microcosm of contemporary society, produces abstract, mundane, spiritually empty space (a vision which recent academic studies of the motorway have questioned; see Edensor 2003, Merriman 2007). It is also complicit in transforming mythical landscapes into consumable heritage sites. The protagonists' motorway drift takes them to 'Camelot', noticed via a motorway sign. Camelot is a theme park travesty of Arthurian legend that, with its blocks of towers and circling rollercoasters, can be read as a microcosm of the motorway landscape of northern Britain through which the rest of the film circles without apparent direction. 'Camelot' in 1994 was also the emblematic incorporation of Arthurian legend in the service of the materialist dream of individual riches as the home of the National Lottery, posters for which adorn the service stations.

By refusing to classify Eunice and her actions as an individual clinical case of monstrous insanity, we can think of her murders as ritual sacrifices without a sacred order within which they might take on meaning, but also as 'insane' disruptions of the meaningless functional circulation of goods and services – her victims are women serving in the stations, or men delivering goods via vans and lorries. Eunice's spiritual quest returns blood sacrifice to these banal landscapes of the motorway network: the filling stations, service stations, lay-bys, car parks and motel baths inhabited by the likes of Mr McDermott, the salesman of vacuum cleaners, in whom, it would seem, there also lurks a masochistic drive (whose erotic fulfilment will lead to his murder by Miriam). The intended ritual significance of these murders is made clear when, on hearing that Miriam has buried one of their victims in the woods, Eunice remarks that the body was to have been left out where 'everyone could see it'. These woods arc the first landscape figured by the film as beyond the borders of the profane motorway network. When, at one point, the pair find themselves at the end of a pier without any obvious way forward, Miriam suggests they could buy a map and navigate. Eunice observes in response that she 'always gets lost and always ends up in the woods, always in the woods, over and over again, it's like déjà vu'. Non-directional drift, a refusal to obey the rules of the road, leads compulsively into the dark woods.

Eunice feels she has no need of maps, because she physically knows these roads from having walked them with her body. The motorway is not constructed as 'a liminal, fluid territory' (Maszierska and Rasaroli 2006: 186); rather it is her encounter with them that produces the liminal landscape. At one point, she provides a visionary mapping of the roadscape at night (through their street lighting) from the roof of Miriam's tower block, whose cage bars suggest that Miriam will move from the disciplinary environment of the tower block to the discipline of the secure unit. 'That's the A558, over there's the A6 and the motorway, they go all the way up to Scotland; and over there where it's pitch black, that's the sea'. 'The sea', Miriam murmurs in reply. The sea is, in Eunice's vision, a dark spot, where the 'enlightened' (secular) space of the road ends, and it is here, and not on the road as Maszierska and Rascaroli claim (2006: 181), is where the film ends.

Indeed, a straightforward reading of the film's narrative arc would see it as concluding 'in the liminal space of the Lancashire sea strand' (Chedgzoy 1999: 56), but this would be to disregard the fact that there are two framings of this seascape, and its liminal connotations, within the film. On the first occasion, Miriam has to walk through the woods to find Eunice on the beach. Freed now of the car and its infrastructural restrictions, they can indulge in a moment of playful intensity, flirting, as it were, with the water, in the tidal space.[1] It is important that this scene sets up the beach as a site of ludic possibility, for this positive reading of the 'liminal landscape' will be apparently radically reversed in the film's conclusion, which again finds the protagonists off the road. The forces of law and order have been strikingly absent throughout the film, other than implicitly present in the disciplined hygenic space from within which Miriam recounts their journey. As a result, there is no sense of pursuit, no sense that the film's conclusion is derived from anything else but the dynamic of the relationship between Eunice and Miriam (whereas in *Thelma and Louise*, the suicidal end is forced by the police pursuit). The car is now parked amidst sheep, off road, and Eunice, unchained by Miriam, sleeps peacefully alongside her. In the morning Eunice effectively stages her own ritual drowning in the tidal waters; the sequence however begins with a reprise of the playful interactions between the two, as if this 'free unstructured play' led naturally to the drowning that is clearly intended by Eunice as a ritual purification, but will be understood as murder by the authorities who will return Miriam to a new kind of secure imprisonment.

Butterfly Kiss reframes any equation of the liminal landscapes of the road and the sea. In *Butterfly Kiss*, the road appears as a secure space where the potential fluidity of transitional states has been sanitized, but this illusory security, as with the illusory security of Miriam's initial domestic situation, her hygienic exclusion of the threat of indifferentiation (Maszierska and Rascaroli 2006: 184), is shattered with the eruption of the sacred, in the form of Eunice, and her transformation of the road into a space of dangerous encounter that leads ultimately, but inevitably, to the sea. Butterfly Kiss ends ambivalently, if pessimistically: the liminal subject, once it has moved beyond the boundaries of the secular, can only be reassimilated within the disciplined order of society, as in the case of Miriam, or returned to a state of oceanic indifferentiation, as in the case of Eunice.

Conclusion: the liminal landscape and the 'liminoid' road movie

The road movie's narrative structure, moving its protagonists from the secure bounds of society's order into a phase of disorder which threatens social cohesion, opens up the road movie's liminal landscape as a potential space of social critique. How are we to understand the relationship between liminality and social critique? The road movies of the late 1960s and early 1970s in America framed the generational conflict which threatened the social structure of the period as a journey through a liminal landscape. The youthful, rebellious protagonists of such films do not respect 'borders, positions, rules'. In his discussion of thresholds and initiation, van Gennep equates the liminal phase of a rite of passage with the production of the sacred: '[in this phase] the novices are outside society, and society has no power over them, especially since they are actually sacred and holy, and therefore untouchable and dangerous' (van Gennep 1960: 114). In these films, the 'harmful effects' of the eruption of the *sacred* (the disruption of the social order) are managed not through a passage to reassimilation, but through either a blank or indeed suicidal resignation on the part of the protagonist (*Two Lane Blacktop, Five Easy Pieces* and *Vanishing Point*) or the eradication of that disruptive power, as illustrated by the violent conclusions of *Easy Rider* and *Bonnie and Clyde*. While both forms of conclusion suggest that the societies represented in these films have few or no productive mechanisms for managing societal transition, the films in themselves can be read as having a ritual function for their spectators, taking them on a journey into a liminal landscape as a kind of rite of passage in which, following van Gennep, the function of *rites* of passage is to grant temporary free play to the sacred, thus reducing its potentially 'harmful effects' by placing it within a structure of ultimate containment (van Gennep 1960: 13).

We can undoubtedly identify a critique of modern Britain in *Radio On, Gallivant* and *Butterfly Kiss*, one that emerges from the encounter with the liminal landscapes opened out by the films' narrative structures. These films negotiate differently with an elemental and dangerous presence that cannot be easily accommodated within a secular Britain that is presented, through its ordered road network, as dominated by circulation, acceleration and the commodification

of tourist experience. In their moments of extremity, Winterbottom's and Kötting's films refuse the faded charm of the ordered seaside and instead takes us
into a liminal landscape beyond the secular roads of modernity. *Butterfly Kiss*
not only maps 'the human psyche onto the physical environment' (Picken
1999: 229), but presents the environment as a psychic force, revealing the death
drive lurking beneath the tarmac of civilization. It may be playful but it is also
dangerous; it is precisely *sub*lime, beautiful and terrible.

As films produced and distributed in the context of a cinematic industry, they
share the positions of their protagonists as marginal to the values and norms of
the society with which they engage. None of these films celebrate landscape in
the conventional visual fashion of the American road movie (Klinger 1997), but
rather offer psychogeographical mappings of terrains on the margins of an industrialized society. These mappings render visible the sacred which is at odds with a
society that, as the films show, carefully polices the boundaries of the proper and
improper (every selected shot of a road sign in these films is evidence for this). If
Gunther Kress defines a genre as 'a kind of text that derives its form from the
structure of a (frequently repeated) social occasion, with its characteristic participants and their purposes' (1988: 183), then it is useful to think of these films
within their function as cinema not as generic 'road movies', but as the ludic
reworking of the social occasion (i.e. ritual) implicit in the exhibition of a generic
'road movie' and its narrative structure. Whereas a generically conventional film
such as *Genevieve* can illustrate how cinema opens out a kind of ritual space in
which an audience's dissatisfaction with everyday domesticity can be played out
in a managed environment, in the other films discussed, the viewer is taken on a
journey beyond the bounds of the road movie's 'generic' home. Presumably in
order to distinguish himself from an industrial mode of production, Kötting
resisted the genre designation 'road movie' for his film (Picken 1999: 224). In
their experimental forms and narrative structures, these films also do not conform
to the industrialized norms of the generic road movie. Indeed there is something
self-consciously artisanal about all three films' modes of production, most explicitly in respect to Kötting's project, but also implicitly in the auteurist modes of
Petit and Winterbottom.[2] The films create a ludic space for the investigation of
social identity, but it is perhaps too much to expect anything more than the *performance* of the 'eruption of the sacred' even from experimental films such as
Gallivant or *Butterfly Kiss*, given that the threat involved in such an eruption will
always be ultimately contained within the structure of cinema itself – although
the responses to Winterbottom's film show how it can provoke the reinscription
of societal boundaries of the proper and improper. Nevertheless, like 'independent' films of the late 1960s and early 1970s such as *Easy Rider* and *Two Lane
Blacktop*, these films can also be read as 'liminoid' phenomena, the term invented
by Victor Turner to describe those domains of contemporary life 'descended from
earlier forms of liminality' (Turner 1977: 39), and particularly artistic production
in an industrial society which 'develop[s] apart from the central economic and
political processes, along the margins, in the interfaces and interstices of central
and servicing institutions ... [and which are] plural, fragmentary, and experimental

in character' (Turner 1983: 155). Turner argues that, in such works, 'far more even than in tribal and agrarian rituals, the experimental and the ludic are stressed' (Turner 1977: 42). If the liminoid excludes the sacred because it emerges in order to define a set of activities produced by a society devoid of the sacred (Crosby 2009: 12), then, as Kötting and Winterbottom illustrate, the playfully liminoid too can still evoke the threat of the sacred.

Notes

1 Winterbottom's employment of Cranberries' tracks here, and elsewhere in the film, could be explained as the kind of music that Miriam would have encountered while working at the service station, and thus the kind of music she would use to soundtrack her reminiscences of her time with Eunice.
2 Winterbottom makes highly conscious use of the technological limitations placed upon his film-making in another (anti-)road movie, *In this World* (2002), and playfully engages with generic convention in the 'road movie' comedy drama, *The Trip*, made for the BBC in 2010.

References

Bonnett, A, (1991) 'The situationist legacy', *Variant*, 9: 28–33.

Chedgzoy, K. (1999) 'Pilgrim through this barren land', in R. Phillips (ed.), *De-Centering Sexualities: Politics and Representations Beyond the Metropolis*, London: Routledge, 47–60.

Crosby, J. (2009) 'Liminality and the Sacred: Discipline Building and Speaking with the Other', *Liminalities: A Journal of Performance Studies*, 5: 1–19.

Edensor, T. (2003) 'M6 – Junction 19–16: Defamiliaring the Mundane Roadscape', in *Space and Culture*, 6 (2): 151–168.

Klinger, B. (1997) 'The Road to Dystopia: Landscaping the Nation in *Easy Rider*', in S. Cohan and I.R. Hark, *The Road Movie Book*, London: Routledge, 179–203.

Kress, G. (1988) *Communication and Culture: An Introduction*. Kensington, NSW: New South Wales University Press.

Kristeva, J. (1982) *Powers of Abjection. An Essay on Abjection*, trans. L.S. Roudiez, New York: Columbia University Press.

Mazierska E. and Rascaroli L. (2006) *Crossing New Europe: Postmodern Travel and the European Road Movie*, London: Wallflower.

Merriman, P. (2007) *Driving Spaces: A Cultural-historical Geography of England's M1 Motorway*, Oxford: Blackwell.

Picken, S. (1999) 'Highways, Byways and Lay-Bys: The Great British Road Movie', in J. Sargeant and S. Watson (eds) *Lost Highways*, London: Creation, 221–230.

Turner, V. (1977) 'Variations on a Theme of Liminality' in S.F. Moore and B.G.Myerhoff (eds), *Secular Ritual*, Assen: Van Gorsum, 36–52.

Turner, V. (1982) *From ritual to theatre: the human seriousness of play*. New York City: Performing Arts Journal Publications.

Turner, V. (1983)'Liminal to Liminoid, in Play, Flow, and Ritual: An Essay in Comparative Symbology' in J.C. Harris and R. Park (eds), *Play, Games and Sports in Cultural Contexts*. Champaign: Human Kinetics Publishers, 123–164.

Van Gennep, A (1960) [1908] *Rites of Passage*. Trans. M.B. Vizedom and G.L. Caffee, Chicago: University of Chicago Press.

13 Threat and suffering

The liminal space of 'The Jungle'

Anita Howarth and Yasmin Ibrahim

Introduction

The border tensions between the UK and France over immigration have been well documented in the media. Much of this centred on the ferry town of Calais with its large transient population of migrants seeking to bypass immigration controls en route to the UK. By 2009 reportedly 700–800 refugees were camped in scrubland near the port and that September the French authorities demolished their 'Jungle' encampment in a dawn raid with bulldozers, vans and up to 500 riot police armed with flamethrowers, stun guns and tear gas (*Daily Mail* 2009b).

The narrative of The Jungle was the latest in long-running tensions and debates about illegal immigration through Calais. In 1999, the former Sangatte Red Cross centre at the entrance of the Channel Tunnel had opened for refugees from the Balkan wars and within three years was housing 1,500 people a day from other wars looking to leap or sneak onto vehicles headed for the UK. Its closure in 2002 had been justified in discourses of protecting the vulnerable migrants from human traffickers and in discourses of blame about lenient asylum rules in Britain and the existence of a permanent structure serving as a magnet for migrants. Most of the refugees were displaced (Freedman 2004) and the flow of migrants into Calais continued (Somerville 2007: 66).

This chapter looks at how collective newspaper coverage of the changing liminal conditions and behaviour at Sangatte's successor, The Jungle, justified its final, violent destruction. It explores this narrative through collective discursive techniques used by British national newspapers. Such techniques frame the story and include the use of metaphors; the ordering of discourses; proximity and distance framing; the invocation of moral paradigms to fuel different kinds of panic; and the justification of material enactments in the form of new policy initiatives, the physical obstruction of migrants and the demolition of their camp.

We contend that these discursive techniques powerfully frame debates about immigration policy failures. Dominant discourses of the threat of illegality, criminality and violence to the social order delegitimize the migrants by constructing them as the source of those threats. Discourses of their suffering are subordinated, the experiences of it de-recognized in claims of degraded living and the sufferers depersonalized through policy failure discourses which reduce their experiences of it to an argumentative abstraction. A moral obligation to act is evoked on pseudo-rational grounds of addressing policy failure, imposing order and minimizing the threat of lawlessness unleashed from The Jungle rather than the amelioration of suffering.

The consensus in media and journalism studies (see Thomas 2005) is that Britain's newspapers are predominantly conservative and right-leaning; however, we found that by 2009 even the liberal, left-leaning titles were using the language of The Jungle and calling for its closure. Thus the focus in this chapter on collective discourses across the British press is valid.

It is well established that the media plays a pivotal role in recreating a public sphere but only recently have the role of emotions in this and the intertwining of politics with popular culture received attention. Furthermore, recent studies have drawn attention to the emotional deficit in the literature on the normative Habermasean public sphere and its valorizing of rationality in public debates (see Lunt 2005; Richards 2004) arguing instead that emotions play an important role in sustaining interest and participation, and in invoking an 'emotional morality' (Barnes 2008).

Richards (2004: 339) argues that rationality and emotions are not antithetical, and neither do the latter necessarily undermine mature, balanced political debate. A growing body of literature on the sociology of emotions and common sense suggests that, rather than being dichotomous, feeling and reason are deeply interconnected and complementary. Richards contends that this 'affective turn has implications for political communication' (2004: 339). This emotionalization of politics – the intertwining of reason and emotion – can serve to connect otherwise esoteric policy debates with the public. Some areas such as education and health resonate with the public because they have a particular emotional salience. We contend that newspaper constructions of the liminal space of The Jungle and the intertwining of reason and emotion in immigration debates – a feature we term pseudo-rationality – is just such a case.

The liminality of The Jungle

Liminality is a useful concept to analyse situations that involve the 'dissolution of the social order' (Szakolczai 2009: 147). This chapter explores what newspaper constructions of just such 'dissolution' of The Jungle reveal about the ideologies, discursive practices and material enactments surrounding immigration issues in Britain and France.

Liminal refers to changes in status and time when individuals become detached from previous social structures but have yet to become attached to new ones and so occupy 'betwixt and between' spaces (Turner 1964; van Gennep 1960). Such spaces are potentially transformative in that liminality operates outside the 'very structure of society' so is able to challenge the hegemonies within it (Szakolczai 2009: 147). However, they are destructive spaces, associated with vulnerability and suffering – physical, psychological and social – as the occupants become 'nameless, spatio-temporally dislocated and socially unstructured' (Thomassen 2006: 322). These challenges and destructiveness evoke powerful human reactions to the liminal subjects and experience so agency becomes foregrounded (Thomassen 2006: 322).

Our analysis of British newspaper 'reactions' to migrants in The Jungle highlights how the liminal served, not as a process of legitimation and initiation into the surrounding community (see Turner 1964; van Gennep 1960), but to delegitimize, de-recognize and justify blocking admission to it. Rather than a 'homogenization of status' (Thomassen 2009: 15), the liminal space of The Jungle was seen as a descent into barbarity, the degrading of the geographical space. This focus on discourses of place is supported by some of the existing literature on the politics of place that views social geography as socially and discursively constructed (see Harvey 1973; Massey 1991; May 1996; Shields 1999). Shields conceptualizes social spatialization as a 'social imaginary' where spatial divisions and distinctions provide the means to ground hegemonic ideologies and social practices (1999, 1991). In these 'social imaginaries' boundaries and stereotypical constructions of others can reflect social practices of exclusion and inclusion.

We theorize liminal space as the creation of a geographical space of de-legitimation and de-recognition through discursive practices that give rise to forms of communal imaginings. Discourses of immigration construct the migrant as 'betwixt and between' their homeland and a new land. In 'Fortress Europe' these communal imaginings designate liminal subjects as illegal entities, transgressing borders and unconstrained by the policies designed to keep them out. Their movement into guarded spaces is seen as endangering peaceful neighbourhoods, threatening security and blighting the landscape. Not only do they taint the civilized, ordered spaces occupied by the legitimate residents, the liminal spaces they use as home bases for these forays become 'jungles' of degradation and debasement, evoking disgust rather than compassion. The use of the jungle metaphor on the one hand de-recognizes the aspirations and suffering of the inhabitants of The Jungle, and on the other hand justifies distinctions between the civilized, rational 'us' and the atavistic, irrational fear of the 'other' – a fear exacerbated by discourses of policy failure to curb the threat by them. Constructions of policy failure move issues of immigration into a pseudo-rational space in which the decisive action of the authorities is not only expected but also reasonable. Human suffering can rationally be banished to the liminal without any attendant guilt. The material enactments that follow, such as the demolition of the camp, can therefore be justified as rational responses of self-protection against the de-legitimized and de-recognized inhabitants of The Jungle.

Liminal is defined in this chapter as the interstitial spaces between socio-political structures and between defined borders. At the borders entrenched ideologies, discursive practices and material enactments seek to govern and repel any encroachment into their spaces by the liminal bodies. These entrenchments guard against moral denigration through enlightenment constructs such as hospitality and humanitarianism (see Boltanski and Burchell 1999; Chouliaraki 2010). In modernity, the nation-state celebrated rationality and order while rendering humanitarian initiatives a selective pseudo-rational tool, capable of creating distance or proximity with a wider humanity depending on what was perceived to be in the interests of the state and its citizens. In post-modernity, the liminal space of 'betwixt and between' becomes a politicized enclave and a repository for unresolved and contested issues. The burden of dealing with the displaced and the irrational fear of the 'other' inform a critical discourse that associates negative human emotions with policy failure rather than primeval emotions or the human condition.

We identify the term 'liminal' as operating at a number of intersections of UK–French border tensions over illegal immigrants and exemplified in the metaphor of The Jungle. First, there is the sphere of discourse, which adopts pseudo-rationality while exhibiting a primal fear of the other. Second, there is an allusion to border spaces where boundaries are tightly controlled and patrolled yet porous so continuously transgressed and contested. Third, The Jungle signifies the occupation of no-man's-land in the midst of civilized suburbia, which over time becomes degraded and the suffering of its inhabitants distanced. Fourth, the policy failure to effectively guard the boundaries with the liminal means the uncouth forces of The Jungle encroach on and threaten ordered, routinized suburbia.

The concept of the post-modern liminal therefore conveys the politics of guarding the margins against encroachment, a space of unresolved tensions where the uncouth threaten ordered peace and policy struggles are concerned with extending and consolidating power and so upholding clearly delineated boundaries.

Contextualizing immigration discourses

Immigration debates in Britain need to be located within an international context where there has been a shift from the discourses of protection and rights to discourses of threat and risk depending on whether the migrant is labelled a refugee, trafficker or terrorist.

Dominant discourses of protection and rights emerged after the Second World War in international agreements on how civilians should be treated in war. These sought to protect civilians displaced by conflict by defining who is a refugee and thus grant certain entitlements, including the right to seek sanctuary and claim asylum, and avoid penalties for illegal entry in search of these. The liminal subject – the refugee – was therefore assumed to have the right of initiation into the societies in which he or she sought sanctuary. However, in Europe these dominant discourses of rights were disrupted by three major developments.

The first was the political upheaval following the breakup of the Soviet Union, the Eastern bloc and the former Yugoslavia in the 1990s. The massive displacement that followed was accompanied by a discursive shift away from rights, protection and sanctuary to threats posed by 'unregulated, unaccountable population shifts' to the political stability and cohesion of the states (Bosworth 2008: 201). The premise of self-protection over the protection of the liminal 'other' began to solidify in policy discourses.

The second development was the growth of transnational criminal networks, including people trafficking. The 2000 United Nations protocol locates trafficked migrants within these networks and thereby justifies the denial of their rights to protection. The presumption of immunity from prosecution for illegal entry was replaced by a new global discourse which criminalized this; the trafficked 'migrant' became not a 'blameless victim', but 'complicit in the act of "illegal migration"' " (Fekete 2003: 3). Thus admission to the sanctuaries of the EU was increasingly obstructed.

The third major development was the growth of international terrorism, in particular the attacks on New York, Madrid and London. A new category of migrant – the terrorist – emerged and presumptions of rights, protection and sanctuary were further eroded.

These global developments were accompanied by discursive shifts: 'illegal migrant', rather than evoking compassion for the displaced and vulnerable, came to be associated with uncontrolled population flows, trafficking and terrorism. The imperative to protect and offer sanctuary was replaced by the imperative to self-protect against overwhelming pressure, criminalization and threat. Traces of the humanitarian imperative were retained in the categorization of migrants into those who were entitled to protection and those who were denied it (see Bosworth 2008; Fekete 2003).

EU policy increasingly drew on these discursive shifts to justify the formation of 'Fortress Europe', a collaborative 'paramilitary system' to manage illegal migrants within its borders and obstruct others from entering (Fekete 2003: 4). Britain's initial reluctance to be part of this was overtaken by a concern about the growth in illegal migrants (Geddes 2003, 2005). New discourses justified co-operation in terms of ensuring 'proper restrictions ... affecting our country' (Tony Blair, cited in Geddes 2005: 726) and in claims about the globalization of trafficking and terrorism. Collaboration was needed for 'effective' management in the best interests, safety and cohesion of the nation (Bosworth 2008: 201). The consequence was an expansion of policing beyond the borders of the UK and the appropriation of socio-legal distinctions between being 'tough on illegal immigrants' and 'fair on legal migrants' (see Bosworth 2008: 201 and Young 2003).

These policy discourses set the tone and content of British public debate on immigration (see Geddes 2005), attracting repeated criticism for 'fuelling negative perceptions' of migrants through constant association with illegality and criminality (Parliament 2007d: 23). The government's message that the presence of asylum seekers was a 'problem requiring control' was seen as exacerbating 'considerable hostility' towards them (JUSTICE, cited in Parliament 2007d: 27).

A decade-long newspaper 'campaign' on immigration

The salience of illegal immigration for the British government was mirrored by a similar salience for British national newspapers. Their discourses on The Jungle can be located within the resumption of a decade-long 'media campaign' against immigration policies (Parliament 2007e). Most of Britain's national newspapers are ideologically conservative (Greenslade 2004), however anti-immigration policy discourses are discernible across the political spectrum of British national newspapers. Even before The Jungle developments a dominant theme across all the newspapers was of policy failure and the need to urgently address this. The most critical, though, were the mid-market titles – the *Daily Express* and *Daily Mail* – which framed this failure in terms of government abdication of moral responsibility to protect Britons and migrants from exploitation by criminal networks.

The newspaper campaign against immigration peaked in 2003, was followed by a lull and then resumed with '2500 articles' between early 2006 and early 2007 alone (Parliament 2007e: 55). The tone of coverage was 'overwhelmingly hostile', drawing on emotive and pejorative language such as 'flood', 'bogus' and 'fraudulent' (Parliament 2007a: 99) and contributing to a 'dehumanizing' of asylum seekers (Parliament 2007f: 98) and a 'misleading picture' of immigration which 'fuel[led] political prejudice … and extremism' in Britain (Parliament 2007e: 55).

Editors justified their coverage claiming, on the one hand, that their coverage was responsive to the legitimate concerns of readers and that it was the responsibility of the media to hold governments to account for failing to address these (see Parliament 2007b). On the other hand they claimed that the continued presence of '400,000 illegal immigrants' was evidence of policy failure; that '12 years of mismanagement' and the 'breakdown in the asylum system have created a political space in which this media campaign is rooted and can flourish' (Parliament 2007e: 55).

Persistent policy failure, the editors claimed, had already risen to an 'unprecedented' scale of immigration (Parliament 2007c: 52) bringing about the 'greatest demographic change … since the Norman invasion' (Parliament 2007b: 52). The scale of the problem was claimed to fuel right-wing extremism (Parliament 2007e), divert limited health and housing resources away from Britons and introduce new criminal elements into the country (Parliament 2007c). This, the *Daily Express* claimed, was evident in the 'proliferation of new ethnic gangs' and the growing attention of the security forces on 'suspected terrorists, many of whom had come through the asylum route' (Fagge 2007: 1). Furthermore, Paul Dacre, editor of the *Daily Mail*, argued that persistent government failure 'to get hold of this' signified a moral failure to protect vulnerable migrants 'risking their lives on trains, at the mercy of gangsters, coming in willy-nilly on boats and trains and planes. It's horrible, it's obscene' (cited in Hagerty 2002: 14).

This rationale and justification by editors coincided with the emergence of discourses surrounding The Jungle in Calais.

National newspapers and The Jungle

The significance of Calais is its status as the main ferry port to Britain, so comprising the main transit route for many migrants. We are concerned to explore the discursive practices of the newspapers that constructed the liminal – that is, the geographical space of The Jungle and its inhabitants – on this transit route and what this reveals about the hegemonies underlying immigration issues.

Discursive practices here refer to the construction of collective meanings around dominant themes, the ordering/prioritizing of certain meanings or discourses over others, and the discursive techniques adopted by newspapers. What emerged with The Jungle was a communal imagining of 'us' and 'them': the surrounding social order and the liminal, which was then used to justify certain material enactments against the liminal such as the demolition of the migrants' camp.

The dominant theme of policy failure and the dominant discourse of threat in editors' defence of their critical coverage of immigration (see above) were also reflected in their coverage of developments in Calais. Discourses of suffering and vulnerability – for instance, the presence of children in The Jungle – were subordinate, the experiences of pain de-recognized. These dominant and subordinate discourses emerged through particular discursive techniques including the use of metaphor to signify the physical and social manifestation of policy failure, the destruction within the liminal and the threat of the spread of this, causing dissolution in the surrounding areas. This we analysed in the shifts in the physical description of the space, its size and conditions; in the actions of its inhabitants; and in their incursions and the encroachment of The Jungle beyond the boundaries of the liminal into surrounding suburbia.

The metaphoric shifts were accompanied by a framing of the proximity of threat from the liminal and the distancing of suffering within it. Threat was constructed in accounts of forays by The Jungle inhabitants into neighbouring areas, the geographical proximity of the border town of Calais to Britain and the spectre of the criminalized reaching Britain's shores. Conversely, the suffering of the migrants was distanced through de-legitimization of the illegal and lawless; de-recognition of their vulnerability by inferring complicity in human trafficking; and a reduction in their suffering to an abstraction in policy arguments of blame between French and British authorities. So the dominant–subordinate discourses were reinforced by proximate–distant framing.

These discursive techniques supported newspaper criticisms and justifications of material enactments against the liminal space of The Jungle. The metaphoric shifts paralleled discursive shifts in material enactments from criticism of French inactivity to the growing problem of The Jungle, to criticism of periodic, 'unsuccessful' raids on the camp and to a justification of its final demolition. This justification was constructed within the pseudo-rationality of a logical response to policy failure, self-protection from a growing threat and a distancing of suffering.

Relevant articles from Britain's main national newspapers were identified through a search on Nexis News of 'illegal immigrants + Calais' (423 articles) and 'The Jungle + Calais' (152 articles) for a date range between February 2007, when discourses of The Jungle first reappeared, and September 2009, when it was demolished. The use of two sets of search terms enabled the tracing of the discourse of The Jungle from incidental mentions to a dominant discourse used by all the newspapers, including more liberal titles such as the *Independent* and *Guardian*. This analysis of discourses across time facilitated the capture of the changing usage of The Jungle as a metaphor for wider problems with immigration policies.

Three key elements were analysed in the articles: changes in the metaphor; accounts of the changing nature of The Jungle as a manifestation of policy failure; and the justification for the destruction of The Jungle.

The evolving metaphor of The Jungle

'The Jungle', which first appeared in February 2007, was 'borrowed' by migrants from an older camp near Sangatte to refer to a new informal settlement near Calais (Tristem 2007). Initially, it was used sparingly but by 2009 The Jungle had become a dominant discourse in all the newspapers, a shift that paralleled accounts of the expanding number of inhabitants of The Jungle from 500 in 2008 to 800 in 2009 (Sparks 2009) and its use as a metaphor for the dissolution of the surrounding order and the degradation within the liminal space.

Initially, The Jungle was described as 'inhospitable' scrubland (Allen 2007) located on a 'discarded industrial estate' on the main transit route to the ferry port of Calais (Allen 2007). Within a year, the location had been redefined as being near 'Gasoline Alley' where illegal immigrants sought to stow away on trucks filling up with petrol on the way to Britain (Peake 2008). The 'once peaceful piece of woodland' had become a 'ghetto' comprising hundreds of shacks (Peake 2008). Within another year it was a 'sprawling shantytown' encroaching on the peaceful suburbs of Calais (Bracchi 2009) and 'just over 20 miles from Britain' (Rawstorne 2009).

These descriptive shifts in the location and growth of The Jungle captured the sense of an expanding population occupying a liminal space, presenting an escalating problem to the surrounding social order and with a geographical proximity to Britain. These discursive shifts paralleled a shift in the metaphor of The Jungle from the relatively benign, into the anarchic and the malevolent, a disintegration within the liminal and dissolution without. What had originally been seen as a 'sanctuary' from the police (Reid 2007) had, within a year, become 'notorious' (Peake 2008), a 'hiding place' for criminals evading the forces of law and order (Allen 2008a). By 2008, there were frequent accounts of violence – 'vicious battles between armed migrants and people smugglers' (ibid.), inter-ethnic 'turf wars' (*Daily Mail* 2008) and 'rampant' criminality (Fagge 2008). The narrative of a descent into anarchy and fear was reinforced by claims that The Jungle had become a 'no-go area' for the police (*Daily Mail* 2008). The apparent indifference of the French authorities and press to the 'problem' (Reid 2008) changed with the rape of a British student (*Daily Express* 2008). This act of violence against one of 'us' was seen as spotlighting 'France's dirty secret', a hidden 'waiting room' for migrants where the lawlessness of The Jungle went unchecked (Peake 2008). The rape thus exposed the murky world of the liminal.

By 2009 newspapers were describing new levels of ferocity and threat, engendered by a 'new breed of immigrant who let nothing stop them coming to Britain' and whose ruthlessness ensured the violence was 'becoming more indiscriminate', less predictable and no longer containable within the confines of The Jungle (Bracchi 2009). The woodland was no longer a 'sanctuary' or 'hiding place' but a menacing 'launch-pad' for criminal attempts to 'smuggle' into Britain or 'attacks' on the legitimate residents of Calais (*Daily Mail* 2009a).

The sense of an impending invasion from the liminal was conveyed in discourses about how the 'law of the jungle ... has now extended beyond the boundaries of this godforsaken "community"' into a 'siege of Calais' (Bracchi 2009). There were accounts of attacks on legitimate French businesses, 'pregnant mothers' and 'British holidaymakers' en route through Calais (Bracchi 2009). The 'wasteland' now signified the loss of functional space for legitimate residents of Calais who could no longer 'take the air ... walk their dogs ... picnic in the summer' (Rawstorne 2009). The 'sprawling shanty town just over 20 miles from Britain that 'grows by the day', had taken over, threatening the everyday activities of ordinary citizens of Calais, a 'situation ... [that was] deteriorating fast' (Rawstorne 2009).

Thus by 2009 The Jungle had become a very powerful metaphor for the cumulative consequences of failed immigration policies. Descriptive shifts in its location paralleled shifts in the metaphor from the relatively benign sanctuary, through an internal descent into anarchy and the external spread of malevolence. Constructions of the physical proximity of Calais and preferred destination of the migrants reinforced the sense of a growing proximity of threat. A powerful argument for decisive action by the authorities was being constructed. However, what action was deemed appropriate depended on how the suffering of the migrants was constructed.

The migrants' suffering was de-legitimatized through discourses of their illegal status and escalating anarchy and distanced in accounts of deteriorating living conditions in The Jungle. In 2007 there was some concern for the inhabitants as temperatures fell below zero and temporary shelters were justified through humanitarian discourses (Allen 2007). However, by 2008 these few expressions of compassion had been subordinated or displaced by the expansion of the metaphor of The Jungle, explicitly linking the anarchic to degraded and deteriorating living conditions. The 'once peaceful piece of woodland' had been 'turned into a filth-ridden, lawless ghetto', sinking into 'a sea of putrid refuse' (Peake 2008), which a year later was polluting the air with the 'smell of human excrement and acrid smoke' (Allen 2009). The debasing 'inhumane squalor' (Allen 2009d) was likened to 'the trenches' of the First World War (Bracchi 2009). The growing congregation of hungry, 'desperate people' (Chrisafis 2009a) would often 'explode into violence' (Sage 2009a). The degradation within The Jungle and the threat of dissolution without were not only proximate but also pervasive. Its dislocated and displaced inhabitants were suspended in the 'waiting room' of The Jungle, looking for opportunities to 'smuggle' themselves into Britain (Fagge 2008).

Thus the evolving metaphor of The Jungle constructed evolving conditions in the liminal: its descent from the relatively benign to the anarchic and malevolent, from sanctuary to squalor. The message conveyed through this discursive strategy was reinforced by the technique of proximity–distance framing and created the sense of an urgent problem in need of addressing. What material enactments were deemed appropriate for dealing with the liminal was circumscribed by the distancing of the suffering of the migrants, constructed through discourses of illegality (in status and actions) and debasement in living conditions that evoked revulsion rather than compassion. Suffering was thereby de-legitimized. Decisive action by the authorities was therefore unmediated by any compassionate obligation to alleviate the suffering of the inhabitants of The Jungle. This was further reinforced by newspapers' de-recognition of suffering in discourses of policy failure.

The Jungle as a discourse of policy failure

The discursive devices of metaphor and proximity–distance framing were reinforced by discourses of policy failure – ineffective material enactments – to curb the threat the liminal space of The Jungle posed to suburban Calais and to stem the flow of illegal migrants into Britain. Discourses of blame attributed failure to misguided humanitarian considerations and added to cross-border tensions. As these discourses escalated, the suffering of the inhabitants of The Jungle became an abstraction in a policy argument – and hence de-personalized and further distanced.

Discourses of French policy failure were grounded in 'visible' manifestations of The Jungle – the size of the camp, the presence of the migrants, crime reports and the smell around Calais. Discourses of British policy failure to stem the flow of illegal migrants were grounded in challenges to Home Office claims of a fall in the number of illegal migrants into Britain from 10,000 in 2002 to 1,526 in 2006. Charities in Calais and newspaper 'investigations' counter-claimed that as many as 200 migrants a week and over 10,000 a year could be entering the UK undetected from Calais, but that the 'true' numbers were unknown (Fagge 2007). Thus, French failures were attributed to a lack of will and were visibly manifest. British ones were attributed to systemic weaknesses and were more difficult to 'detect'. Visible developments in Calais therefore became critical signifiers of the more elusive 'problem' in Britain.

Newspapers also linked these constructions of what constituted policy failure to claims about the causes of it such as the lack of French resolve to solve the problem of The Jungle. The French media and authorities were accused of 'ignoring' the mounting violence until the rape of a British student (see above), an incident which triggered more direct, forceful action by the French police. Thereafter, there were a number of reports about raids on the camp that 'flatten[ed the] immigrant shantytown (*Daily Mirror* 2008) and strategies 'at long last' to '[get] tough on people traffickers' (*Daily Mail* 2009b). However, the newspapers claimed that within days the arrested migrants had been released, The Jungle rebuilt and that policy was still failing (see Bracchi 2009).

The newspapers attributed this ineffectiveness to contradictory humanitarian considerations. French politicians – on the insistence of the British government – claimed to have blocked the construction of any permanent structures that would service the needs of migrants so act as a magnet for more (see Ford 2007). However, within a year newspapers claimed a 'massive u-turn' with the opening of a charity centre for 'British-bound migrants' to meet their basic needs of food, clothing, blankets and basic healthcare, but not of shelter (Allen 2008b). The appointment of a new 'hard-line' French immigration minister coincided with a declaration of 'war on The Jungle' and the resolution to demolish the makeshift tents (Mackay 2009) but the plans were delayed amid fears that the inhabitants would decamp to a nearby chemical works with health implications for the migrants (*Daily Mail* 2009c). Within these discourses of vacillating material enactments a distinction was made between unacceptable and acceptable human-itarian provision, between shelters that would serve as a 'magnet' for more migrants thereby exacerbating the problem, and food, clothing and basic medical aid provided on the basis of human decency. Thus the liminal subject was frag-mented in these discourses; the meeting of basic needs that would alleviate suf-fering was apportioned according to the differing political objections or sensibilities of the French and British authorities.

The negotiation of these contradictions within limited humanitarian sensi-tivities became a major source of cross-border tension, placing strain on col-laborative attempts to resolve the problem. For instance, in 2009 joint French–British plans to repatriate migrants to their countries of origin faltered after a legal challenge in the French courts on humanitarian grounds (Reid 2009). The British newspapers concluded that decisive French action to solve the problem of The Jungle was being undermined by humanitarian concerns, while the 'waiting room' for migrants to slip into Britain remained open (Reid 2009).

As tensions over The Jungle escalated, discourses of blame escalated. French politicians claimed British policies were to blame for 'their migrant camps crisis' (*Daily Express* 2009a), that 'the generous allowances on offer', the opportunities to work and the availability of legal aid served as a magnet for migrants (Allen 2009e). Britain, it was claimed, was seen by migrants as a 'promised land', an 'El Dorado' (Flanagan 2009) that had to be reached before they applied for asylum (Sparks 2009). The French also claimed illegal migration was 'funda-mentally a British problem' in that the migrants had come from former colonies, shared a common history, spoke English, had family in Britain and were drawn to the country (Allen 2009a).

Thus, not only did policy failure debates prioritize discourses of illegal immi-gration and render humanitarian ones fragmented and contentious, they also de-personalized the suffering of the inhabitants of The Jungle, reducing it to an abstraction in pseudo-rational discourses of policy failure and blame. This de-recognition of inhabitants of The Jungle further entrenched their liminality. The way was paved for the discourses of policy failure and proximity of threat to drive the material enactments taken to address this.

Justifications for destroying The Jungle

These discursive techniques of metaphor and proximity-distance framing formed the basis of newspaper justifications and accounts of the violent destruction of The Jungle.

The first major justification was the need for radical action to deal with crime. The French immigration minister was quoted as saying 'the "law of the jungle will reign no longer" … [that this was] an operation to root out people-traffickers' who exploited the migrants (Chrisafis 2009b). Thus within this discourse of the removal of threat was a moral justification of acting to protect the vulnerable. This was reinforced by claims that the women and children had already left the camp 'leaving a hard core of young men' (*Daily Mail* 2009b) to face the demolition squad, so absolving the authorities of any trauma the demolition may cause.

The second justification claimed that the 'sheer squalor … the stench of rotting food and human waste … [was] one reason for its closure' (*Daily Mail* 2009b). However, there was a general silence on the absence of alternative accommodation or shelters for the displaced inhabitants, the inference being therefore that the destruction of the camp was about the removal of a blight on the landscape rather than concern for the well-being of the camp's inhabitants.

The third justification extended the de-personalization of the migrants in the policy discourses by suggesting that the demolition was a media event, constructed to appease journalists and convey decisive political action. 'Left-wing activists … suggested the demolition was "just a photo opportunity to show the Government is tackling people-smuggling"' (Sage 2009a). An imminent raid had been flagged up weeks in advance (see Reid 2009), a significant proportion of the inhabitants had already fled into Calais (Taylor 2009) and there was a large number of camera crews and journalists on site for the event (Sage 2009b: 14).

The stage was thus set for the destruction of The Jungle; the discursive conditions had been created to legitimize violent means to deal with its anarchy. The narrative of the demolition reiterated this as newspapers claimed there had been a 'police crackdown' to 'clear the Jungle' (Sage 2009a) but the dominant metaphor on the day was a military one. The French authorities, it was claimed, had declared 'war on the jungle at last' determined to 'clear the infamous Calais Jungle camp which shelters illegal migrants bound for Britain' (Mackay 2009). The demolition itself was labelled an 'armed operation' (Sage 2009a) and a 'bulldozer blitz' on the camp (Peake 2009a; 2009b). It was a 'dawn raid', in 'no-man's land' (Chrisafis 2009b) against inhabitants whose suffering had been systematically de-legitimized and de-recognized over three years.

What also became apparent with the demolition of the camp was the effectiveness of the discursive techniques of subordination and silence. Few articles in the three years we surveyed mentioned the presence of children. When they did it was often with reservations. One narrative of the demolition recounted that 'Camp dwellers, many of whom were children, were dragged away by police officers and put into waiting buses but because few have papers there is little way of verifying if those who claim to be minors are telling the truth' (*Daily Mail* 2009b). Others such as the *Guardian* claimed children of between 10 and 15 had been living on their own in the camp and were displaced by the demolition of The Jungle (Topping 2009). There were also 'protests as children held in "Jungle" migrants swoop' (Hodge 2009). What is puzzling is that even the more liberal or left-leaning newspapers had paid relatively little attention to the presence and vulnerability of the children inhabiting the liminal space of The Jungle prior to its demolition. This general silence becomes even more apparent when compared to a warning from the UN Refugee Agency (UNHCR), given even before the camp was demolished, that very young children, some as young as three, were in the camp and were particularly vulnerable to traffickers (Spindler 2009). There was a little more attention to this in the aftermath of the raid, with some newspapers claiming that it left the most vulnerable even more so as 'children sleep rough on the streets of Calais' and 'unaccompanied minors make dangerous trips' to Britain (Topping 2009).

Within weeks the newspapers were claiming the raid had failed to address the problem. New migrant camps had sprung up in Calais (Gammell 2009) and the 'traffickers were defying the law of the Jungle' (Sage 2009c). They also warned that the 'tide of despair has only just begun', that the 'desperate scenes at the Calais Jungle have shone a grim light on Britain's immigration problem' but that 'ineffective policies and porous borders of the EU mean that much worse is to come' (Johnston 2009). The consensus was that Europe 'needs to face up to the migration challenge' (*Independent* 2009); The Jungle had gone but 'the issue has not' (Taylor 2009).

Conclusion

This chapter used the concept of the liminal to analyse the discursive techniques used by newspapers in covering The Jungle and the wider issues of immigration this raised. Liminal here refers to the interstitial spaces between socio-political structures, between defined borders and, in discourses of immigration, between the civilized, rational 'us' and the atavistic, irrational fear of the 'other'. These 'betwixt and between' spaces have potential for transformation yet are also destructive, both in terms of the suffering of the liminal subjects – the migrant inhabitants of The Jungle – and in communal imaginings of the dissolution of the surrounding social order.

These geographical spaces are also discursive spaces of de-legitimation and de-recognition. On the one hand the evolving metaphor of The Jungle and proximity-distance framing served as discursive techniques for tracing shifts from benign sanctuary, through squalid degradation to anarchy and expanding malevolence. This created a dichotomy between 'them' and 'us', between the uncouth, illegal inhabitants and the peaceable, legitimate residents of Calais; between the degraded, debased conditions of the camp and the civilized, ordered spaces of suburbia; between disintegration within The Jungle and threatened dissolution of the surrounding order; between distanced vulnerability and suffering and the proximity of threat.

This polarization evoked newspaper reactions of disgust, fear and anger at the failure of the authorities to adequately address the problem. The discourses of policy failure facilitated a pseudo-rationality in which the suffering of the liminal subjects was seen as an abstraction; their basic needs fragmented and apportioned according to policy imperatives of appearing to meet humanitarian concerns while preventing any mechanism that would serve as a magnet for more migrants. Communal imaginings of dissolution and threat posed by the liminal supported a self-protective rationale for material enactments such as periodic raids and the ultimate demolition of The Jungle without an attendant guilt over the suffering of the displaced.

Turner (1964) and van Gennep (1960) argued that the liminal would ultimately be resolved through admission to the social order. We have argued that, on the contrary, post-modern liminal spaces of immigration become geographical and politicized enclaves of unresolved contestation over who should deal with the burden of the liminal subjects – the displaced migrants – and where fear of 'other' justifies the denial of admission to all but a few. Such negative human emotions evoked by the liminal are displaced into a pseudo-rational sphere of 'policy failure' where violent material enactments against the 'threat' can be justified in discourses of self-protection and problem-solving rather than admit to the primeval emotions that are part of the human condition. The migrant whose suffering has been distanced – de-legitimized and de-recognized – is displaced into another liminal orbit. The liminal spaces of immigration thus remain perpetually unresolved.

References

Allen, P. (2007) 'French go ahead with "Sangatte 2" despite warning', *Daily Telegraph*, 14 April: 17.

Allen, P. (2008a) 'Police target migrants heading for Britain', *Daily Telegraph*, 24 October: 13.

Allen, P. (2008b) 'Calais opens shelter for British-born migrants', *Daily Telegraph*, 30 December: 13.

Allen, P. (2009a) '"Inhumane" UK blamed for French migrant woes', *Daily Telegraph*, 10 January: 14.

Allen, P. (2009d) 'France promises to clear migrant camp near Calais', *Daily Mail*, 24 April: 4.

Allen, P. (2009e) 'France sparks diplomatic row after cancelling flight deporting England-bound illegal immigrants', *Daily Mail*, 18 November: 4.

Barnes, M. (2008) 'Passionate participation: Emotional experiences and expressions in deliberative forums', *Critical Social Policy*, 28 (4): 461–88.

Boltanski, L. and Burchell, G.D. (1999) *Distant suffering: media, morality and politics*, Cambridge: Cambridge University Press.

Bosworth, M. (2008) 'Border control and the limits of the sovereign state', *Social & Legal Studies*, 17 (2): 199–215.

Bracchi, P. (2009) 'The bloody siege of Calais', *Daily Mail*, 25 July: 6.

Chouliaraki, L. (2010) 'Post-humanitarianism: humanitarian communication beyond a politics of pity'. *International Journal of Cultural Studies*. 13 (2): 107–26.

Chrisafis, A. (2009a) 'Refugee crisis: trapped in "le jungle"', *Guardian*, 16 June: 12–13.

Chrisafis, A. (2009b) 'The view from no man's land: riot police clear Calais camp as UK ministers close the doors', *Guardian*, 23 September: 3.

Daily Express (2008) 'British student raped by migrants in Calais camp', 29 August: 11

Daily Express (2009a) 'Now French blame us for their migrant camps crisis', 10 January: 6.

Daily Mail (2008) 'Riots in Calais as 50 freed Afghans prepare to resume illegal journeys to Britain after failed bid to deport them', 19 November: 6.

Daily Mail (2009a) 'French MP blames UK for "misery of migrants"', 10 January: p. 50.

Daily Mail (2009b) 'At long last, Calais gets tough on people traffickers', 22 April: 10.

Daily Mail (2009c) 'Shanty town migrants invade Calais houses', 28 July: 4.

Daily Mirror (2008) 'Cops flatten immigrant shantytown: cleanup', 24 October: 18.

Fagge, N. (2007) 'Rival refugees "bloody battle" to get to Britain', *Daily Express*, 16 August: 4.

Fagge, N. (2008) 'Riot police in "clean-up" of 1,000 illegal migrants', *Daily Express*, 14 October: 31.

Flanagan, P. (2009) 'How saying the word "family" got four Iraqis into Eldorada Britain', *Daily Express*, 13 February: 7.

Fekete, L. (2003) *From refugee protection to managed migration: the EU's border control programme*. Unpublished Paper for the European Race Bulletin.

Ford, R. (2007) 'Calais welfare centre "will lure more migrants to Britain"', *The Times*, 14 February: 27.

Freedman, J. (2004) *Immigration and insecurity in France*, Aldershot: Ashgate Publishing.

Gammell, C. (2009) 'Migrants defiant as "Jungle" is cleared', *Daily Telegraph*, 23 September: 5.

Geddes, A. (2003) *The politics of migration and immigration in Europe*, Oxford: Oxford University Press.

Geddes, A. (2005) 'Getting the best of both worlds? Britain, the EU and migration policy', *International Affairs*, 81 (4): 723–44.

Greenslade, R. (2004) *Press gang: How newspapers make profits from propaganda*, Basingstoke: Pan Macmillan.

Hagerty, P. (2002) 'Paul Dacre: the zeal thing', *British Journalism Review*, 13 (3): 11–22.

Harvey, D. (1973) *Social Justice and the City*, London: Edward Arnold.

Hodge, K. (2009) 'Protests as children in "Jungle" migrants swoop', *Independent*, 22 September: 11.

Johnston, M. (2009) 'Flow of migrants will continue however many tents are torn up', *The Times*, 22 September: 14–15.

Independent (2009) 'Europe needs to face up to the migration challenge', 23 September: 16.

Lunt, P. (2005) 'The Jerry Springer Show as an emotional public sphere', *Media, Culture & Society*, 27 (1): 59–74.

Mackay, D. (2009) 'We'll clear the jungle: French vow to shut Calais camp', *Daily Mirror*, 24 April: 14.

Massey, D. (1991) 'The political place of locality studies', *Environment and Planning A*, 23: 267–81.

May, J. (1996) 'Globalization and the politics of place: place and identity in an inner London neighbourhood', *Transactions of the Institute of British Geographers*, 21 (1): 194–215.

Parliament (2007a) Commission for Racial Equality. Written evidence to Joint Committee on Human Rights. *The Treatment of Asylum Seekers*, London: The Stationery Office.

Parliament (2007b) Esser, R. Oral evidence to Joint Committee on Human Rights. *The treatment of asylum seekers*, London: The Stationery Office.

Parliament (2007c) Hill, R. Oral evidence to Joint Committee on Human Rights. *The Treatment of Asylum Seekers*, London: The Stationery Office.

Parliament (2007d) Joint Committee on Human Rights (2006–7) *Treatment of Asylum Seekers*. Tenth Report, London: The Stationery Office.

Parliament (2007e) Travis, P. Oral evidence to Joint Committee on Human Rights. *The Treatment of Asylum Seekers*, London: The Stationery Office.

Parliament (2007f) United Nations High Commissioner for Refugees. Written evidence to Joint Committee on Human Rights. *The Treatment of Asylum Seekers*, London: The Stationery Office.

Peake, A. (2008) 'Inside jungle rape camp', *Sun*, 30 August: 6.

Peake, A. (2009a) 'Jungle warfare: Bulldozer blitz on immigrants' Calais camp', *Sun*, 23 September: 12–13.

Peake, A. (2009b) 'Migrants' camp is bulldozed', *Sun*, 23 September: 2.

Rawstorne, T. (2009) 'Hundreds of illegal immigrants armed with knives and crowbars swarm round Calais trucks heading for Britain', *Daily Mail*, 11 May: 5.

Reid, S. (2007) 'Return of Sangatte – Countless immigrants plot to slip into UK', *Daily Mail*, 13 April: 11.

Reid, S. (2008) 'Hard men who live hard lives in camp they call The Jungle', *Daily Mail*, 29 August: 5.

Reid, S. (2009) 'They're back: Mass of migrants queue up at Calais to reach "Promised Land" UK', *Daily Mail*, 13 March: 5.

Richards, Barry (2004) 'The emotional deficit in political communication', *Political Communication*, 21 (3): 339–56.

Sage, A. (2009a) 'Police crack down to clear migrants from their "jungle"', *The Times*, 24 April: 44.

Sage, A. (2009b) 'Dawn raid on the Jungle to end migrants' stay', *The Times*, 23 September: 14–15.

Sage, A. (2009c) 'Traffickers defy law of the Jungle', *The Times*, 26 September: 37.

Shields, R. (1991) *Places on the Margins: Alternative Geographies of Modernity*, London: Routledge.

Shields, R. (1999) 'Culture and the economy of cities', *European Urban and Regional Studies*, 6 (4): 303–11.

Somerville, W. (2007) *Immigration under New Labour*, London: The Policy Press.

Sparks, I. (2009) 'Britain is NOT the promised land, the UN tells immigrants in Calais', *Daily Mail*, 28 May: 6.

Spindler, W. (2009) 'UNHCR draws road map to help people out of Calais "Jungle"', 17 July, www.unhcr.org/4a6091846.html (accessed 1 June 2010).

Szakolczai, A. (2009) 'Liminality and experience: structuring transitory situations and transformative events', *International Political Anthropology*, 2 (1): 141–72.

Taylor, J. (2009) 'Migrants flee ahead of police crackdown', *Independent*, 22 September: 12.

Thomas, T. (2005) *Popular newspapers, the Labour Party, and British politics*, London: Routledge.

Thomassen, B. (2006) 'Liminality', in A. Harrington, B. Marshall and H.-P. Muller (eds) *Routledge Encyclopaedia of Social Theory*, London: Routledge.

Thomassen, B. (2009) 'The Uses and Meanings of Liminality', *International Political Anthropology*, 2 (1): 5–27.

Topping, A. (2009) 'Very young children heading for Britain, warns refugee agency', *Guardian*, 25 September: 6.

Tristem, A. (2007) 'The return of Sangatte', *Sunday Express*, 18 February: 23.

Turner, V. (1964) 'Betwixt and Between: The Liminal Period in Rites of Passage', in J. Helm (ed.) *Proceedings of the American Ethnological Society for 1964*, Seattle: American Ethnological Society.

Van Gennep, A. (1960 [1909]) *Rites of Passage*, Chicago: Chicago University Press.

Young, J. (2003) 'To these wet and windy shores: recent immigration policy in the UK', *Punishment & Society*, 5(4): 449–62.

14 Shards in the landscape

The dispersed liminality of contemporary slaveries in the UK

Pietro Deandrea

The number of enslaved people living in contemporary Britain is difficult to estimate. Their existence is extremely isolated, and rarely documented. They have access to few rights and are often referred to as 'invisibles', 'ghosts', 'non-persons', 'unpersons'.

In a number of previous essays I sought to emphasize the fragmented, scattered nature of this phenomenon, due to its illegal and hidden nature. Some works identify these new forms of slavery with specific sites: namely, they present the private house as equivalent to a gaol or prison (Deandrea 2009a: 403–412; 2009b: 667–668, 674, 677–678). Other works show how not only the apparently respectable British[1] house, but also the cultivated field, the truck container and the picturesque beach (to mention but a few) have all become potential sites for these new forms of bondage, thus intensifying the haunting presence of these undocumented migrants throughout the country (Deandrea forthcoming). The liminal spaces where these forms of slavery are found, then, are far from being contained within specific areas; they are dispersed, atomized throughout the country – what I tentatively call a 'concentrationary archipelago'.

Referring to fictional works, films and studies on migration issues, this chapter analyses an analogous surfacing of the same concentrationary archipelago in other case studies. These case studies represent a good range of what is defined with the umbrella term 'genre fiction': humour (Lewycka's *Two Caravans*), crime (Rankin's *Fleshmarket Close*) and dystopia (P.D. James's *The Children of Men* and its film version by Cuarón). I also want to show how they occupy and undermine some *loci* traditionally associated with British tourism, such as bucolic landscapes, coastal resorts and historic city centres.[2] In my conclusion, I discuss the relation between the phenomenon of new slaveries and some facets of the concept of liminality.

Marina Lewycka: United bloody Nations

The first example analysed here, Marina Lewycka's *Two Caravans* (2007), represents humour. Its characters compose a multifarious bunch of migrant workers, coming from Ukraine, Poland, Moldova, Malawi, Malaysia and China. They live in two caravans provided by farmer Leapish, and for a living they pick the strawberries of his nearby fields. The beginning of the novel presents readers with a sort of bucolic picture:

> There is a field – a broad south-sloping field sitting astride a long hill that curves away into a secret leafy valley. It is sheltered by dense hedges of hawthorn and hazel threaded through with wild roses and evening-scented honey-suckle. ... In fact so delightful is the air that, sitting up here, you might think you were in paradise. And in the field are two caravans, a men's caravan and a women's caravan.
>
> (*TC* 1)[3]

The reality of these people's lives, however, contrasts sharply with the tourist-friendly image that they had formed in their imagination. Lewycka provides abundant detail about the business. Pickers are paid 30 pence a kilo before deductions – meaning that 'half you fork out in wages you can claw back in living expenses' (*TC* 31). In contemporary Britain, agriculture is one of the sectors (together with care, construction and contract cleaning) where forced labour constitutes a particular concern, where the problem of gangmasters is most present, and with the highest rate of fatal injuries (Anderson and Rogaly 2005: 11, 22, 33):[4]

> Press coverage have [*sic*] ... identified a range of food production, horticulture and agriculture outlets that supply some major supermarkets and food outlets, which depend on migrant workers who are being paid less than £3 per hour for 72-hour weeks and living in substandard housing conditions.
>
> (Craig *et al.* 2007: 42)

In *Two Caravans*, the image of the English countryside as a pastoral paradise is further undermined when unfortunate circumstances scatter the characters into several places and jobs. The Polish Tomasz finds himself on a poultry farm where 40,000 chickens are crammed together:

> a thick carpet of white feathers;... so tightly packed you can't make out where one chicken ends and the next begins. And the smell!... a rank cloud of raw ammonia that makes his eyes burn and he coughs and backs away from the door, his hand over his mouth. He has seen paintings of damned souls in hell, but they are nothing compared with this.
>
> (*TC* 120)

The wished-for paradise, then, turns into a hell for chickens, with their own excrement burning their buttocks and legs.

The ideal England undermined by the encounter with reality is not an image exclusive to literature about migrant workers. The Anglophone literature produced by post-colonial migrants in the UK and their descendants (usually labelled as 'Black British literature') has been presenting it as a recurrent trope, historically rooted in the educational structures of the colonial enterprise and their exaltation of British values (Dawson 2007: 2). The clash between dream and reality is one of the main sources of humour in *Two Caravans*, as in Tomasz's ordeal: it surfaces in his dialogues with his teenage colleague, the white British Neal. Their linguistic misunderstandings play on the ambiguous similarities between intensive poultry raising and British mainstream life and popular culture:

> 'Don't you know Big Brother? What do they have on telly where you come from? It's where they lock'em all up together in a house, and you can watch'em.'
> 'Chickens?'
> 'Yeah, yeah, just like chickens. I like that.'
> [...]
> 'They [the farmers] keep the light on low, so they never stop for a kip – just keep on feeding all night. Bit like eating pizza in front of the telly.'
>
> (*TC* 121–122)

Against the background of Black British literature, *Two Caravans* brings to the fore the continuity of the expectations raised by dream-England in the lives of those contemporary economic migrants who do not necessarily come from former British colonies. This continuity can be accounted for by the lure exercised by Western culture, especially in former Communist countries. This involves another tourist facet of Britain, namely cultural tourism. The gang-master Vulk is very explicit as soon as he picks Irina at Dover: 'England is not like in you [sic] school book' (*TC* 7). Irina's expectations about England had indeed grown from her studies at home, building an ideal landscape merging with culture:

> In fact I was particularly looking forward to meeting a gentleman in a bowler hat like Mr Brown in my *Let's Talk English* book, who looks supremely dashing and romantic, with his tight suit and rolled-up umbrella, and especially his intriguing bulge in his trouser-zip area, which was drawn very realistically in black ink by a previous owner of that textbook. Who wouldn't want to talk English with him?! Lord Byron looks romantic, too, despite that bizarre turban.
>
> (*TC* 20–21)

The deflating irony of these lines will be complemented by Irina's work in Leapish's fields, with the physical pain involved in bending and picking (*TC* 30).

A miner's son, Andryi is much less cultured compared to Irina, but he too has an idyll to dream of: a 'blond-haired Angliska Rosa ... packed with high-spec features. ... And a rich pappa' (*TC* 17). When he is unexpectedly and abruptly seduced by a woman closely fitting that description, she soon turns out to be the farmer's wife thirsty for revenge on her husband for his adultery:

'What the hell...? You bitch! You bloody bitch!'

The farmer strides towards them. The Angliska Rosa looks up over Andryi's shoulder and with her free hand, not the one that is fumbling with his fly zip, she gestures at the farmer with two fingers. Andryi tries to seize the moment to escape, but the blonde holds him fast, and now the enraged farmer runs forward with a roar, and flings himself onto Andryi's back. Holy whiskers! This is not turning out at all according to plan. He is trapped between the two of them like the meat in some mad sandwich.

(TC 49)

In the ensuing brawl, the woman runs over her husband with her luxury car, breaking his leg. The whole group will consequently have to leave for fear of trouble with the police.

As for Tomasz's fantasizing, he dreams of ideals of freedom instilled in him by his passion for Bob Dylan's songs, which led him to come to the West. During breaks, he is half-horrified and half-amused by his Portuguese-Brazilian colleagues squeezing chickens in order to hit one another with spurts of excrement. When the workers start playing football with a chicken as ball, he grabs it, runs to the fence, puts it down, sees the animal go away and explains to his puzzled fellow workers: 'Rugby. I score.' *(TC* 131) The following day, he will notice the same chicken squashed on the road. Altogether, his experience triggers some bitter reflections:

[Titchington, near the poultry farm] turns out to be no more than a cluster of quaint steep-gabled cottages with gardens full of roses, clustered around a pretty medieval church. He wonders whether the villagers know the horror that is happening on their doorstep. It was said that the villagers who lived near Treblinka had only a hazy idea of what was happening behind the barbed wire fence a few kilometres away. They, like the villagers of Titchington, must have been bothered by the smell when the wind blew in a certain direction.
[...]
Is he freer here in the West today than he was in Poland in the years of communism, when all he dreamt of was freedom, without even knowing what it was? Is he really any freer than those chickens in the barn, packed here in this small stinking room with five strangers, submitting meekly to a daily horror that has already become routine? Tormentor and tormented, they are all just damned creatures *in hell*. There must be a song in this.

(TC 132, 134; emphasis mine)

By linking the horror of concentration camps to brutalized chickens and migrant labour, Tomasz's thoughts reinforce my main assumption, what I call 'Britain's concentrationary archipelago': namely, the presence of a palimpsest constituted by Second World War concentration camps beneath the forms of imprisonment to which new slaves are subjected.

Two Caravans develops its plot in many sites of exploitation: cultivated fields, farms, factories, restaurants (being a kitchen hand is described by Andryi as 'being a slave with ten masters', *TC* 212), old people's homes where African nurses work. This landscape is populated by a 'human wasteland' (*TC* 172): the novel's migrant protagonists are always in danger of becoming part of it. Their flashbacks often convey a home background marked by the violence of poverty and squalor – a needed complement for a fully developed character. The gruesomeness of the sex trade is probably most representative of this wasteland reducing humans to commodities or beasts; when chased by the pimp and would-be rapist Vulk, Irina feels like 'a hunted animal' (*TC* 61; see also 179).

In this context, Lewycka struggles to maintain the balance between tragedy and humour, and she is often successful. At some points the harshness of reality seems to necessarily take centre stage, whereas her final chapters take a picaresque direction leading to an unlikely happy ending, probably in tune with the overall humorous mood.

On the other hand, it must be conceded that there is one brilliant passage where the cynicism of an employer succinctly conveys all of the exploitative attitude ingrained in the British economic system, and the particularly wrenching ordeal of Chinese migrants, who occupy the bottom rung:

> six quid an hour. The other hour is voluntary, like I said. You don't have to do it. There's always plenty that do. Ukrainians, Romanians, Bulgarians, Albanians, Brazilians, Mexicans, Kenyans, Zimbabweans, you lose track. Jabber jabber jabber round here. Day and night. It's like United bloody Nations. We used to get a lot of Lithuanians and Latvians, but Europe ruined all that. Made 'em all legal. Like the Poles. Waste of bloody time. Started asking for minimum wages. Chinesers are the best. No papers. No speekee English. No fuckin' clue what's goin' on. Mind you, some folk do take advantage. Like them poor bleeders down at Morecambe. Jabber jabber jabber into the mobile phone, tide comin' in, and nobody's got a clue what they're on about. What's the point of having foreigners if you got to to pay 'em same as English, eh? That's why we went over to the agency. Let them take care of all that.
>
> (*TC* 117; the novel is dedicated 'To the Morecambe Bay cockle-pickers')

'United bloody Nations': the speaker's half-voluntary humour (including a pun on 'bloody') replicates the general strategy on which the irony of the whole novel is based, that is to say the contrast between the ideal and the real. In this case, these two poles hint at equality versus slavery, universal rights versus total lack of rights. And in some parts of *Two Caravans*, as shown above, this contrast revolves around traditional tourist sites or cultural attractions, be they pastoral or cultural or both, turned by the phenomenon of new slaveries into liminal zones where exploitation is the order of the day, and potentially dotting every part of the UK. As the following section shows, these zones are unexpectedly extended, to the point of including institutional places.

Ian Rankin: chasing the overworld

Ian Rankin's *Fleshmarket Close* (2004) is a popular crime novel which alludes to new forms of slavery from the double meaning of its title: 'More than one kind of flesh market', goes DS Siobhan Clarke's comment after a visit to a lap-dance club (*FC* 157).[5] Like Lewycka, Rankin tackles this subject by playing on the ambiguous relationship between sites of tourist attractions and the liminal places of contemporary slaveries. Moreover, he adds in the picture a new space for the latter, i.e. legal detention centres. In Britain, the turn of the century was marked by radical policy changes in this regard; a major expansion of detention centres was announced by the government in the year 2000:

> Some 15 per cent of applicants (of about 10,000 per year) are currently detained, or 700–1,000 at any one time ... The leader of the opposition went one step further, to prove he could be more vicious in his compassion than the government, and promised that all asylum-seekers would be detained if he came to power.
>
> (Harris 2002: 39)

In *Fleshmarket Close*, when the corpse of an unidentified immigrant is found stabbed, DI John Rebus gets involved in a complex investigation, leading him also to wonder about his own Polish ancestry, of which he knows very little. He happens to work side by side with the black Immigration Official Felix Storey from London, who illustrates the bigger picture to the inexperienced Rebus:

> My own parents arrived here in the fifties: Jamaica to Brixton, just two among many. A proper migration that was, but dwarfed by the situation we've got now. Tens of thousands a year, coming ashore illegally ... often paying handsomely for the privilege. Illegals have become big business, Inspector. Thing is, you never see them until something goes wrong.
>
> (*FC* 210)

Similarly to Lewycka, then, Rankin does not elude – or rather, makes more explicit – the continuities and discontinuities with the issues confronting many Black Britons. Storey's last sentence is yet another reference to contemporary enslaved migrants as invisibles, ghosts. Rebus, too, realizes: 'I haven't seen any of these people, the people everyone is so angry at.' (*FC* 68) Consequently, the first big obstacle for him consists in identifying the corpse found in the ghetto of Knoxland, in the western outskirts of Edinburgh. The place is made of high-rise blocks 'Reaching skywards with all the subtlety of single-digit salutes.' (*FC* 4) It is:

> A dumping ground for tenants the council found hard to house elsewhere: addicts and the unhinged. More recently, immigrants had been catapulted into its dankest, least welcoming corners. Asylum-seekers, refugees. People

nobody wanted to think about or have to deal with. Looking around, Rebus realised that the poor bastards must be left feeling like mice in a maze. The difference being that in laboratories, there were few predators, while out here in the real world, they were everywhere.

(*FC* 5–6)

Rankin's description through Rebus's thoughts clearly points at the responsibility of political authorities who place foreigners in a prison-like, or jungle-like, nightmarish environment, turning them into prey. This national dispersal scheme, which began at the start of the twenty-first century and denied refugees the right to choose where they live (see Mynott 2002: 114–117),[6] is emblematic of how institutions do not always work against the atomized exploitation of undocumented migrants.

More specifically, Rankin's Knoxland seems to be inspired by the aftermath of the national dispersal scheme which took place in Glasgow in 2001; a great number of asylum-seekers were housed in Sighthill, 'one of Scotland's "sink estates" ... the poorest constituency in Scotland, the second most unhealthy in Britain ... [with] the highest male unemployment rate in Britain'[7]; this resulted in stabbings, angry demonstrations by the immigrants and counter-protests by rampaging far-right movements (McGhee 2005: 82–85). Since asylum-seekers were in many cases sent to 'the poorest areas with high levels of empty housing stock' (Mynott 2002: 119–122; see also Robinson *et al.* 2003: 166), like Rankin's Knoxland, such actions were bound to spur racist violence and asylophobia in the interested areas. As for the dispersed migrants themselves, only if they agreed to be dispersed could applicants receive the very controversial allowance in vouchers:

> In practice, many applicants just disappear – giving up the supposedly lavish benefits from the public purse – rather than be separated from friends and relatives. Once disappeared, they can become ordinary illegal immigrants, able to look for work and thus much better off than when trapped in the misery of asylum-seeking.

(Harris 2002: 39)

In his vehement pamphlet against British immigration policy, Steve Cohen (2006: 105) compares this national dispersal to the nineteenth century workhouses for the 'undeserving poor': he defines its contemporary version 'a national, punitive scheme based on isolating the undeserving/undocumented from the rest of the community and keeping them in a position of impoverishment/degradation and powerlessness.'

In Rankin's Knoxland, where a 'venerable piece of graffiti had been altered from JUNKIE SCUM to BLACK SCUM', the so-called natives resort to angry protests, the lawyer Mo Dirwan gets beaten up and asylophobic questions abound, even from some of Rebus's colleagues (*FC* 61, 115). Highly perplexed at the course of events, Rebus silently questions the state of contemporary Scotland as a whole:

'What in Christ's name is happening here?' he found himself asking. The world passed by, determined not to notice: cars grinding homewards; pedestrians making eye contact only with the pavement ahead of them, because what you didn't see couldn't hurt you. A fine, brave world awaiting the new parliament. An ageing country dispatching its talents to the four corners of the globe ... unwelcoming to visitor and migrant alike.

(*FC* 204)

Surrounded by a wall of 'white' resentment and migrant fear, Rebus is unable to discover the victim's real identity, until a call comes from Whitemire, an old prison recently turned into a so-called 'Immigration Removal Centre' (as fictitious as Knoxland, but based on the real Dungavel). The call is from a woman who works at the centre, and who has recognized the photo of the victim because his wife and children are held in Whitemire. She is calling anonymously, a detail which casts doubts on the legal activities in Whitemire since its very first appearance in the novel. As is often the case, Whitemire is run by a private security company.[8]

During his visits there, DI Rebus sees for himself the appalling state to which its 'guests' are reduced: 'families, individuals scared out of their wits ... people who know that to be sent back to their native land is a death sentence' (*FC* 124). In Whitemire, inmates are not given a humane environment, but are kept with 'a bare minimum of education and nourishment' (FC 167).[9] The place still resembles a prison, with its 'twelve-foot perimeter fence ... augmented by runs of pale green corrugated iron' (*FC* 132), uniformed guards with sets of keys, tight security measures and regulations (*FC* 134, 139). Rankin's setting is obviously based on real places. Lindholme Removal Centre, for example,

holds up to 112 men ... staff routinely impose random strip-searches after visits. Detainees are also strip-searched on admission to the centre as a matter of routine, without any reason given. Staff at this former prison treat detainees as offenders, though they have not been convicted of any crime. There is a prison atmosphere with detainees being made to wear prison clothes.

(Cohen 2006: 97)

In Whitemire, Rebus meets harrowed, hollowed-out human beings – one of them resorting to a suicide attempt (*FC* 247–249). These include Mrs Yurgi and her two children, to whom Rebus bears the news of the murder of their husband and father. They will all be taken to the mortuary, children included,[10] to identify the body of Stef Yurgi (a human rights Kurdish journalist persecuted by Turkish authorities);[11] they are taken in a custodial blue van 'with bars on its windows, a toughened grille between the front seats and the benches in the back' (*FC* 175–176).

More importantly for this analysis, Rebus is increasingly made suspicious by the barely suppressed lack of collaboration from Whitemire Centre's manager.

In the end, the full picture will prove his doubts true. On one hand, authorities stack immigrants in God-forsaken ghettoes where they become easy prey to modern slavers and exploiters. In addition, Whitemire's officials allow these slavers to bail immigrants out for their criminal purposes, and thus help them strengthen their empire with the bonus of the perfect blackmail: 'Any of them complain, Whitemire's hanging over them like a noose' (*FC* 423). In other words, Rebus's investigation discloses how far the two supposed opposites on the legal/illegal axis, the ghetto of Knoxland and the Centre of Whitemire, are connected, to the point that illegal dens of enslavement and official sites of removal inevitably blur, becoming indistinguishable. Faced with the sheer inhumanity of the living conditions in Whitemire, Rebus tries to respond to the consequent frustration of one of his colleagues:

'That's the problem though: who is it I *am* pissed off with?'
'The people in charge?' Rebus guessed. 'The ones we never see.' He waited to see if she'd agree. 'I've got this theory,' he went on. 'We spend most of our time chasing something called 'the underworld', but it's the *overworld* we should really be keeping an eye on.'

(*FC* 142)

As far as the complementariness of the institutional and criminal dimension is concerned, the ending of *Fleshmarket Close* is unsparing. Felix Storey jails the whole criminal organization, but (as Rebus finds out) only thanks to anonymous tips coming from an even more powerful slaver and migrant-smuggler who managed to use the Immigration Service (although they 'wielded more power than the police', *FC* 387) to get rid of his rival. Rebus concludes to Storey:

'But here's the thing – all the glory you're going to get, it adds up to the cube of bugger-all, because what you've done is smoothed Caffery's path. It'll be *him* in charge from now on, not only bringing illegals into the country, but working them to death too.' Rebus paused. 'So thanks for that'.

(*FC* 475)

The merging of institutional and criminal persecution of migrants takes place on a palimpsest constituted by some of Edinburgh's tourist attractions – in this case, Gothic and historical tourism. Two skeletons, a woman and an infant, are found buried under a concrete cellar floor in Fleshmarket Close. They are soon revealed to be old samples which had disappeared from the School of Medicine, University of Edinburgh. Nevertheless, in a very short time, thanks to the sly promptness of the cellar's owner who is turning his pub into a 'theme bar' (*FC* 173), the place is included in the city centre ghost tour along the Royal Mile. The same skeletons, however, were being used by the same criminal organization as real victims of slaughter, to threaten any exploited migrant who turned rebellious. They were fake, but part of the terrifying atmosphere on which new slaveries works.

Through this narrative turn, Rankin seems to be implying a few important points. First of all, even though Knoxland and Whitemire are two liminal places far from the bustling, tourist city centre, the Royal Mile is involved in the migrants' suspension of human rights; thus, the liminality linked to new slaveries is yet again shown as more and more dispersed.

Second, a gap is evident between the frivolity of 'ghost tours' and harsh reality: in the case of the two skeletons, the tourist routes become a mere gloss for the depth of new slaveries, hiding the real ghosts, the real skeletons, the real fleshmarkets of our age. Faced with the 'enticements to experience "Edinburgh's haunted past"', Siobhan feels 'more concerned with its haunted present' (*FC* 81). The liminal sites occupied by the Gothic, then, need revision in the light of the context provided by new slaveries.

Third, Rankin links new slaveries in contemporary Edinburgh to the serious issues from Scottish history underlying today's Scottish tours. One of the two skeletons might be that of the eighteenth century Mag Lennox – a woman accused of witchcraft and burned by citizens (*FC* 78). Her descendant Judith Lennox works as a ghost-tour guide and as a consultant to that bar owner (FC 173). The implication is obvious: who are the witches being burned *today* by respectable citizens? At Whitemire, when told that Stef Yurgi's family is to be deported because 'they hadn't proved they weren't economic migrants', Detective Sergeant Ellen Wylie replies: 'Tough one ... Like proving you're not a witch...' (*FC* 137).

Alfonso Cuarón: a liminal centrality

P.D. James's *The Children of Men* is set in the year 2021, when mankind has mysteriously lost its ability to reproduce. Extinction looming ahead, with a population of 36 million and 20 per cent of them over 70 years old (*CM* 126),[12] Britain has turned into a bizarre society which, as is often the case with dystopian narratives, could be construed as a hyperbolic projection of our present – in this case, of our present incapability of conceiving our future. In the words of the protagonist, Theo Faron, 'We can experience nothing but the present moment, live in no other seconds of time, and to understand this is as close as we can get to eternal life.' (*CM* 9)

The lack of any hope for the future has worsened citizens' indifference to active participation in politics and decision-making. Parliament only meets once a year; everything is ruled by decree of the Council of England, composed of five members including Xan Lyppiatt, 'Warden of England' and Theo's cousin:

> The system has the merit of simplicity and gives the illusion of democracy to people who no longer have the energy to care how or by whom they are governed as long as they get what the Warden has promised: freedom from fear, freedom from want, freedom from boredom.
>
> (*CM* 89)

It is not by chance that one of the members of the Council, when reminding Theo of the rise in crime during the 1990s, declares: 'The other freedoms are

pointless without freedom from fear' (*CM* 96). P.D. James's near future resonates with the emptying out of values and ideals in contemporary politics and
social debate. Slavoj Zizek aptly points out that fear has become today 'the main
mode of politics ... how you mobilize people ... fear of immigrants, even left-
ists, fear of too-strong state, fear of taxation.' The Slovenian thinker also connects this issue with the main narrative device of James's novel: 'This is the
definition of infertility: when your mobilizing principle is just pleasure and fear'
(Cuarón and Elías 2006: no page reference).

A related aspect of fear-based policies is the increasing criminalization of
sectors of Western societies, what the language of contemporary political studies
defines 'crime deal' (Palidda 2009: 8). In Britain, from 1998 the Labour government policies constantly introduced an attitude of deterrence which was bound
to create an atmosphere of suspicion and prejudice towards asylum-seekers
(McGhee 2005: 65–77); this was effected principally through nine Bills which
introduced detention for an increasing number of immigration cases (Bosworth
and Guild 2009: 132–137).

The 'crime deal' answers the needs to both scapegoat and enslave a new class
of easily exploitable migrants (Palidda 2009: 9–10). James dystopically projects
this dominant political ideology onto her novel: criminals (even petty ones) are
given a life sentence in the penal colony of the Isle of Man, where anomie and
violence reign (*CM* 61–64; 95–96). Migrants, here called 'Sojourners', are
employed for menial jobs such as caring for the elderly, road repairs and rubbish
collecting, and then sent back (sometimes 'forcibly repatriated') when they reach
the age of 60: 'They work for a pittance, they live in camps, the women separate
from the men. We don't even give them citizenship; it's a form of legalized
slavery' (*CM* 58). In order to justify this system, one of the Council members
makes reference to the 1990s, speaking the language of asylophobic demagogy
and racial superiority:

> People became tired of invading hordes, from countries with just as many
> natural advantages as this, who had allowed themselves to be misgoverned
> for decades through their own cowardice, indolence and stupidity and who
> expected to take over and exploit the benefits which had been won over cen-
> turies by intelligence, industry and courage.
>
> (*CM* 97)

Nevertheless, 'sojourners' are not given a prominent role in the novel. They are
mentioned only nine times, sometimes as fleeting presences in the background,
casually noticed by the protagonist. The second part of the book turns into a
fugitive plot where Theo and a group of radicals protecting a pregnant woman
are chased through the English countryside, which depopulation has turned into
an empty, liminal and dangerous no-man's-land gradually consuming
civilization.

In his film *Children of Men*, Cuarón shifts James's perspective onto this dys-
topic world, thanks to a series of radical changes involving plot, characters,

liminal spaces – changes which in many cases seem to revolve around a marked centrality assigned to migration issues in British society. Cuarón's changes are mainly based on three elements: the carefully woven background, the figure of the pregnant woman and the setting of the final part of the movie.

The protagonist Theo is followed against a background teeming with references to migrants. This background presents an accumulation of details which are much more imposing than James's spare references: loudspeakers saying that 'to hire, feed or shelter illegal immigrants is a crime. ... Protect Britain'; groups of people caged along train platforms, lamenting their fate in a Babel of languages and guarded by fully armed soldiers; coaches with grills on their windows taking refugees to detention camps ('our government hunts them down like cockroaches'). Theo is initially apathetic to the world around him; thanks to his meetings with his former wife Julian and with his old friend Jasper, his awareness seems to re-awaken. Accordingly, the director's camera focuses more and more on the suffering faces of these people: Slavoj Zizek calls this procedure 'anamorphosis ... the true focus of the film is there in the background ... This fate of the individual hero remains a kind of a prism through which you see the background even more sharply' (Zizek 2006: no page reference). What emerges very clearly, certainly more than in the novel, is that citizenship makes the important difference between life and death, human dignity and total denial of rights.

Thanks to Julian, who leads a radical group called 'The Fishes', Theo becomes involved in a journey to the southern coast aiming at protecting the pregnant woman Kee. In the novel, the pregnant woman is the white Briton Julian, who thanks to her deformed hand has been exempted 'from the six-monthly, time-consuming, humiliating re-examinations to which all healthy females under forty-five were subjected' (*CM* 39); the child's father, Luke, was also excluded because he had mild epilepsy as a child; hope, then, seems to reside in those who are, generally speaking, excluded. The film places this hope in a more specific category – Kee is a black refugee – thus emphasizing the crucial importance of migrants for contemporary British society. As outlined in the preceding discussion, I believe this is the key to Cuarón's transposition of the novel, which can be accounted for by his personal history, but also by the increasing centrality of migrations in the 14-year period between the publication of the book and the release of the film.

The same perspective helps to make sense of the setting of the film's final parts, very different from the novel's abandoned countryside. The refugee camp of Bexhill is a dilapidated town which is controlled on the outside by ruthless soldiers provided with all kinds of high-tech equipment, and left to total anarchy inside (possibly a development of the penal colony on the Isle of Man described in passing in the novel).

Bexhill is situated on the coast of southern England: this would-be tourist place is turned into a battlefield, and its dark 'entrails' are reminiscent of a slave castle on the West African coast. Paradoxically, Theo and Kee must enter this hellish landscape in order to reach the ship that will rescue them: the detention camp, a liminal site par excellence, the place where all rules are suspended or violated, is presented as an unavoidable ordeal to understand British society.

Cuarón's interpretation of P.D. James's novel replicates what Giorgio Agamben argues theoretically. His writings offer a number of possible theoretical paradigms which could be employed to analyse the British concentrationary archipelago shaped by new slaveries. Starting from classical societies, his *Homo Sacer* is centred on the genealogy of the figure of the prisoner in Nazi concentration camps, seen as someone who was deprived of any of the rights usually pertaining to humankind, and thus reduced to 'bare life'. Some of Agamben's definitions are highly appropriate to the new forms of slavery studied here, and its legalized equivalents such as detention centres. The concentration camp, for instance,

> is the space that is opened when the state of exception begins to become the rule. In the camp, the state of exception, which was essentially a temporary suspension of the rule of law on the basis of a factual state of danger, is now given a permanent spatial arrangement, which as such nevertheless remains outside the normal order.
>
> (Agamben 1998: 168–169)

According to Agamben, the camp's 'vocation is precisely to realize permanently the exception' (2000b: 40). He sees the concentration camp as the emblematic paradigm of our times, the 'hidden matrix ... of the political space in which we are still living' (Agamben 1998: 166). Agamben's words resonate with the conditions of those undocumented migrants for whom the suspension of human rights has become so common. This scenario is very similar to what happens in detention centres, where the suspension of human rights becomes normative – where the liminal, I would add, becomes central. As I have argued, the state of exception of new slaves becomes normative, systemic, and constitutes a pillar of the British economy.

My argument rests on the validity of this theorization by Agamben; at the same time, through an analysis of fictional products side by side with studies on migration issues, this chapter shows how, in today's Britain, the concentration camp has been atomized, vaporized into a myriad of ever-changing, ever-shifting different places, thus embodying the features of trans-national capitalist mobility.

Conclusion: new slaveries and the liminal

The case studies examined in this chapter demonstrate that the liminality of new slaveries in the UK is not only dispersed, but has paradoxically become systemic, central. It is a *systemic* liminality for three main reasons:

1   It can be found anywhere, including institutional, legal places, and is enforced by British laws: Rankin's *Fleshmarket Close* offers an effective translation of this phenomenon.

2   It forms a pillar of the British economy, and capitalist power relations thrive on its existence: in their different generic frames, Lewycka's and James's novels convey the indispensability of migrants in the British labour system.

3   It has seeped into traditional, identitarian forms of tourist attractions: the three case studies of this chapter lay bare the dark, exploitative side of bucolic land-scapes, cultural attractions, historic city centres and coastal resorts.

Considering my literary field of investigation, I am aware that I have been employing the term 'liminality' in a rather broad way which does not strictly conform to its original, anthropological meanings. I have been wondering, for instance, what kinds of 'rite of passage' could be embodied in new slaveries, given the state of permanent exclusion in which most new slaves are trapped; in other words, what might their liminality be a prelude to, besides the better life they obviously strive after? In this regard, I would like to refer again to Giorgio Agamben, and to his seminal essay 'Beyond human rights'. This work focuses on the pivotal role played by the figure of the refugee as a development of the con-centration camp prisoner; in the wake of Hannah Arendt's essay 'We refugees' (1943) which called refugees 'the vanguard of their people', Agamben wrote:

> the figure that should have embodied human rights more than any other ... marked instead the radical crisis of the concept. ... If the refugee represents such a disquieting element in the order of the nation-state, this is so prima-rily because, by breaking the identity between the human and the citizen and that between nativity and nationality, it brings the ordinary fiction of sover-eignty to crisis. Single exceptions to such a principle, of course, have always existed. What is new in our time is that growing sections of humankind are no longer representable inside the nation-state – and this novelty threatens the very foundations of the latter. Inasmuch as the refugee, an apparently marginal figure, unhinges the old trinity of state-nation-territory, it deserves instead to be regarded as the central figure of our political history. [...the refugee is a] limit-concept that at once brings a radical crisis to the princi-ples of the nation-state and clears the way for a renewal of categories that can no longer be delayed.

Only when this renewal is effected, he concludes, 'only in such a world is the political survival of humankind today thinkable' (Agamben 2000a: 20–22, 26). Agamben, then, theorizes how migrants can offer a possibility for a collective, rather than personal, transformation: Tomasz's comic misunderstanding with his white British workmate (*Two Caravans*), Rebus's bitter reflections on the con-dition of Scotland (*Fleshmarket Close*) and Theo's descent into the hell of Bexhill Detention Centre (*Children of Men*) are all to be seen, I argue, as fic-tional translations of Agamben's voicing of this need for a radical renewal inspired by the tragedy of new slaveries.

Curiously, Agamben's words resonate with Victor Turner's analysis of limi-nality in *The Ritual Process* (Turner 1969: 94–130), in which he identifies an alternative to societal structures which he calls 'communitas', 'where secular distinctions of rank and status disappear or are homogenized' and '[i]t is rather a matter of giving recognition to an essential and generic human bond, without which there could be *no* society' (Turner 1969: 95, 97, emphasis in original). Turner applies the same ideas to certain modern manifestations where examples of communitas are usually affected by what he calls 'the powers of the weak' (Turner 1969: 108–111), such as court jesters, outsiders (in literature and cowboy movies), millenarian movements and hippie communities:

> In closed or structured society, it is the marginal or 'inferior' person or the 'outsider' who often come to symbolize what David Hume has called 'The sentiment for humanity', which in turn relates to the model we have termed 'communitas'.
>
> (Turner 1969: 111)

In the light of this, I cannot help wondering what Turner would have written on Britain's new slaves.

Notes

1 See Kumar (2003) for a full exploration of the complexities and contradictions associated with the use of the term British.
2 See Arranz (2006a and 2006b) for the different identities woven by aspects of the tourism industry in relation to the urban and rural landscapes.
3 Quotations from the novel will be referred to with *TC* followed by page number.
4 For a description of individuals harshly exploited in this sector, see Pai 2008: 120–157. In the same pages, the author narrates the weeks she spent undercover, pretending to be an undocumented agricultural labourer.
5 Quotations from the novel will be referred to with *FC* followed by page number.
6 On the issue of clustering and dispersal, see also Robinson *et al.* 2003: passim, and McGhee 2005: 68–71.
7 According to a World Health Organization report (August 2008), there is a 28-year gap in the life expectancy between the poorest and the richest suburbs in Glasgow; available at www.who.int/mediacentre/news/releases/2008/pr29/en/index.html (accessed 1 February 2011).
8 Dungavel House Removal Centre, for example, is run by Premier Detention Services Ltd: 'A substantial degree of immigration controls is enforced by private security firms, many of which are part of multinational companies ... Now for the price of a share everyone can be a stakeholder in immigration controls' (Cohen 2006: 78).
9 As for the lack of educational and medical facilities in detention centres, see also Crawley and Lester 2005: 14.
10 Since 2001 refugee children, both with and without a family, can be detained under the same policy as adults. Similarly to the general phenomenon of new slavery, figures are extremely hard to determine (Crawley and Lester 2005: 5), even though we are dealing with institutional places only.
11 'Turkey is a difficult country. The evidence of torture is notorious, but Turkey is a friend, a member of NATO, a potential member of the EU. The claims of those in flight from Turkey, mainly Kurds, are treated with suspicion' (Harris 2002: 38).
12 Quotations from the novel will be referred to with *CM* followed by page number.

References

Agamben, G. (1998 [1995]) *Homo Sacer: sovereign power and bare life*, trans. D. Heller-Roazen, Stanford, CA: Stanford University Press.

Agamben, G. (2000a [1993]) 'Beyond human rights', in *Means without End*, trans. V. Binetti and C. Casarino, Minneapolis and London: University of Minnesota Press.

Agamben, G. (2000b [1994]) 'What is a camp?', in *Means without End*, trans. V. Binetti and C. Casarino, Minneapolis and London: University of Minnesota Press.

Anderson, B., and Rogaly, B. (2005) *Forced Labour and Migration to the UK*, Oxford: Centre for Migration, Policy and Society (COMPAS) in association with the Trades Union Congress.

Arendt, H. (1996 [1943]) 'We refugees', in M. Robinson (ed.) *Altogether Elsewhere: writers on exile*, Houghton Mifflin: Harcourt. Available at http://www-leland.stanford.edu/dept/DLCL/files/pdf/hannah_arendt_we_refugees.pdf (accessed 6 November 2010).

Arranz, J. (2006a) 'Rural, White and Straight. The ETC's Vision of England', *Journal of Tourism and Cultural Change*, 4 (1): 19–52.

Arranz, J. (2006b) 'BTA's Cool Britannia: British national identity in the new Millennium', *PASOS*, 4 (2): 183–200.

Bosworth, M., and Guild, M. (2009) 'Gran Bretagna: governare attraverso il controllo delle migrazioni', in S. Palidda (ed.) *Razzismo democratico: la persecuzione degli stranieri in Europa*, Milan: Agenzia X.

Cohen, S. (2006) *Deportation Is Freedom! The Orwellian world of immigration controls*, London and Philadelphia: Jessica Kingsley.

Craig, G., Gaus, A., Wilkinson, M., Skrivankova, K. and McQuaide, A. (2007) *Contemporary Slavery in the UK: overview and key issues*, York: Joseph Rowntree Foundation.

Crawley, H., and Lester, T. (2005) *No Place for a Child – Children in UK immigration detention: impacts, alternatives and safeguards*, London: Save the Children.

Cuarón, A. (writer, director, 2006) *Children of Men* (film), Universal.

Cuarón, A., and Elías, J. (writers, 2006) 'The Possibility of Hope', *Children of Men*, DVD bonus disk, Esperanto Filmoj Productions, interviews by R. Romani, Universal.

Dawson, A. (2007) *Mongrel Nation: diasporic culture and the making of postcolonial Britain*, Durham: University of Michigan Press.

Deandrea, P. (2009a) 'Human bondage in contemporary UK and its generic transformations: from Bridget Anderson's *Britain's Secret Slaves* to Ruth Rendell's *Simisola* and Kazuo Ishiguro's *Never Let Me Go*', in V. Cavone, C. Corti and M. Trulli (eds) *Forms of Migration, Migration of Forms: literature (proceedings of the 23rd AIA conference, Bari 20–22 September 2007)*, Bari: Progedit.

Deandrea, P. (2009b) 'Unravelling unpersons: inscribing the voices of contemporary slavery in the UK', *Textus: English studies in Italy (Marginal Textualities)*, eds C. Dente and S. Orgel, XXII/3: 665–680.

Deandrea, P. (forthcoming) 'Contemporary slavery in the UK and its categories', in F. Giommi and A. Oboe (eds) *Black Arts in Contemporary Britain: literary, visual, performative*, Rome: Aracne.

Harris, N. (2002) *Thinking the Unthinkable: the immigration myth exposed*, London: Tauris.

James, P.D. (2006 [1992]) *The Children of Men*, New York: Vintage.

Kumar, K. (2003) *The Making of English National Identity*, Cambridge: Cambridge University Press.

Lewycka, M. (2008 [2007]) *Two Caravans*, London: Penguin.

McGhee, D. (2005) *Intolerant Britain? Hate, citizenship and difference*, Maidenhead: The Open University Press.

Mynott, E. (2002) 'From a shambles to a new apartheid: local authorities, dispersal, and the struggle to defend asylum seekers', in S. Cohen, B. Humphreys and E. Mynott (eds) *From Immigration Controls to Welfare Controls*, London and New York: Routledge.

Pai, H.-H. (2008) *Chinese Whispers: the true story behind Britain's hidden army of labour*, London: Penguin.

Palidda, S. (2009) 'Introduzione', in S. Palidda (ed.) *Razzismo democratico: la persecuzione degli stranieri in Europa*, Milan: Agenzia X.

Rankin, I. (2004) *Fleshmarket Close*, London: Orion.

Robinson, V., Andersson, R. and Musterd, S. (2003) *Spreading the 'Burden'? A review of policies to disperse asylum seekers and refugees*, Bristol: The Polity Press.

Turner, V.W. (1969) *The Ritual Process: structure and anti-structure*, Chicago: Aldine.

Zizek, S. (2006) 'Comments by Slavoj Zizek', *Children of Men*, DVD bonus disk, Universal.

15 Afterword

David Crouch

Across the chapters

Can landscape be anything but liminal?

I will seek to fill out an answer to this awkward question through this sketch of themes and diversities emergent in this rich collection of new writing.

A number of threads work through and across these chapters. Some of the contributors work closely to the orienting concepts of Victor Turner and Arnold van Gennep; others make their entries through as diverse authorities as Benjamin, Agamben and even de Certeau. The plurality of arrivals into a discussion concerning landscape and liminality are welcome; they render the growing richness and contested character of the matter of the liminal, what is liminal and how is it so, that has emerged over recent decades. Perhaps, for me, there is less attention in this volume to the matter of landscape: what 'is' landscape; how does it *occur*? And so on. These curiosities form a later section of this Afterword, as landscape, like its particular potentiality towards uncertainty and complexity, has re-emerged problematically in cutting edge cross-disciplinary and multi-disciplinary discussions in the recent period, most particularly in the current century so far. Putting these complexities together with the unsettled matter of liminality draws these chapters into an intense series of inter-related debates.

Across this book a number of very different situations, liminal landscapes, are critically engaged and considered. Some of our chapters examine and wrestle with the 'harder edges' of the liminal character of landscape. These are tackled in relation to individuals' lives, and in their hegemonic wielding of their sometime-production. Rather than journeys of progressive productivity or recovery and openness, liminality can be marked on the ground, in lives, by closure and oppression, and speak of the hardest politics and their events, rather than rites of passage and possibilities. Yet rites of passage may even surface in closure or hegemonies other than human, as exemplified in discussions of risk and fear. Elsewhere across these chapters liminality happens in practices of resistance and its possible hope; there may be hope in the very identity of the liminal. Another fascinating theme in the book is the use of ritual, with implicit irony, in reaching 'the liminal', in becoming; an approach that is close to Buddhist ideas and similar leanings.

Other chapters' debates take place in engagement with the presented-re-presented character of artwork and media; film and writing. Van Gennep's 'sacred' may be open to numerous and more diverse meanings when we engage contemporary culture and meanings; contemporary life and its cultures. The matter of time frequently occurs in this collection, in relation to artwork, sea reaches and mires, as well as in ancient caves. In each case, there is an engagement of feelings of materiality and of 'other than human' in our lives.

Talking and writing liminality is always open to being problematised, perhaps made ironic, in terms of our wielding our own 'cultural capital'. There is a tendency to 'read' and to grade what may be liminal along a particular aesthetic that may implicitly guide and determine our critical reflections. Aesthetic, hierarchy: the 'run down', the 'makeshift', the un-planned. I have argued elsewhere that at least the last two of these three aesthetic possibilities (and perhaps, for some, the first also) there is a positive and progressive aesthetic in the liminality of community gardens, allotments and their use of materials, working of the ground and so on (2003; with Ward 2007). Similarly, in Tim Edensor's fascinating account, ruins may not be end points, or even sites (landscapes?) awaiting replacement, but liminal sites of emergence (2005). Drab coastlines marked by consumer paraphernalia and plastic beach playthings for children maybe deeply valued in assisting enjoyment; being there; enabling the comfort of a family together (Miller 2008). Wandering by uninvolved, unconnected, we may find this fits ill with our holiday heritages (*sic*). Thus we can mis-read the engagement of sites, landscape; practice, feeling and value.

In familiar literature landscape has been considered as pre-given in one way or another: through cultural representations; by virtue of the mixture or assemblage of particular objects, materiality; features, as it were, 'out there'. Landscape is a word that has considerable popular purchase. The 'stuff' that is often substituted for what is meant by landscape tends to be more in terms of countryside, but it can also include broadly the assemblage of landforms, concrete shapes, fields, gutters, designed spaces, and serendipitous collections of things. Implicitly included are our own bodies that are now enlivened into the 'landscape'. It is to the character of that 'enlivening' that my following remarks attend.

The notion of landscape as ever-liminal

In his marvellous story *The Unbearable Lightness of Being*, Milan Kundera asks what flirtation is:

> One might say that it is behaviour leading to another to believe that sexual intimacy is possible, while preventing that possibility becoming a certainty. In other words, flirting is a promise of sexual intercourse without a guarantee.

> (Kundera 1984: 174)

Such pregnancy of possibility, and possibility of becoming; the implicit if possibly agonising playfulness; the very combination of contingent enjoyment, uncertainty, frustration, anxiety and hope would seem to thread across living. Along with these, living holds a felt possibility of connection, meaning, change. To fix may be assurance, certainty or entrapment, closure or a mix of these.

The more explorative, uncertain and tentative ways in which our being part of a world of things, movements, materials and life; openings and closures, part openings mixed with part closures; engaged in living suggests a character of flirting; spaces of possibility. It can be exemplified in the way in which we can come across very familiar sites finding new juxtapositions of materials, materialities and feelings, as it were, 'unawares'. The unexpected opens out. Ordinary, repetitive, extraordinary, we find that we can 'look ... for the first time'; feel the world anew. (Bachelard 1994: 156). Our emotions become alive in the tactility of our thought; we discover our life and its spaces anew. Time and emotion can deliver the change. However modest these feelings of vitality may be this quiet dynamic can unsettle familiar and expected cultural resonances and the work of politics. What was felt ordinary, mundane and everyday changes; changes in texture and in a feeling of what matters. Encounters like this can happen in diverse, nuanced, complex ways amongst moments of doing things, across different spaces and journeys of our lives and different intensities of encounter. Familiar and habitual rhythmic engagement, meaning and relationships with things can change in register. In these ways flirting is a creative act. My particular concern in this book surrounds cultural and geographical knowledge of fluidities, contingencies and complexities: a practical, embodied ontology of living and the feeling of its doing and becoming (Crouch 2001; Harre 1993; Shotter 1993).

Milan Kundera's observations on flirting seem prescient to our efforts to grasp the tentative, explorative and emotional character of landscape. In recent years, in art theory, social anthropology and cultural geography, there has been a number of innovative contributions that auger fresh approaches to landscape thinking (Cresswell 2004; Lorimer 2006; Matless 2003; Mitchell 2002; Merriman *et al.* 2008; Massey 2006; Rose 2006; Tilley 2006; Wylie 2006). Landscape has become exemplary of the critical debates between representational and so-called non-representational theories affecting debates in the humanities and social science, from art theory to cultural geographies. Here, I seek to engage what landscape 'is', or may be, in terms of its relation with something called 'space', to which, I argue, landscape is inevitably related. I consider landscape as the expressivity and poetics of flirting (with) space.

Flirting is not something in passing, superficial, or an alternative to the *flâneur*, or the much-overstated 'gaze', or linked with any particular high-intensity, long-distance (in Euclidian terms) travel (Urry 2002; Urry 2007). Of course, long journeys of measured distance can be almost leitmotifs for the liminal as superficial and fleeting (Shields 1993). However, flirting offers a means through which to explore the character of living spacetime through a number of threads that connect everyday living and our feeling and thinking. It serves as a means to articulate life in its negotiation, adjustment, disorientation and becoming. Whilst it may be caught in more widely dispersed influences and affects of the contemporary, flirting is not offered as a twenty-first century emergence. Flirting with space is a vehicle to explore the dynamics of what is happening and how that flirting can affect things. Yet what is 'space' in this context?; do we flirt 'with' it or is space of the flirting itself, only engaged, not detached or semi-detached from us?

Shifting thinking

Before re-engaging space, flirting and landscape, I briefly remind us of two particular orientations that have been of significant ongoing resonance in several disciplines, these two emerging from cultural geography. As Wylie has extensively presented, there are numerous 'landscapes' or conceptual stories concerning it (Wylie 2007). The first of the two I select was a more humanistic geography of phenomenology; the other a very English and critically Marxist reading of the ideological power of landscape making (big gardens and nineteenth century painting in particular). The former offered a means to relate life and a materiality of landscape in practice (Seamon 1980). The latter worked between art history and historical landscape geographies with regard to the interpretation of power as expressed in the representation of ideas, in art and in the construction of large landed estates, especially in Renaissance to early nineteenth century European painting (Cosgrove and Daniels 1988; Daniels 1989). It is representation's capacity to frame and prefigure the world that is open to use in pursuit of particular ideologies of power (Matless 1999), focusing upon representations forged in the particular reading of artwork. Humanistic geography offered an alternative to the work of representations in the emphasis on landscape in experience, yet found limits in acknowledging too the work of representations, i.e. the broad cultural significances felt to influence experience (Seamon 1980). The work on representations developed the more strongly. Alongside cultural studies, and continuing a long sociological perspective on material culture Benjaminian philosophies of streets and shop windows, amongst others, these approaches broadened to a contemporary application to designs of products, streets and 'grand views' (Benjamin 1982; Pred 1995).

It is interesting to observe that much of the work on art/representation in discussions on landscape has concerned the deterministic meanings and significances of landscape in the form of values, relationships and influences including ideology, significantly examined in terms of the way place or space is experienced and consumed (Duncan and Ley 1993). Baudrillard's hyper-reality provided a postmodernism that disrupted deterministic imagery, at least detached it from rational moorings (Baudrillard 1988). Something as everyday and ordinary about community gardening, little plots and everyday life appealed as it threw together strong political histories, contexts, with everyday practice and its phenomenologies. A more contingent and flexible landscape became evident in the material patterning of the ground through working it, with nature and with diverse recycled materials, re-figuring their previously mediated content. Emerging through these was significant displacement of apparent consumer culture and passivity that is now acknowledged in material culture studies critical understanding of consumption; and the insights of performativity, becoming; emotion, self and intersubjectivity. Landscape flows.

With significant exceptions conceptual debate on landscape has emphasised a relative stability, marked more recently by Ingold's articulation of dwelling, an articulation in which he refers both to habitual practices and their representation in Breugel's art (Ingold 2000). Important work on the ideology and power of particular landscapes in representation emphasise their persistent consumption and longevity (Cosgrove and Daniels 1988). Whilst the intended political power of the use or doing of landscape is difficult to contest, the way it works is less clear yet no less important (Mitchell 2002). Familiarly presented in terms of powerful ideologies as sites of representation imposing of social relations even to the point of claiming national identity (Cosgrove and Daniels 1988; Matless 1999), or more recently in contested presences, or in Mitchell's unambiguous phrase 'a form of social regulation' landscape begins to bear more nuanced critical challenge (Mitchell 2002: 241). Olwig's more flexible treatment of landscape remains soundly of materiality with social, political, cultural, ethics and everyday practices and not confined to fields of vision. Any 'position' on landscape changes over the trajectories of these components (Olwig 1996).

My critique of particular arguments for landscape captured in and as ways of seeing combines with an acknowledgement of the continuing contingency of romance in our landscapes as process (Edmonds 2006). Romance may be one emergent feeling in landscape. Landscape is informed through combinations of different times and life durations, memory and rhythms, different registers and intensities of experience (Paterson 2001). Landscape emerges as continual process, emergent in the expressive and poetic character of spacing: creative, contingent, awkward and not blocked in representations. Landscape may be present or it may *present* itself in artwork variously on the ground (for example in landscape design), on canvas or in any other form.

Anything but liminal?

Landscape is not merely encapsulated in a detached 'gaze'. It is, rather, fleshy, felt, imagined, affected and affects. It is of presence, bodily, and as Wylie elucidates, absence too, 'a fracture forbidding any phenomenological fusion of self and world, entailing instead an *opening-to* and *distancing from*', anything more a constant dream. (Wylie 2009). It is not only referred to social constructivism, or phenomenology, but across the more reverberant and active of its character the moments of shift and fluidity are performative, not merely of habitual performance. Landscape can collide with something else that resonates a sense of our own lives, and has the power to re-assemble it. Such intensities of significance, or merely calm moments of reassurance, happen across the range of performativities and their circulation in representations. Landscape resonates a capacity of belonging, disorientation and disruption. Landscape is not perspective and horizon, or lines, but felt smudges, smears, kaleidoscope, a multisensual expressive poetics of potentiality, becoming and poetics.

Space may be at once considered a loose entity or mixing of features, movements, energies; ideas, myths, memories, actions; an active ingredient in processes of feeling. Amidst these energies is a rearrangement of energies and the spaces we feel can arise, that we felt we knew but that emerge in new ways different in assemblages of power and meaning. Thus, *space* is increasingly recognised to be always contingently related in flows, energies and the liveliness of things; therefore always 'in construction', rather than fixed and certain, let alone static (Massey 2005). What space 'is' and how it occurs is crucially rendered unstable and shifting; matter and relations in process. It may be *felt* to be constant, consistent and uninterrupted, but that feeling is subjective and contingent.

The energy and vitality of space is articulated in the work of Deleuze and Guattari that has helped unravel and unwind familiar philosophies of the vitality of things; the multiplicities of influences and the way they work; and in a world of much more than the result of human construction. Their term *spacing* introduces a fresh way of conceptualising the process-dynamics of the unstable relationality of space/life. Spacing occurs in the gaps of energies amongst and between things; in their commingling. Their interest thus emerges 'in the middle', the in-between.

Landscape as signified through spacing can have a gentle yet cumulative politics, profound in its feeling and ideas, as the community gardener expressed. Landscape as practice or *art* practice is forwarded into process, as dynamic rather than either 'outside' experience or only focused through the physical character of encounters. In this article I have placed emphasis upon efforts to articulate the dynamic and complex character of landscape in process, working away from the particularly fixed character familiarly associated with landscape in and as representation. Landscape as the performative expressive-poetics of spacing is a way that makes possible an always emergent dynamic relationality between representations, practices and identities. By so doing, I hope to have rendered landscape's purported fixed and steady character as instead shuffling, unstable and lively.

Of course, as noted earlier in this chapter, contexts obtain and persist, sometimes become changed, contested, removed; they are malleable. Their power can assert at particular moments and in particular situations and sites. Thus, whilst noting the relationality, fluidity, contingency and perhaps above all complexity of the emergence or occurrence of 'landscape', as discussed here, there is always the potentiality, to phrase with Deleuze, of coercion of particular contexts and their distinctive character and wield of power. Perhaps more explicitly is Selwyn's engagement with landscape concerning the entangled complexity of the emergence of liminality and how it can be felt and experienced in life.

Thus, to re-engage the other 'L' of the book title and chapters' efforts, if landscape is ever-lively, as Massey argues of space, ever contingent, uncertain, then is it ever not 'liminal'? Is landscape of its character, its emergence, its process, ever but liminal? A painting may of its expressive-poetics of the artist's encounter in flirting with space offer a momentarily-held landscape; that may affect our flirting with it, amongst and across our multitude of moments of experience, their performativities and so on. Yet contexts, amongst them; 'representations' inflect; flicker rather than determine. Perhaps the moments of liminality vary in duration, in intensity, exemplified in its occurrence and feeling in individuals' lives. Landscape emerges in our performativities, now and of other times. Landscape occurs, then, in, amongst our (shared) expressive-poetics, in performativities through which we engage, recall, exaggerate, seek to gear, and desire our feelings to be.

Cultural resonance emerges as one way in which landscape is informed. Landscape erupts in this process as an expressive and poetic act of which artwork is unexceptional. Representations are borne of the performativity of living. The liveliness of performativity is available to individuals who encounter these representations. Thus in no sense are representations fixed or closed to change. They are open to further interpretation and feeling. Representations and their projected cultural significance remain open too, 'available' for further work. The certainty of representations can be disrupted in this complex/multiple process of spacing: available, open and flexible, with a permanent possibility of re-inscription and gentle politics as well as purposive resistance. Landscape is informed through combinations of different times and life durations and rhythms, different registers and intensities of experience. Landscape is full of liminalities.

Note

The key themes of this chapter are drawn from Crouch (2010a, 2010b).

References

Bachelard, G. (1994) *The Poetics of Space*. Boston, Mass.: Beacon Press.

Baudrillard, J. (1988) 'Simulacra and Simulations', in M. Poster (ed.), *Selected Writings*, Stanford, CA: Stanford University Press.

Benjamin, W. (1982) *Das Passagen-Werk*. Edited by R. Tiederman, Frankfurt: Suhrkamp Verlag.

Cosgrove, D. and Daniels, S. (eds) (1988) *The Iconography of Landscape: Essays on the Symbolic Representation, Design and Use of Past Environments*. Manchester: Manchester University Press.

Cresswell, T. (2003) 'Landscape and the Obliteration of Practice', in K. Anderson, M. Domosh, S. Pile and N. Thrift (eds), *Handbook of Cultural Geography*, London: Sage.

Crouch, D. (2001) 'Spatialities and the Feeling of Doing', in *Social and Cultural Geographies*, 2 (1): 61–75.

Crouch, D. and Ward, C. (2007) *The Allotment: Its Landscape and Culture*, Nottingham, Five Leaves Press, sixth edition; first edition, Faber and Faber 1988.

Crouch, D. (2003) *The Art of Allotments: Culture and Cultivation*, Nottingham, Five Leaves Press.

Crouch, D. (2010a) *Flirting with Space: journeys and creativity*, Aldershot: Ashgate.

Crouch, D. (2010b) *Flirting with Space: thinking landscape relationally, Cultural Geographies*, 17(1): 5–18.

Daniels, S. (1989) 'Marxism, Culture and the Duplicity of Landscape', in N. Thrift and R. Peet (eds), *New Models in Geography II*, London: Unwin Hyman.

Deleuze, G. and Guattari, F. (2004) *A Thousand Plateaus*, London: Continuum.

Duncan, J. and Ley, D. (eds) (1993) *Place/Culture/Representation*, London: Routledge.

Edensor, T. (2005) *Industrial Ruins: Space, Aesthetics and Materiality*, London: Berg.

Edmonds, M. (2006) 'Who said romance was dead?', in *Journal of Material Culture*, 11(1/2): 167–88.

Harre, R. (1993) *The Discursive Mind*, Cambridge: Polity Books.

Ingold, T. (2000) *The Perception of the Environment: Essays on Livelihood, Dwelling and Skill*, London: Routledge.

Kundera, M. (1984) *The Unbearable Lightness of Being*, London, Faber and Faber.

Lorimer, H. (2006) 'Herding Memories of Humans and Animals', in *Environment and planning D: Society and Space*, 24 (4): 497–518.

Merriman, P., Revill, G., Cresswell, T., Lorimer, H., Matless, D., Rose, G. and Wylie, J. (2008) 'Landscape, Mobility, Practice' in *Social and Cultural Geography*, 9 (2): 191–212.

Massey, D. (2005) *For Space*, London: Sage.

Massey, D. (2006) 'Landscape as a Provocation: Reflections on Moving Mountains', in *Journal of Material Culture*, 11(1/2): 33–48.

Matless, D. (1999) *Landscape and Englishness*, London: Reaktion Books.

Matless, D. (2003) 'The Properties of Landscape', in K. Anderson, M. Domosh, S. Pile and N. Thrift (eds), *Handbook of Cultural Geography*, London: Sage.

Miller, D. (2008) *The Comfort of Things*, London: Routledge.

Mitchell, D. (2002) 'Dead Labour and the Political Economy of Landscape – California Living, California Dying Practice', in K. Anderson, M. Domosh, S. Pile and N. Thrift (eds), *Handbook of Cultural Geography*, London: Sage.

Olwig, K. (1996) 'Rediscovering the Substantive Meaning of Landscape', in *Annals of the Association of American Geographers*, 86 (4): 630–53.

Paterson, M. (2001) 'On Bachelard and Bergson and the Complexity of Memory', in *Philosophy in Review*, 21(3): 159–62.

Pred, A. (1995) *Recognizing European Modernities: a Montage of the Present*, London: Routledge.

Rose M. (2006) 'Gathering "Dreams of Presence": a Project for Cultural Geography', in *Environment and Planning D: Society and Space*, 24 (4): 537–54.

Seamon, D. (1980) 'Body-subject, Time-space Routines and Space Ballets', in A. Buttimer and D. Seamon (eds), *The Human Experience of Space and Place*, London: Croom Helm.

Shields, R. (1993) *Places on the Margin*, London: Routledge.

Shotter, J. (1993) *The Politics of Everyday Life*. Cambridge: Polity Press.

Tilley, C. (2006) 'Introduction: Identity, Place, Landscape and Heritage', in *Journal of Material Culture*, 11 (1/2): 7–32.

Urry, J. (2002) *The Tourist Gaze*, 2nd edition; first edition 1999, London: Sage.

Urry, J. (2007) *Mobilities*, London: Polity.

Wylie, J. (2006) 'Depths and Folds: on Landscape and the Gazing Subject' in *Environment and Planning D: Society and Space*, 24 (4): 519–35.

Wylie, J. (2007) *Landscape*, London: Routledge.

Wylie, J. (2009) 'Landscape, Absence and the Geographies of Love', in *Transactions of the Institute of British Geographers*, 34 (3): 257–289.

Index